New
Progress
to Proficiency

Teacher's Book

Leo Jones

CAMBRIDGE
UNIVERSITY PRESS

CAMBRIDGE UNIVERSITY PRESS
Cambridge, New York, Melbourne, Madrid, Cape Town, Singapore,
São Paulo, Delhi, Dubai, Tokyo, Mexico City

Cambridge University Press
The Edinburgh Building, Cambridge CB2 8RU, UK

www.cambridge.org
Information on this title: www.cambridge.org/9780521635523

First published 1986
Third edition 2002
5th printing 2011

Printed in the United Kingdom by Short Run Press, Exeter

A catalogue record for this publication is available from the British Library

ISBN 978-0-521-63552-3 Teacher's Book
ISBN 978-0-521-63553-0 Students's Book
ISBN 978-0-521-00789-4 Self-study Students's Book
ISBN 978-0-521-63551-6 Audio Cassettes (3)

Contents

Introduction

New Progress to Proficiency is for any group of students preparing for the 'University of Cambridge Local Examinations Syndicate Certificate of Proficiency in English' examination – better known as Proficiency or CPE, for short. It is also suitable for students preparing for an exam of similar level and scope, such as a university examination. It contains a wide variety of tasks, practice activities and exercises which increase in difficulty and complexity unit by unit until, towards the end, students are tackling tasks of exam standard.

Students using this course will have passed the Cambridge First Certificate (FCE) exam – or reached an equivalent level – and may also have taken the Cambridge Certificate in Advanced English (CAE) exam, perhaps using *New Cambridge Advanced English* by Leo Jones.

This book has two main aims:

- to help students to improve and refine their language skills so that they can do their very best in the Proficiency exam
- to help students to improve the language skills that they will need in real life: in social situations and in their work or studies

This book's varied and interesting activities, tasks and exercises increase students' confidence and flexibility. It also allows them to discover what aspects of their English they still need to improve in order to become more accurate and fluent users of English.

Why a new edition?

The First and Second editions of *Progress to Proficiency* have been outstandingly popular and effective coursebooks, used with great success in Proficiency classes all over the world. But, in the meantime, some of the original material seemed to be getting rather dated, new ideas have come along, major changes have been made to the exam syllabus – and teachers requested a full-colour book.

New Progress to Proficiency incorporates all the strengths of the Second edition but is much easier for students and teachers to use. Many of the reading texts, recordings, tasks, activities and exercises are completely new, but all the features that teachers and students have appreciated have been retained. All the skills and techniques that exam candidates need to master are covered. The favourite texts and activities which have been retained from the Second edition have been modified so that they work better and are more user-friendly. The new colourful layout and clear organisation of the pages make the course easier to use – this helps the students to get the maximum benefit from their work.

The revisions and changes are based on detailed comments and reports from teachers who had been using the Second edition successfully for many years. *New Progress to Proficiency* is easy for both students and teachers to use and find their way around. The format of each unit provides a more balanced lesson structure and increased flexibility.

New Progress to Proficiency

The 18 topics in *New Progress to Proficiency* have been selected not just because they 'come up' in the Proficiency exam but because they are important for advanced learners, and include themes which any educated person should be confident enough to read about, hear about and discuss – not as an expert or as a professional, but as an informed layperson.

Teachers familiar with *New Progress to First Certificate* or *New Cambridge Advanced English* will notice that this book includes many of their more effective and enjoyable features. However, thanks to the higher level of the Proficiency exam, students are set free to explore topics and ideas that are more intellectually demanding, and go into greater depth and detail.

As you work through the book, you will become aware of a progression from unit to unit:

FROM exercises, tasks and activities where
      the questions can be discussed . . .   TO exam-style questions and tasks

FROM exercises, tasks and activities with
      problems to be solved with a partner . . .   TO exercises which have to be done alone

FROM exercises, tasks and activities where
      guidance is given . . .   TO exercises and tasks where students
                                                       have to use the knowledge and skills
                                                       they have acquired

FROM exercises, tasks and activities which
      help students to learn . . .   TO exercises which, like the exam,
                                                       test their knowledge

FROM exercises, tasks and activities where
      students work at their own speed . . .   TO exercises which have to be done
                                                       within exam-style constraints of time and
                                                       length.

Hence the title: *New **Progress** to Proficiency*.

To do all the sections in one unit will take about 5 hours – longer if a lot of time is devoted to discussion. The whole course thus requires around 90 hours to complete, though students who spend time preparing exercises at home may not need so long. Any substantial pieces of written work (i.e. compositions, written tasks and summaries) as well as reading the longer passages through for the first time will, it is assumed, be done as homework in any case.

It is advisable to SELECT certain parts of each unit to concentrate on with your class, which means that some parts may be omitted. This is left to your discretion, as it is dependent on each class's strengths and weaknesses, as well as on their interests.

For example, if there isn't enough time to do one of the reading passages in a unit, it can be set for homework. Or if a particular grammar point is easy for your students, it can be left out altogether. Or if your class find listening comprehension fairly easy, then it may be a good idea to omit one of the listening sections in a unit. The material in this book is designed to be used selectively, though some sections in a unit do depend on previous sections.

Exam preparation and exam practice

Examination practice tests, though they are certainly helpful to accustom students to the kinds of tasks they will encounter in the exam, should not be over-used in class for a number of reasons:

- the questions in tests are based on a random selection of different language points, which is confusing for students
- many of the questions in tests seem impossibly hard (only the best candidates will get them right) while others seem very easy (even the weakest candidates will get a few marks on these), and this is frustrating for students
- in tests the reading passages and the recordings are chosen because they are suitable for testing purposes, not because they are intrinsically interesting or enjoyable, and not because they provoke discussion
- no help whatsoever is given to help students to improve their performance, since the purpose of the test is only to assess candidates' proficiency, not to help them

By contrast, *New Progress to Proficiency* provides comprehensive and, above all, systematic coverage of the wide range of language skills required in the Proficiency exam. Some of the exercises and tasks are simply designed to help students to learn, some provide a challenge so that they will 'stretch' their English, some provide opportunities for discussion. The texts have been chosen because they are likely to interest, entertain, inform, provoke or intrigue students. The entire course is designed to help students to improve their skills progressively in the different areas tested in the exam.

In a Proficiency course there has to be a realistic balance between exam preparation (after all, everyone wants to do well in the exam!) and improving language skills that will be useful in the real world. Using the material in this book will help you to make sure that this balance is maintained throughout the course.

The teacher and the students

The role of the teacher in a Proficiency class cannot be over-stressed. The best source of explanations and advice on grammar, usage, style and writing skills is not a book but the teacher. The teacher is the person who knows the students personally: only the teacher knows what their strengths and weaknesses are, what they know already and what their interests and enthusiasms are. Only the teacher knows what kind of action to take when difficulties arise – perhaps action as straightforward as suggesting better ways of saying or writing things, or more complex such as introducing suitable supplementary material.

No textbook can replace the teacher because the problems of any particular group of students are individual and unpredictable. Lengthy explanations of grammar points, detailed advice on how to write a good essay or exhaustive analyses of appropriate style which are general enough to be relevant to every student would be unwieldy and time-consuming in a textbook – but the teacher can tailor such explanations and advice to the needs of each class.

The teacher therefore has an essential creative contribution to make – not just by regulating the pace and intensity of each lesson and deciding which sections to concentrate on, but by adapting the material to the students' needs and interests, by giving the right kind of advice and by maintaining a friendly, cooperative working atmosphere in class.

Proficiency students can't expect to sit back and be 'taught', they have to LEARN – by asking questions, by finding things out for themselves, by reading widely, by drawing on each other's knowledge, by discovering what they can do well and what they are weak at, but above all by improving their ability to use the English they already know in a flexible, confident way to perform a wide range of tasks.

It's a sad fact that students at this level find it difficult to appreciate that they are making progress: you can give them encouragement by keeping a permanent record of their work throughout the course. Each student's work can be sub-categorised into the different skills that will be assessed in the exam: vocabulary, composition writing, reading comprehension, use of English, listening comprehension and speaking skills (communicative ability, grammatical accuracy and pronunciation). These individual 'profiles' can be kept up to date and shown to students from time to time, so that they can see what improvements they have made and also what aspects of their English they still need to work on. Make sure they realise that the purpose of this is to help, not intimidate them!

Working in pairs or groups

Many of the exercises and tasks in *New Progress to Proficiency* are designed to be done by students working together in pairs or in small groups of three or four, and not 'round the class' with each student answering one question.

There are several advantages to this approach:

- students get an opportunity to communicate their ideas to each other while they are discussing each exercise or task
- students are more likely to remember answers they have discovered or worked out by themselves than answers other students give – or answers the teacher announces to the class
- students working in groups are more active than if they are working as a class: they talk more and do more thinking too. If a class of, say, 20 were doing a 10-question exercise 'round the class' half of them wouldn't get the chance to answer a single question

One drawback of doing exercises in pairs or groups is that it does take time. However, as many of the exercises can be done as homework, time can be saved by setting some exercises to be done at home. Then, back in class next time, students can begin the session by comparing their answers in pairs or groups, and discussing as a class any problems they encountered.

Another possible problem is that errors may go uncorrected and that students might even learn 'bad habits' from each other. This can be dealt with by vigilant monitoring of students as they are working together and encouraging students to correct each other's mistakes – which they should be able to do quite efficiently at this level. (See also **Mistakes: marking and correction** on page 15.)

The following symbols are used in the Student's Book:

    = 'Join another person to form a pair'

    = 'Work in pairs' – if you have an odd number of students in the class there will have to be one group of three students

⣿→⣿ = 'Join another pair to form a group'

⣿⣿ = 'Work in groups of three or four' (whichever size seems to be more convenient) – sometimes you might prefer to form groups of five

◀)) = 'Listen to the recording'

✏ = 'Students write'

What's in each unit?

A typical unit starts with a warm-up discussion activity, followed by work on Topic vocabulary and a Reading passage to introduce the topic of the unit. Most units continue with sections on Grammar review, further Reading passages, Vocabulary development, Advanced grammar, Writing skills, Listening and Composition writing. Eight of the units end with a Verbs and idioms exercise.

But there is no fixed sequence of sections: each unit looks and feels rather different from the one before. For students and teachers it is reassuringly easy to find your way round each unit, but each unit contains a few surprises and unpredictable elements.

Topic vocabulary

Each unit has a section covering some of the vocabulary connected with the topic of the unit. There are various types of exercises, tasks and activities in these sections, including warm-up discussion questions and a follow-up activity. Some of these are open-ended discussion activities (e.g. 1.1) where discussion among the students leads them to discover the gaps in their vocabulary and encourages them to ask questions or use a dictionary. Some are activities which encourage students to explore and exploit vocabulary in intriguing ways (e.g. 5.1 and 9.1).

Some of these sections contain exercises with gaps to fill (e.g. 4.1). An exercise of this type is to some extent a test, if only because no two students share the same knowledge of English. However, different students will benefit from different parts of each exercise: learning new words, being reminded of words they don't actively use, finding words with similar meanings and determining how they are used. Such exercises cover the skills required for Part 1 of the Reading Paper in the exam, with discussion activities which foster the kind of communication skills tested in the Speaking Paper.

There is a progression in the book:

FROM activities which introduce and practise vocabulary without reference to the exam

   TO exercises where students have to choose three words that are …
      appropriate ✓   correct ✓   suitable ✓   good   authentic

     TO exercises with exam-style multiple-choice questions where only … alternative is correct.
        one ✓   two   three   four

       TO exercises where there are also questions on grammar and usage, as in the exam.

Besides the sections dedicated to Topic vocabulary, students will encounter relevant vocabulary in other sections in a unit, particularly in the Reading sections, many of which contain special vocabulary exercises.

For the teacher, it's not easy to help students to learn new vocabulary because:

– Students find it hard to remember vocabulary items. Giving them a large amount of controlled oral practice in class is no guarantee that they will remember everything a week later!
– Students need to develop a sensitivity towards the kinds of contexts and situations in which each vocabulary item can be used: which words are formal or informal, which are used jokingly or seriously, which are used in a derogatory or complimentary sense, and what collocations the words are used in. Students also need to develop an awareness of the connotations or associations of different vocabulary items, since many broadly synonymous expressions may have quite different connotations.

Unfortunately, there are no easy solutions. What will certainly help is:

- DISCUSSION of the meanings, connotations and usage of vocabulary introduced or encountered in class
- encouraging students to use a DICTIONARY intelligently, particularly by studying the EXAMPLES given after the definitions
- encouraging students to highlight unfamiliar vocabulary items which they want to remember
- making sure that students get plenty of EXPERIENCE in reading English, not just the texts in this book, but wider reading in English for pleasure and information
- a REALISTIC approach to the problems: it's the students who have to do the remembering – all the teacher can be expected to do is encourage students to experiment with new vocabulary and not play safe by using simple words
- systematic use of NOTEBOOKS to store useful new vocabulary items, preferably devoting separate pages to each topic. Students should be encouraged to discuss which systems of vocabulary storage they consider most effective. (See 1.3E in the Student's Book and **Vocabulary development** below.)

Vocabulary development

Most units contain a section on Vocabulary development, which is designed to expand students' vocabulary in various ways. The following aspects are covered in these sections:

1.5 Adjective + noun collocations
2.3 Words easily confused
3.7 Opposites
4.8 Forming adjectives
5.5 Adjectives and participles
6.4 One word – different meanings
7.8 Compound nouns
8.6 Prefixes
9.6 Abstract nouns
10.9 Different styles
11.6 Collocations: idioms
12.7 Suffixes
13.6 Underlying meanings
14.2 Collocations: verb phrases
16.7 Synonyms and homonyms
17.3 Modifying adjectives and participles

Vocabulary exercises can't 'teach' students new vocabulary, they can only introduce them to new words and phrases, and remind them of what they have come across before. The students themselves are the only people who are fully aware of what they already know, and of what they need to learn. The exercises in *New Progress to Proficiency* should be viewed as a SOURCE of new vocabulary and revision of vocabulary students may have encountered previously. It should not be assumed that doing the exercises in this book will magically 'teach you everything you need to know'. Learning new vocabulary is not such a simple process.

Whenever students come across a potentially useful new word or phrase in this book (or in their reading generally), they should use a dictionary to look it up, paying particular attention to the example sentences given and any information given about collocations. Next time they come across the word, they should notice the collocation.

If a word or phrase seems unusual or specialised, they shouldn't necessarily try to remember it – often they can guess its meaning from the context anyway.

Using a dictionary is best done in private and in their own time outside class. This means that it is essential to prepare work before each class and spend time alone following it up afterwards. Just 'doing their homework' is not enough – they should make time for this sort of preparation and follow-up work.

Students should use a fluorescent highlighter to highlight useful new words so that the words stand out whenever they flip through the book. (If preferred a pencil may be used instead to underline or put rings round words – but a highlighter is more effective.) Then as the course progresses they should be reminded to flip regularly through the units they have covered so far to revise the vocabulary they've encountered – this could easily be done in spare moments between classes or when using public transport on their way to or from class, for example. This will help them to assimilate new words so that eventually they can incorporate them into their own active vocabulary, and use them in their writing and conversation. As the weeks go by, if the highlighting fades, they should re-highlight the words they still want to be reminded of.

Writing new words in a notebook is another good way of memorising new words, particularly their spelling. It usually helps to store words in categories (e.g. under topic headings), or alphabetically, rather than make a chronological list. The best kind of notebook for this is a loose-leaf personal organiser or Filofax, into which new pages can easily be inserted.

Every student must also possess a good English–English dictionary, so that they can look up the meanings of words and find other examples of their uses.
The following are recommended:

Cambridge International Dictionary of English
Longman Dictionary of Contemporary English
Oxford Advanced Learner's Dictionary of Current English
Collins COBUILD English Language Dictionary

A bilingual dictionary is NOT sufficient for Proficiency students.

The Teacher's Book contains answer keys and suggestions for handling the exercises.

Reading

New Progress to Proficiency contains a wide variety of authentic texts taken from newspapers, magazines and from fiction and non-fiction books. The questions focus on different reading skills: reading for gist or reading to extract specific information, as well as recognising and appreciating the style of the passage and the writer's attitude or intention. The passages are all chosen as springboards for discussion.

Before many of the reading comprehension tasks there are pre-reading tasks, preliminary discussion questions or questions about the theme that students may be able to answer from their own previous knowledge. These tasks help students to approach the text with more interest and curiosity than if they merely had to 'Read the text and answer the questions'.

It is essential for students to realise that they don't have to be able to understand every single word in a passage to perform the tasks in this book, or even to answer the questions in the exam. They should concentrate on what the writers are trying to say and the information they are communicating. Unfamiliar words in a reading text may be distracting but students should not assume that every single one is important and 'worth learning'.

There are many exercises where students have to highlight certain vocabulary items in a passage. This encourages them to deduce meanings from the context and also to notice the contexts in which particular words are used. Many of the reading passages have numbered paragraphs, rather than numbered lines, to help students to search for words and to make it easier to refer to parts of the text in discussion or follow-up work.

After the reading comprehension questions there are usually further discussion questions, to encourage students to use some of the new words they have encountered in the text and share their reactions to its content with each other. In some cases there is a Communication Activity or a writing task, arising from the content of the passage.

There is a progression unit by unit:

FROM exercises where students are asked questions like this:
　　　Who made the first move?　*Harry*

　or The person who made the first move was ..*Harry*........
　or true/false questions:
　　　Holly was the one who made the first move.　✗　*False*
　TO exam-style multiple-choice questions:
　　　The one who made the first move was . . .
　　Harry ✓　　Henry　　Holly　　Hetty

In the exam candidates' understanding is 'sampled' only, so there are fewer questions on each reading text to answer than there are in this book. To save time in class, students should be asked to prepare the reading passages by reading them through at home beforehand.

The Teacher's Book contains background information on the literary writers whose work is reproduced. Most of the texts from works of fiction are the opening paragraphs of a book – this is intended to whet the reader's appetite and encourage further reading.

Students also need to be encouraged to read widely for pleasure and information, selecting material that suits their own interests and tastes – fiction and non-fiction, books, newspapers and magazines in English. Weekly news magazines like *The Economist*, *The Guardian Weekly*, *Newsweek* or *Time* are particularly recommended. These publications also have their own websites where students can read each week's main articles.

Here is a list of the reading texts in the book:

Prescribed reading

New Progress to Proficiency does not contain questions on particular books, as these change each year. Choosing one of these books not only gives students an extra topic to choose from in the Writing Paper, but also gives them a good chance to improve their reading skills and enrich their vocabulary. It's a really good idea to recommend one of the books to your students and discuss it regularly in class. One of the others might also be recommended as reading for pleasure. A wide range of tastes is catered for in the selection of texts, as this list for 2002 shows:

Anne Tyler: *The Accidental Tourist*
John Wyndham: *The Day of the Triffids*
Graham Greene: *Our Man in Havana*

(Actually all of those books are entertaining and well worth reading!)

Written work should be set on the particular book chosen: the kinds of questions that might be asked would relate to the characters, plot, style and relevance of the particular book. For examples of typical questions, see the most recent *Cambridge Proficiency Examination Practice*.

The latest Examination Regulations booklet obtainable from your local Examinations Secretary contains each year's list of prescribed books.

Grammar review and Advanced grammar

The Grammar review sections cover the main problem areas of English grammar that cause difficulties for advanced students. The Advanced grammar sections cover areas of grammar which students may not have dealt with before, though they are likely to have encountered them in their reading. Particular attention is given in the Advanced grammar sections to points that 'come up' in the Proficiency exam, and to structures which students will find useful in their composition writing.

Both types of sections contain a variety of exercises: contrasted sentences where students have to discuss the differences in meaning, error correction exercises, cloze exercises, transformation exercises, gap-filling exercises and sentence-completion exercises, together with other more open-ended tasks. Many of these exercises reflect the kinds of questions that students will encounter in the Use of English Paper.

Towards the end of the book more emphasis is placed on the techniques students will require in Part 1 of the Use of English Paper, with annotated exam-style exercises and hints for dealing with different kinds of test items.

The points covered in these sections are as follows:

1.2 Comparing and contrasting
1.7 Using participles
2.2 Articles and determiners
2.7 Position of adverbs
3.2 Reporting – 1
3.5 Using inversion for emphasis
4.4 *–ing* and *to* . . .
4.6 *Wh–* clauses
5.4 The passive – 1
5.7 *should* and *be*
6.3 The future
6.7 Revision and exam practice
7.2 Prepositions – 1
7.4 Past and present
7.7 Further uses of *–ing*
8.2 Modal verbs
8.7 *There* . . .
9.5 Question tags and negative questions
9.8 Reporting – 2
10.4 Conditionals – 1
10.6 Uses of the past
11.5 Conjunctions and connectors – 1
11.8 *It* . . . constructions
12.4 Verbs + prepositions
12.5 The passive – 2
13.2 As the saying goes . . .

If you feel that a particular Grammar review section covers points which present no difficulties for your students, you should leave out that section, or maybe recommend that it is done as homework with a short follow-up discussion in class.

Students should realise that if they require more detailed rules or guidelines and further examples, they should refer to a reference grammar book, such as *Advanced Grammar in Use (with Answers)* by Martin Hewings (CUP) or *Practical English Usage* by Michael Swan (OUP). They should be encouraged to ask questions if they are unsure about any points in the grammar sections.

Summary-writing

In Part 5 of the Use of English Paper, candidates have to answer questions and write a summary of two reading passages. The questions may include explaining the meaning of certain words used in the passage, explaining the reference of cataphoric and anaphoric devices (such as *it* or *this*) or general comprehension questions. Writing the summary requires the students to select relevant information and then write 50–70 words.

Many students find summary-writing particularly difficult, as it often requires skills they haven't used before. Special attention is given to these skills in *New Progress to Proficiency* and students are given ample practice in rephrasing quotations from texts in their own words and in summarising passages within a fixed word limit.

Often these exercises are done orally by students working together before they write their answers down, probably for homework.

The Teacher's Book contains Model summaries which you may photocopy, if you wish, for your students to compare with their own.

Listening

The recordings in *New Progress to Proficiency* include many broadcasts, authentic interviews and discussions. The exercises and tasks are designed to help students to develop their skills in finding the important information in the recording, listening for gist, listening for specific words, note-taking, interpreting a speaker's attitude, etc. Some of the longer recordings are split into shorter sections, with different tasks.

The listening comprehension tasks are often preceded by pre-listening tasks, preliminary discussion questions or questions about the theme which students may be able to answer from their own previous knowledge. These tasks help students to approach the recording with more interest than if they merely had to 'Listen to the cassette and answer the questions'.

As the exam may include a variety of question types, the tasks include exercises with true/false questions, exercises with open-ended questions, exercises where the answers have to be shown graphically, exercises where a form or chart has to be completed and exercises with multiple-choice questions.

There is a progression unit by unit:

FROM recordings that are relatively easy to understand, with straightforward questions on the content, or questions for discussion

TO recordings that are more difficult to understand, with more demanding exam-style questions that may catch out the unwary student

It may be helpful to 'set the scene' for students before they hear the recording by explaining where the speakers are and what their relationship is (colleagues, good friends, etc.). Remember that students will be trying to understand disembodied voices coming out of a loudspeaker without the aid of a Transcript, and this is much more difficult than being in the same room as a real person who is speaking to you, and who can adapt what they are saying according to your reactions.

In some of the listening exercises, students may need help with vocabulary. It is a good idea to read through the Transcript in your copy of the Teacher's Book before the lesson, and highlight any vocabulary that you wish to draw your students' attention to.

Most students will need to hear each recording at least twice to extract all the required information. In some classes, where students are weak at listening, you may need to pause the tape frequently and play certain sections again to help them to understand more easily. The Transcripts for some of the longer recordings contain suggested 'places for pausing' indicated with ★★★.

However, it is essential for students to realise that they don't have to be able to understand every single word to answer the questions. Generally, they should concentrate on what the speakers are trying to say and the information they are communicating, NOT the actual words they are using. Occasionally, however, there are questions where students are required to write down the exact words used.

Generally, there is a difference between the recordings in which authentic interviews are used, and the ones based on broadcasts. In the former, where people are talking about their experiences, it is usually easier to absorb the information they give, thanks to the naturally-occurring repetition, emphasis and redundancy that happens in conversations. In the latter, a lot of information is sometimes given in a short time, and students may need to hear the recording more than twice to pick up all the information. This means that although some of the authentic interviews last over ten minutes, they will actually take less time to do in class than some of the shorter passages.

After the listening comprehension task there are often further discussion questions, to encourage students to share their reactions with each other and discuss the implications of what they have heard. In some cases there is a Communication Activity, related to the theme of the listening text.

In some units there is a listening activity which leads in to a discussion, providing students with an opportunity to hear native speakers giving their views on the topic before they take part in their own discussion.

Some Listenings are linked to a Composition which the students have to write, where the information given in the recording provides information or ideas which will stimulate students to put their own ideas in writing.

The Teacher's Book contains a complete Transcript of the recordings and answers.

Here is a list of all the recordings:

1.4 'You've got to be selfish' – Allison Curbishley
2.5 'If something goes wrong …' – Alastair Miller
2.8 Be prepared! – Walking in the mountains
3.4 Who's talking?
3.8 'Not waving but drowning' and 'Bloody men'
4.2 Meanings and translations: The Interpreter
4.7 The English-speaking world
5.8 Describing a process: Margarine manufacture
6.8 The impact of tourism
7.1 Amanda Hooper, store manager
7.5 Enhancing customers' lives – Mitsukoshi
8.4 '. . . that is part of the job' – Jayne Evans
8.8 Hitting the headlines
9.1 Happy days?
9.4 'It's just the most wonderful thing' – Sarah Wilson and Claudine Kouzel
9.8 Reported speech
9.9 Summerhill School
10.2 'Our cousins in the ocean' – Ray Gamble
11.1 Enjoying reading
11.2 'My last novel is the best work I can do' – William Boyd
12.2 The Freedom Ship
13.1 Friends . . . and enemies
14.1 Work and business
14.7 Looking for a job?
15.2 'You're being paid to be a child!' – Simon Russell Beale
16.4 Good health
16.6 Was Freud a fraud?

Writing skills and Composition

The Writing skills sections are designed to develop students' writing skills by focusing on various aspects of writing compositions, and encouraging students to develop their own personal repertoire of styles.

The following points are covered in the Writing skills sections:

Many of the Composition tasks are linked to listening or reading input, where students will already have heard or read related ideas and information and had an opportunity to discuss them. This means that they don't have to approach the composition tasks 'cold', searching for inspiration, nor do they need to spend too long working out their ideas or finding out information before writing. Instead they can concentrate on the main task of actually planning and writing their composition.

These exercises cover all the types of composition and essay required in the Proficiency exam: descriptive, narrative, discursive – as well as shorter, more specific tasks where students are expected to write a report or a letter, based on specific information. The composition tasks are designed to be discussed beforehand and afterwards – not just written in isolation and handed in for the teacher to evaluate.

In the Composition sections there is a progression from unit to unit towards exam-style exercises where students write compositions of exam length and against the clock.

The Teacher's Book contains Model versions of the composition tasks, which you may photocopy, if you wish, for your students to compare with their own.

Make sure you do allow your students time to read each other's written work. This is particularly important if composition writing is to be considered as more than 'just an exercise'. Any piece of writing should be an attempt to communicate ideas to a reader. If students know that their partners, as well as you, are going to read their work, they are more likely to try to make it interesting, informative and entertaining! If you, their teacher, are the only reader, the process of writing seems less realistic. Students can learn a great deal by reading each other's work – and from each other's comments on their own work. A piece of written work should be regarded as a piece of communication, not simply an opportunity to spot the grammatical errors that students make.

You may have your own views on whether or not to award a mark for each composition – if you do, allow scope in your system for students to see an improvement over the months: it's pretty discouraging if you're still getting the same mark even at the end of the course! Instead, you may prefer to write a few appreciative and helpfully critical comments. (See **Mistakes: marking and correction** below.)

In an advanced class, each individual student may to a greater or lesser degree be 'good at writing'. It is essential to regard the Writing skills exercises in *New Progress to Proficiency* as a starting point. Further remedial work may be necessary for students whose writing skills are especially weak. In particular, the feedback you give to students when handing back their written work should take into account each individual student's strengths and weaknesses.

Mistakes: marking and correction

Mistakes in written work

In marking students' written work, it is important to remember how discouraging it is to receive back a paper covered in red marks! It's better for students to locate and correct their own mistakes, rather than have corrections written out for them. This is particularly important when you believe that a student has made careless mistakes or slips of the pen.

In many cases, once mistakes are pointed out to students, they can often correct them themselves. A 'marking scheme' like the following is recommended, but whatever scheme you do use make sure your students are conversant with your system.

✗ = 1 ERROR	'Somewhere in this line there is a mistake of some kind that you should find and correct.'
✗ ✗ = 2 ERRORS	'Somewhere in this line there are two mistakes that you should find and correct.'
An incorrect word or phrase underlined = ERROR	'This particular word or phrase is not correct and you should correct it.'
G = GRAMMAR	'Somewhere in this line there is a grammatical mistake that you should find and correct.'
V = VOCABULARY	'Somewhere in this line there is a vocabulary mistake that you should find and correct.'
Sp = SPELLING	'Somewhere in this line there is a spelling mistake that you should find and correct.'
P = PUNCTUATION	'Somewhere in this line there is a punctuation mistake that you should find and correct.'
WO = WORD ORDER	'Some of the words in this sentence are in the wrong order; please rearrange them.'
ST = STYLE	'The style or register you have used here is not really appropriate to the task – it may be too formal, or too informal.'
? = ??	'I don't quite understand what you mean.'

And equally important, remembering that all learners need encouragement and praise as well as constructive criticism, some more positive or encouraging marks should be included:

✓ = 'Good, you have expressed this idea well!' or 'This is an interesting or amusing point.'

✓✓ = 'Very good, you have expressed this idea very well!' or 'Very interesting or amusing point!'

As the symbols shown here would appear on the side of the page in the margin, make sure your students do leave a wide enough margin for your comments!

Mistakes in oral work

In speech, although work on improving students' accuracy is essential, it is far more important for learners to be able to communicate effectively. It is very difficult to develop confidence if one is afraid of making mistakes. In real life, after all, people have to communicate with each other IN SPITE OF the mistakes they may be making and their less-than-complete command of English.

Students should certainly be corrected when they make serious errors, but it is usually best to point out any mistakes that were made *after* the groups have completed an activity, rather than interrupting the flow of the activity. While students are working together in pairs or groups, and you are going from group to group listening in, you may be able to make the occasional discreet correction without interrupting the flow of the discussion, but normally it is better to make a note of some of the errors you overhear and point them out later.

You may hear your students making mistakes in pronunciation, grammar or style, but rather than mentioning every mistake you have heard, it is more helpful to be selective and to draw attention to specific points that you think your students should concentrate on improving. It may be less confusing to focus on just one type of error at a time by, for example, drawing attention to pronunciation errors after one activity and then to grammatical errors after another. Accuracy is something that takes a long time to develop and it cannot be achieved overnight!

There are no exercises in *New Progress to Proficiency* specifically devoted to pronunciation. This does not imply that phonology is unimportant. Indeed, it requires constant attention, particularly when you are giving students feedback on their performance in spoken activities. At this level, CORRECTION is likely to be the most effective method of dealing with phonology. In the Speaking Paper in the Proficiency exam, pronunciation is one of the aspects that will be assessed.

Speaking: discussion & Communication Activities

Every unit contains a variety of questions for students to consider and then discuss in small groups. These should be regarded as 'discussion opportunities', and if they have a lot to say, these discussions may go on for quite a long time. Conversely, if your students have little to say about some of these questions, they may be omitted. In other words, the amount of time that should be devoted to these is unpredictable and you will need to 'play it by ear' when deciding when to move on to the next section. If a particular topic is especially popular, you may decide to ask students to do some supplementary written work, outlining their own ideas or summarising the discussion they have been involved in. This option is not included in the Student's Book rubrics, and is left to the teacher's discretion. Besides the discussion activities, there are photographs to talk about and Communication Activities, which provide students with plenty of preparation for the Proficiency Speaking Paper. Many of the activities reflect the kinds of tasks expected of candidates in the exam, but there are also some sections specifically devoted to preparing for the Speaking Paper.

The Communication Activities involve an information gap, where each participant is given different information which has to be shared with a partner. In some cases, each student reads a different part of a reading text or has some information to study, which they have to tell their partner(s) about in their own words.

The Communication Activities are 'scrambled' at the back of the Student's Book, so that the students (working in pairs or groups of three) cannot see each other's information. Exchanging information and ideas using this technique tends to be very realistic and motivating for students.

Guide to the Communication Activities

4.2 C	14 + 24 + 31	dictionary extracts
5.8 B	2 + 15	How wine and beer are made
6.2 C	4 + 16	continuation of passage
7.1 D	3 + 10 + 26 + 29	How to handle customers
8.7 D	8 + 17 + 27	News items
12.9 A	6 + 19 + 28	User-friendly design
13.1 B	7 + 20	Just imagine: Edward Hopper paintings
15.4 C	1	*Musée des Beaux Arts* by W.H. Auden
15.6 B	5 + 18	Movie clichés
16.2 A	11 + 21	Exam practice: Conversation with interlocutor
16.2 B	12 + 22	Exam practice: Conversation about pictures
16.2 C	13 + 23	Exam practice: Long turns and discussion
17.2 C	9 + 25 + 30	More information about three war poets

Verbs and idioms

At the end of eight of the units there are exercises on idioms or verbs and idioms. These sections concern phrasal verbs, idiomatic phrases and also the collocations in which certain common verbs are used. The exercises needn't be done at the end of the unit: they can be fitted in when there is a little spare time during the lesson, or set for homework and checked in class later.

These sections deal with the idioms, collocations and phrasal verbs connected with the following words:

2.9	*keep* and *hold*	10.8	*put* and *set*
4.9	*make* and *do*	12.6	*give* and *take*
6.9	*come* and *go*	15.10	*good* and *bad*
8.12	*bring* and *get*	16.12	*mind, brain* and *word*

In addition, there is work on prepositional verbs and phrasal verbs in 12.4 and 14.4 respectively.

The exercises are not intended to provide comprehensive coverage of phrasal verbs or idioms. Students should make a note of any phrasal verbs or idioms that they come across and look them up in a dictionary, paying particular attention to the examples given there. *The Cambridge International Dictionary of Phrasal Verbs* is recommended for students with a particular interest in this area of vocabulary.

Exam practice

Towards the end of the book, some sections are specially devoted to examination practice, helping students to develop confidence in all the kinds of tasks they will have to cope with in the exam.

Here is a list of the exam practice sections:

10.10	Use of English Part 1	16.11	Use of English Part 5
14.8	Use of English Parts 1 and 2	17.1	Reading Part 2
15.5	Use of English Part 5	17.1	Use of English Part 1
15.7	Writing Part 2	17.6	Listening Part 3
15.8	Reading Part 1	17.7	Listening Part 4
15.9	Use of English Part 4	17.8	Writing Parts 1 and 2
16.2	Speaking	17.9	Speaking
16.4	Listening Part 1	18.1	Reading Part 2
16.5	Use of English Part 2	18.2	Use of English Part 3
16.6	Listening Part 2	18.3	Use of English Part 4
16.8	Writing Part 1	18.4	Reading Part 3
16.9	Reading Part 3	18.5	Use of English Part 5
16.10	Use of English Part 3	18.6	Writing Parts 1 and 2

Exam advice and tips

Some advice boxes are in the margin, like this one.

Students will come across advice boxes like this scattered through the book. These sections contain advice which students may find helpful in the exam as well as tips to help them with their studies. These are offered to students as ideas that 'might work for you' and are not intended to be followed unquestioningly. Students should be encouraged to build on their experience of previous exams they have prepared for, refining techniques that have worked well before and discarding ones that may have restricted their success in the past.

The Proficiency exam

The University of Cambridge Local Examinations Syndicate (UCLES) Certificate of Proficiency in English (CPE) examination is held twice a year: in June and in December.

Paper 1 Reading – *1 hour 30 minutes*

Part 1 Three short texts (total 375–500 words), each with 6 gaps. There is a choice of four possible answers for each gap.

> Candidates have to choose the best .... to fit in each gap in the text.
>
> **A** guess   **B** idea   **C** thing   **D** word ✓

Part 2 Four short texts on the same theme (total 600–900 words) with two multiple-choice comprehension questions per text. Candidates have to choose the best answer.

> How many texts are there in Part 2?
>
> **A** one   **B** two   **C** three   **D** four ✓

Part 3 One long text (800–1100 words) from which seven paragraphs have been removed and placed in jumbled order on the next page. Candidates have to decide from where in the text the paragraphs have been removed. There is one paragraph which doesn't fit anywhere.

Part 4 One long text (700–850 words) with seven multiple-choice comprehension questions.

(Total: 40 questions = 40 marks)

Paper 2 Writing – *2 hours*

In both parts of the Writing Paper candidates have to write 300–350 words. Each part carries equal marks.

Part 1 This part is compulsory. After reading the instructions, candidates read a short text (maybe a short letter, article or advertisement) and then write an article, essay, letter or proposal. The focus is on presenting and developing arguments, expressing and supporting opinions, and evaluating ideas.

Part 2 There are four questions from which candidates choose one. One of the choices includes a question on each of the set texts. The following formats are included here: an article, an essay, a letter, a report or a review. The tasks may involve any of the following functions: describing, evaluating, giving information, making recommendations, narrating, persuading, summarising.

(Examiners' marks scaled to 40 marks)

Paper 3 Use of English – *1 hour 30 minutes*

Part 1 One text with 15 gaps to fill, testing grammar and vocabulary. Candidates have to think of a suitable word to fill each gap. (15 questions, each worth 1 mark)

Part 2 One text with 10 gaps to fill. Each gap corresponds to a word. The 'stems' of the missing words are given beside the text and candidates have to transform them to provide the missing word. (10 questions, each worth 1 mark)

| This part tests candidates' .*knowledge*. of word formation. | **KNOW** |

Part 3 Six groups of three sentences, each with a word missing. Candidates have to decide which single word fits into all three gaps. This tests collocation, phrasal verbs, idioms and meanings. (6 questions, each worth 2 marks)

Part 4 Eight key word transformations. Candidates have to rewrite each sentence using the word so that it has a similar meaning. Candidates mustn't change the word given and have to use between three and eight words only. (8 questions, each worth 2 marks)

> This is an example of a key word transformation sentence.
>
> **kind**
>
> This is an example ......*of the kind of sentence*......... candidates may have to transform.

Part 5 Two short texts with two questions on each, and one summary task. The questions focus on the style and tone of the text, and on vocabulary. For the summary candidates have to select relevant information from both texts and write 50 to 70 words. (4 questions, each worth 2 marks. Summary, worth 14 marks)

(Total: 75 marks, scaled to 40 marks)

Paper 4 Listening – *about 40 minutes*

Each text is heard twice. Candidates have time to read the questions and to check their answers afterwards.

Part 1 Candidates hear four short extracts, with two multiple-choice questions per extract. They have to choose the best of three alternative answers for each question. (8 questions)

Part 2 Candidates hear a monologue or interview. They have to complete gaps in sentences with information from the recording. Each sentence has to be completed with a word or short phrase. One longer extract with nine sentence completion questions. (9 questions)

Part 3 Candidates hear a discussion or interview. There are five multiple-choice questions. They have to choose the best of four alternative answers for each question. (5 questions)

Part 4 Candidates hear a discussion between two people. They have to match each of a list of six opinions or statements to the names of the speakers, according to who said what. If the speakers agreed about something, candidates write both names. (6 questions)

(Total: 28 marks, scaled to 40 marks)

Paper 5 Speaking – *about 20 minutes*

There are two candidates and two examiners. One is the assessor (who listens and assesses but doesn't join in) and the other is the interlocutor (who sets up the task, joins in sometimes, and also assesses). The interlocutor also has to make sure that one candidate doesn't dominate the conversations, so that candidates both have an equal amount of time to show how good they are at speaking English.

Part 1 The interlocutor encourages each candidate in turn to give information about themselves and to express personal opinions. This part involves general interaction and social language. (3 minutes)

Part 2 The candidates are given visual and spoken prompts, which generate a discussion between them. They'll have pictures to talk about (but not actually describe): the interlocutor will tell them what they have to do. This part involves comparing, decision making, evaluating, giving opinions and speculating. The interlocutor only joins in if one candidate is speaking too much. (4 minutes)

Part 3 Each candidate in turn is given a written question to respond to. They have to talk for two minutes on the theme of the question, uninterrupted. After each candidate has spoken, the interlocutor asks them questions to encourage a discussion on the same topic. This part involves organising a larger unit of discourse, developing topics, and expressing and justifying opinions. (12 minutes)

(Assessors' marks scaled to 40 marks)

For more information, visit the UCLES website: www.cambridge-efl.org.uk
For general information about CPE:
www.cambridge-efl.org.uk/exam/general/bg_cpe.cfm
To order the CPE Handbook: www.cambridge-efl.org.uk/support/publicit.htm
To download sample exam papers:
www.cambridge-efl.org.uk/support/dloads/ums.cfm

If you haven't taught a Proficiency class before, you should also study the current CPE Handbook an CPE Examination Regulations, which also includes the list of books for **Prescribed reading** (see page 11). These are obtainable free of charge from your Local Examinations Secretary, or directly from UCLES, 1 Hills Road, Cambridge, CB1 2EU.

Acknowledgements

The author and publishers are grateful to the authors, publishers and others who have given permission for the use of copyright material identified in the text. It has not been possible to identify the sources of all the material used and in such cases the publishers would welcome information from copyright owners.

8.8 extract based on *'Bad Time for Talking'* by Paul Sussman *'Death by Spaghetti'*, ©1993–6 The Big Issue/©1996 Paul Sussman; **11.4** extract from the *UCLES CPE Revised Specifications* ©UCLES, 2000; **17.4** *'Everyone Sang'* by Siegfried Sassoon ©Copyright Siegfried Sassoon by kind permission of George Sassoon. *'Everyone Sang'* copyright 1920 by E.P. Dutton, copyright renewed 1948 by Siegfried Sassoon, from *Collected Poems Of Siegfried Sassoon* by Siegfried Sassoon. Used by permission of Viking Penguin, a division of Penguin Putman, Inc.

For permission to reproduce photographs:

p.148 Edward Hopper, American, 1882–1967, *Nighthawks*, 1942, oil on canvas, 84.1 × 152.4 cm, Friends of American Art Collection, 1942–51 '©The Art Institute of Chicago. All Rights Reserved'; p.163 ©Superstock.

Time to spare?

1

See page 12 of the Introduction for more information on the **Topic vocabulary** sections, and page 20 for information on **Mistakes: marking and correction**.

A Arrange the class into pairs. If you have an odd number of students, there can be a group of three.

These questions form the basis of a warm-up discussion. If you suspect your students may not have too much to say about these questions, you may prefer them to do this in groups of three or four, rather than in pairs.

After a few minutes' discussion, call on selected pairs to report back to the class on the most interesting things they found out from each other.

Encourage questions on vocabulary connected with the topic while the students are taking part in their discussions, and afterwards. (The photos show three genuine sports: bog diving – swimming in snorkels in muddy water, synchronised swimming – an Olympic sport since 1984, and snow kayaking – going down a snowy slope in a kayak.)

B **1** A short discussion in pairs about the hobbies shown in the pictures will help everyone to approach the next section more confidently and with some previous knowledge.

2 This is an exercise in listening for gist. Students who are good at listening may only need to hear it once. To help students with the task, pause the tape after each speaker (at the places marked with ★★★ in the Transcript below) so that everyone has time to make notes before the next speaker begins.

3 After the pairs have compared notes, play the recording again. This time ask everyone to note down the drawbacks and difficulties of each hobby.

4 The discussion could continue in pairs, or this could become a whole-class discussion.

SUGGESTED ANSWERS

Ruth:	**a**	Baking – cakes, tarts, cookies, etc.
	b	Being creative – almost like painting a picture
		Everybody enjoys the end product
		Watching a cake rise in the oven
Bill:	**a**	Scuba diving
	b	Like flying underwater
		Wonderful things to see
Sarah:	**a**	Surfing
	b	Satisfaction of doing what only the boys did
		'hanging ten' – standing with ten toes over the edge of the board
		Cruising the surf
Emma:	**a**	Looking after other people's children
	b	A warm feeling
		The smile she sees when they've had a good time
		Building a relationship
		Watching them grow up
Jonathan:	**a**	Going to the gym
	b	Not a lot – but it does keep him healthy

TRANSCRIPTS   *6 minutes*

INTERVIEWER: Ruth, what do you do in your spare time?

RUTH: I bake, actually. Uh…it's something I've done kind of for years and years. Er…I started off by making apple crumble, that was the first thing I ever made, but…um…I've kind of progressed a bit now and I really like…er…making things like a Bakewell tart, which…you know, a really massive one. And…er…I'll make it and kind of…er…call the family, and…er…the neighbours all call in or whatever, and it goes in about three seconds! Um...there's just something really creative about...about getting all these ingredients together. And...um...it's like sort of almost like painting a picture or something and you have this end product and everybody really enjoys it. And I like mak...making...um...scones and Welsh cakes and...um...and cookies for the children, because they really love those. Er...the...the sh...the only shame about it really is that...um...you put all this sort of hard work into it and they go really really quickly. Er...but it...there's nothing more satisfying than watching a Victoria sponge rise in the oven!

★★★

INTERVIEWER: Bill, what hobbies do you have?

BILL: Actually, er...I am a diver, a scuba diver. And that happened...er . . . Strangely, when I was very young I did diving, when I lived in California, and I had an aqualung then for about a year. And then I went to college and sold it, and then years and years and years went by and I didn't dive, and then I went to holiday in Greece and I was...happened to be on a beach next to a diving school. And I thought, 'This is the best time. If I'm ever going to get my qualifications I will do it.' And I spent the week diving and studying diving and I got my certification, and now I dive whenever I can. I've dived on the Great Barrier Reef, I've dived on the islands off Santa Barbara in California, I've dived all around the Mediterranean. I love it, it's like flying through the water, and you have all those wonderful things to see.

★★★

INTERVIEWER: Sarah, do you have any hobbies?

SARAH: Yes, I do. I love surfing, I'm a typical Aussie [Australian] girl, and...er...when I was growing up my brother, because he was the boy, got the surfboard and I was saying, 'That's not fair! I got a boogie board,' which is the little foam thing, 'And he gets a proper surfboard. This is sexist, this is all wrong.' And I thought, 'No, I'm going to learn to surf.' And the next lesson I learnt is that the boys at high school don't want to let you have their board because they're convinced the girls will ding it up [damage it]. And they spend hours waxing their boards, but the girls aren't allowed to touch them. I thought, 'I'm going to save my money and I'm going to get one of these things and I'm going to be better than them all.' And...er...the next thing I know I...I saved my money and I got my own surfboard, which I said, 'Only girls can use.' So I got there...out there on the surfboard and I was terrible! I was absolutely terrible! I fell off every time I stood up, and it was the hardest thing I had ever done! But I kept at it, and eventually I got really cool, that I can now actually get to the front of the board and I can 'hang ten', which is where you get your ten little toes over the edge of the board. Then I fall off, I'm not that great, but...er...I am getting there. And whenever I go home I make sure I get my wetsuit on, so I don't get sunburnt, and I get out on that board and I just love cruising the surf.

★★★

INTERVIEWER: Emma, do you have any hobbies?

EMMA: It's not really a hobby, but...um...I like to look after children. Um...I think...I was the youngest of six, so I never had anybody younger than me to look after. Um...and so once I got old enough to look after other people's children, I...even if I didn't get paid, I used to always offer to help out. And anything ranging from babies to older children. I've worked at nursery schools. I know a friend who owned...who started a nursery school once and I spent my summer working for her for free. Um...and pretty much whenever anybody I know has a baby, I'm sort of the first one in going, 'I'll look after it! I'll baby-sit!' Um...which is a very bizarre thing but there's something...um... there's something quite warm when you . . . I mean it depends...depends on how big the child is, but even a bigger child when you've got them interested in something, or you've managed to do their homework with them, or...er...had a good day with them and they've really enjoyed themselves, and the smile they sort of give you at the end of the day when you say goodbye or anything is...is...is very exciting. And can be also quite un...un...stressing. I looked after a...two children once, a four-year-old and a...and an eighteen-month-old for about...mm...five months... um...lived with their family. And when I had to go to the airport to say goodbye...um...the four-year-old started absolutely screaming and she wouldn't let go. It was absolutely heart-breaking. So it can be quite upsetting if you really get a bond with a child and then you have to say goodbye. But other...um...that's sort of a rare...you know, normally, don't have to say goodbye, so that's quite nice otherwise to have a relationship that lasts. You can watch them grow up.

★★★

INTERVIEWER: Jonathan, what do you do to fill your spare hours?

JONATHAN: Well, one of the things I try to do regularly is drag myself down to the gym, which I've only been doing for the last three or four years, really at my girlfriend's encouragement. Um...I find it deadly boring but it's good for me. So I try and go. I'm supposed...haha...I'm currently supposed to be going four times a week, which is the biggest joke you've ever heard. If I get down there twice a week it's a real achievement. And I do...what do I do? About twenty minutes on the running machines or the cycling or the rowing or something. And then all these weight-lifting machines. And it's supposed to be more each time and it's supposed to make me big and butch and look gori...look glori...gorgeous, but...um...I must say it's...er...I find it mind-numbingly dull.

INTERVIEWER: And...er...how long do you think you'll continue before you expect to see some serious results?

JONATHAN: Er...wh . . . Can you not see any serious results?

INTERVIEWER: Well, I mean, you know, you're looking fit and . . .

JONATHAN: I don't know it's something you never really complete.

INTERVIEWER: It's an ongoing process.

JONATHAN: I think so, yes. It's good for your overall health, keeps the heart healthy.

INTERVIEWER: And do you have a...a figure that you're aiming to replicate?

JONATHAN: Um...well, the trouble with the gym is that everyone else is more gorgeous than you are. So really anyone else's figure would be fine!

1 👥 Arrange the class into an even number of pairs, or groups of three.

Again, encourage questions on relevant vocabulary. During this kind of activity, students may also use their dictionaries. However, it may be best to ban the use of bilingual dictionaries in this kind of activity, in favour of English–English dictionaries. (There is no clear distinction between a *hobby* and an *interest*, though *hobbies* tend to be activities that are creative or involve collecting things.)

> **SUGGESTED ANSWERS**
>
> | | |
> |---|---|
> | Hobbies: | *painting   playing the violin   making model aircraft* |
> | Interests: | *reading   watching football   computers* |
> | Indoor games: | *draughts   Scrabble   bridge* |
> | Team sports: | *baseball   hockey   basketball* |
> | Individual competitive sports: | *badminton   squash   golf* |
> | Non-competitive sports: | *water-skiing   skiing   sailing* |
> | Outdoor activities: | *walking/hiking   gardening   riding.* |

2 👥→👥 Combine the pairs into groups of four or five. Encourage everyone to make notes of useful vocabulary they find out from the other pair before they begin the discussion.

Point out the function of the question *Why?* in the discussion questions: asking *Why?* encourages the other person to justify their opinions and explain their reasons.

1.2 Comparing and contrasting GRAMMAR REVIEW

See page 11 of the Introduction for more information on the **Grammar review** sections.

 A 👥 This is a discussion task to be done in pairs. The matched sentences in this section illustrate some of the ways in which different structures are used to convey different meanings or to imply something different.

With this kind of exercise, encourage everyone to do the easier ones first, and come back to the trickier ones later. If a pair is having difficulty with a particular question, they should ask another pair for help.

At the end spend a few minutes on a feedback session, discussing any questions that arise. Note that these are **Suggested answers**, which may be open to discussion. Other interpretations may be possible, particularly if a sentence is given an unusual intonation, or if particular words are stressed.

> **SUGGESTED ANSWERS**
>
> 1 Water-skiing is less difficult than sailing. —— Both sports are equally hard.
> Sailing is as difficult as water-skiing. —— Sailing is harder than water-skiing.
>
> 2 Like you, I wish I could play the piano. —— Neither of us can play the piano.
> I wish I could play the piano like you. —— You can play the piano, I can't.
>
> 3 Your essay was most interesting. —— No one's essay was better than yours.
> Your essay was the most interesting. —— It was a very interesting essay.
>
> 4 The cliff was too hard for us to climb. —— We were able to climb it.
> The cliff was very hard for us to climb. —— We were unable to climb it.
>
> 5 She is a much better pianist than her brother. —— They both play quite well.
> Her brother is a much worse pianist than she is. —— Neither of them play well.
>
> 6 She swims as well as she runs. —— She is equally good at both sports.
> She swims as well as runs. —— She takes part in both sports.
>
> 7 Bob isn't as bright as his father. —— Bob is less intelligent than his father.
> Bob's father is bright, but Bob isn't that bright. —— His father is more intelligent than Bob.
> Bob isn't all that bright, like his father. —— Neither of them is particularly intelligent.

B   Many alternatives are possible.

> **SUGGESTED ANSWERS**
>
> 2   are far more strenuous than
>   require a great deal more skill than
> 3   takes a lot longer than
>   requires considerably more time and effort than
> 4   I'd rather go out for the evening
>   I prefer to go to a club with my friends rather
> 5   as fast as anyone else in her class
>   so fast that she invariably laps me
> 6   is a great deal less energetic than
>   is not at all energetic – unlike
> 7   the least interesting hobby
>   is one of the most expensive hobbies

C

> **CORRECTIONS IN BOLD**
>
> 1   It isn't true to say that London is **as large as** Tokyo/**larger than** Tokyo.
> 2   He's no expert on cars: to him a Mercedes and a BMW are **alike/the same**.
> 3   Her talk was most enjoyable and much more informative **than** we expected.
> 4   Don't you think that the **more difficult something is, the less enjoyable it is**?
> 5   **Fewer** people watched the last Olympics on TV than watched the soccer World Cup.
> 6   Who is the **least** popular political leader **in** the world?
> 7   My country is quite **different from/to** Britain.
> 8   She's such a **fast** runner **that** I can't keep up with her.

D   👥 This is an open-ended speaking activity, but if you prefer, all or part of it could be done as written work and/or set for homework.

At the end, allow time for feedback and questions. Maybe point out that this section has only covered certain aspects of Comparing and contrasting, and that students who still feel uncertain may need to refer to a grammar reference book, such as *Advanced Grammar in Use* or *Practical English Usage*.

Extra activity   As a follow-up, this **Comparison game** may be appropriate:

👥 Working in pairs (or teams), students note down some pairs of things that are similar in some ways and different in others.

👥→👥 Then the other pair (or team) has to explain the differences and similarities. Like this:

What's the difference between a chair and a table?
— They both have four legs, but a chair is for sitting on and a table is for sitting at. A table is usually higher and heavier than a chair.

Examples of other suitable pairs:

police officer · judge   tree · bush   fountain pen · pencil   knife · scissors
computer · typewriter   tea · coffee   violin · piano

1.3   **Learning a musical instrument**   **READING**

See page 9 of the Introduction for more information on the **Reading** sections.

If time is limited, and you would like everyone to prepare the reading passage before the next lesson, discuss section **E** first, moving on to **A** later.

A   👥👥 This warm-up discussion gives everyone time to prepare themselves by considering the theme of the passage before starting to read it.

The instruments shown are: piano   violin   maraca   harmonica   drums   French horn accordion   guitar   saxophone – though there may be some discussion about some of these.

B **1** Generally, with a reading passage of this length, students should be asked to read it through at home before the lesson, and perhaps also answer the comprehension questions and vocabulary questions. If this is done there is more time in class for everyone to DISCUSS the answers and for any follow-up work. (Question 5 is in 8 parts.)

Students should answer the questions in note form – full sentences are not required in this case.

2 👤→👤 Comparing answers encourages everyone to share their ideas and cooperate, rather than feeling they are being tested by the questions.

> **SUGGESTED ANSWERS**
> 1 piano   violin   maraca   harmonica   drums   brass (e.g. French horn)   guitar   electric accordion   saxophone
> 2 a sense of accomplishment   a creative outlet   an absorbing pastime
> 3 low back pain   shoulder strain   bleeding   unsightly swelling
> 4 You get depressed because you can't play it well enough – or you get depressed because you spend so long practising that there's no time for anything else
> 5 **a** piano: expensive, difficult to play, not sexy
>   **b** violin: notoriously difficult
>   **c** maraca: mildly entertaining but only to babies
>   **d** harmonica: you quickly get bored with it
>   **e** drums: very difficult to learn, but people think it's easy and fun
>   **f** guitar: too popular, most people will play it better than you
>   **g** electric accordion: anti-social
>   **h** saxophone: playing it in public may destroy your credibility
> 6 Brass instruments (e.g. French horn) – if you like making rude noises. And the saxophone – if you really do learn to play well.
> 7 The drummer attacked someone who came up to him, and there was a fight.

C This exercise draws attention to some of the vocabulary in the passage. Make sure everyone has time to highlight the words, as only this can focus on the use of the words in context. Just matching the words and phrases is not enough.

> **ANSWERS**
> grudge = *dislike*
> syndrome = *condition*
> maudlin = *self-pitying*
> endeavour = *effort*
> be misled = *get the wrong idea*
> physical co-ordination = *control of one's movements*
> nuance = *subtle variation*
> unruffled equanimity = *perfect calmness*
> charisma = *charm and magnetism*

D **1** The passage is full of humour, but not everyone may appreciate it. Nevertheless, it's important to be aware when a writer is not being serious, even if you don't share his/her sense of humour.

2 👥 You might prefer to arrange the students into larger groups to compare their reactions.

E **1** 👥 This little task just encourages everyone to read the tips through carefully.

> **SUGGESTED ANSWERS**
> 1 attention   2 meaning   3 writing   4 spelling   5 space/room   6 example

2 👥 You might prefer to arrange the students into larger groups to compare their reactions. Allow enough time for discussion and comparing ideas. Everyone has their own methods of learning vocabulary items, and students may be able to learn from each other some useful techniques which might work for them. There is, of course, no 'best way' of memorising vocabulary, and you and your students may disagree with some of the ideas in this section.

An extra point:
As time passes, if the highlighting ink fades, students can re-highlight the words they still want to be reminded of.

1.4 'You've got to be selfish'

LISTENING

A **1** Allow time for everyone to discuss any previous knowledge they have of the subject and to make some suppositions about the answers to the questions. Reading the questions through in advance and anticipating some of the answers will make it easier for them to follow the interview when they listen to it. It's also something the students will have to do in the exam, before they listen to the recordings.

2 Play the recording, pausing it at the places marked ★★★ in the Transcript to give everyone time to think, write and relax for a moment.

This is an exercise in listening for specific information. The questions don't cover every point made. It may be necessary to reassure students that even if they can't catch every word the speaker says (and she does speak rather fast some of the time), it won't stop them getting the answers to the questions.

ANSWERS

1 400 metres and 400 metre hurdles
2 $\frac{1}{2}$ to $1\frac{1}{2}$ hours (but with warm-up and warm-down: from 9 to lunchtime)
3 She has to conserve her energy (for the training session the next day)
4 excited (not frightened, not nervous)
5 relieved (and proud to be there)
6 winning ✓ flying training ✓ travelling ✓ socialising ✓
  standing on the winners' podium ✓ being applauded by the crowd
7 being injured (and not able to run)
8 confident, selfish (but never forget you're part of a team)

B This is an open-ended vocabulary exercise – the answers are a matter of opinion.

TRANSCRIPT *6 minutes 20 seconds*

NARRATOR: You'll hear an interview with Allison Curbishley. She's a professional athlete, and she's been a member of the British team at two Olympic Games.

ALLISON: My name is Allison Curbishley and I do 400 metres and 400 metre hurdles.

INTERVIEWER: What about, I mean…um…on a typical day, if you can have a typical day, what would…how would it start?

ALLISON: Um…well, if you take sort of at the moment, what we are now sort of coming into the season in…in… May…um…which is pretty much a hectic time for us, training is pretty intense. Um…I'd get up, I'd train round about…I go down to the track about nine. Um…we, you know, Coach would always, say, be at the track for about nine for ten, which would mean nine o'clock we'd be there to warm up, takes about an hour…um…and would be ready to run and start the session at ten, this is if we're on the track. And the session would usually take sort of somewhere in between half an hour and an hour and a half, depending on what we were doing. Um…and then it would be a…a gradual warm-down, stretch, have lunch straight away…um…replace all the…the lost energy, and then basically the rest of the day is pretty much…um . . . We might have another session to do later on in the evening, which would be a light circuit, or, you know, er…if we've done a heavy session in the morning we might just rest. Um…and it's a very easy-going lazy day for the rest of the day. Uh…we try, I mean, I try and keep myself busy. I read, I, you know, I love listening to music, and obviously TV and what . . . It just depends where we are, and you just keep yourself busy. And, you know, the group that I train with is very social, so we often spend time together, we love sitting around in coffee shops in Bath, you know, that's what we do, that's what we spend our time doing most of the time.

INTERVIEWER: Work hard, play hard?

ALLISON: Well, this is it, you know, we've basically got to spend the afternoon…uh…doing very little, because you've got to conserve the energy for the training session the next day.
★★★

INTERVIEWER: Do you think there's still that attitude in Britain or overall that…um…it's the winning that counts, it's not the playing?

ALLISON: Yes, yeah, definitely, and I think…but I also think that, you know, as an athlete, you're in the wrong because, you know, I don't think any athlete would settle for silver if they had the chance of gold. Um…I think in general, yeah, the journalists do kind of take…they can't seem to see any good out of coming back with a silver medal from a…an Olympic Games. They don't see that as success they see it as a, you know,…pretty much a failure.

INTERVIEWER: From where I'm sitting even to be at the Olympic Games would be…er . . .

ALLISON: Oh, yeah, isn't it!

INTERVIEWER: . . . I mean, what was it like at…?

ALLISON: Oh, I mean, it was…er…it was very good for me because I'd gone as a…as a…um…relay member, and so there wasn't the pressure on me as an individual athlete, and I was sort of eighteen at the time. And…and, you know you just I think just the feeling of stepping out onto the track on the sort of second last day just to compete in the . . . I'd been there the whole…I'd gone three weeks preparation with all the team, just to do that one relay leg at sort of pretty much the end of the Games. And it was quite…um…it…it was awesome, it really was. I never got frightened, which I thought I would, I thought I'd get very very nervous, but I just got excited. And you walk onto the track, and walk down the home straight and, you know, there's like a crowd of 80,000 people. Um…and the noise is…is just…just phenomenal, oh, it really was. And it's just, there's very little to describe…there are very few words that can describe the feeling that you, you know, you feel, just running down the back straight, and…um…you know, passing the baton on to the next . . . But I mean there was big relief…sigh of relief once you've passed the baton. But, you know, it was…and…and…it was just great for me to sort of experience that as a first major, then to go on to Athens sort of last year, and sort of pick up from there, you know, it was . . .

★★★

INTERVIEWER: What do you really love about your job?

ALLISON: Um…I love the feeling of a successful training session, I love the feeling of a successful race…um…and of achievement full stop. I mean, there's…um…last year, which was my most successful year…um…in which I gained two championship golds: um…one at European level and one at World Student level. And there's nothing like sort of standing on a podium watching the Union Jack going up, knowing it's for you, and listening to the National Anthem. You know, no matter whether you are patriotic or not you…you get a buzz from that. Um…you know, I…I love the travelling…um…although we don't see a lot of the countries that we go to we see pretty much, you know, a 400-metre track looks the same wherever you are. Um…but it's nice having the opportunity to sort of taste different cultures and…and sort of . . . And, you know, I've been to so many more countries that I…at the age of sort of 21, 22 than I could ever have dreamed of. You know, and I…um…I just…I…I…I like coming back and relaying it to my parents, who haven't been able to travel with me, and have just been there on the other end of the phone, you know. And it's nice to be able to make them part of it. Um…I love the socialising, the social aspect of it. I've made some…you know, all my best friends are part of my sport now, although going through University and…and friends at home that I've grown up with, it's nice to have sort of the…the friends that bring you back down to reality, and . . .

INTERVIEWER: What do you not enjoy so much?

ALLISON: Um…obviously when you're injured, it can get you down, you know, you…you're not doing what you want to be doing. You…you know, somebody is actually stopping you from doing something that you love. Um…and there's the worry of now it's full time for me, you know…um…what do I do if I did get injured, you know?

INTERVIEWER: I'm just thinking of what att…human att…attributes would make a good sports person.

ALLISON: You've got to be confident, you've got to be selfish, you've got to be . . . Uh…but team work is just so important, and although, yeah, athletics is individual…um…you're constantly out for your team. You're constantly looking out for . . . A training group's a team, you know. Um… wherever you are, you know, you…you are part of a team, nobody ever neglects the fact that you are individual, and leaves you on your own, you know, there's always somebody there, just you yourself and your coach that…that partnership is a team.

   Um…I keep saying selfish, you have to be very selfish. A lot of people don't like to admit that but you do. You are very very selfish and purely because, you know, if you're not getting sleep, the food that you need, the…you know, your training's going to fall to bits, you know, if you need to be in a perfect condition to turn up at the track for training, to turn up at the track to race.

1.5 Adjective + noun collocations

VOCABULARY DEVELOPMENT

See page 8 of the Introduction for more information on the **Vocabulary development** sections.

Draw everyone's attention to the advice on using dictionaries in the left-hand margin of the page.

A This short section is an introduction to the subject of collocations. Discuss any variations that the pairs come up with: are they also suitable collocations?

> **SUGGESTED ANSWERS**
> a **deep** lake   a **close/dear/great** friend   a **nearby/handy** shop
> a **noisy** room overlooking the street   a **quiet/peaceful** room overlooking the garden
> a **loud/deafening** noise   a **deep** silence   a **valuable** piece of advice
> an **expensive/exorbitant** meal   a **profound/learned/difficult** book

B **1** 👥 The aim of this section, and of section **C**, is to encourage everyone to be creative, to pool ideas, and to use a dictionary for inspiration whenever necessary. As you can see from the **Suggested answers** there are very many possible combinations, but the students would only need to come up with one or two for each noun.

SUGGESTED ANSWERS

exciting/great/thrilling **adventure**
attractive/beautiful/delightful/ferocious **animal**
gifted/talented **athlete**
absorbing/entertaining/exciting/great/serious **book**
attractive/delightful/funny/gifted/hard-working/naughty/talented **boy**
exciting/great/serious/thrilling **game**
great/serious/slight **interest**
delicious/delightful/great **meal**
beautiful/great **painting**
gifted/great/talented **photographer**
attractive/beautiful/delightful **place**
great/serious/slight **problem**
beautiful/catchy/delightful/great **song**
absorbing/exciting/funny/thrilling **story**
delightful/gifted/hard-working/serious/talented **student**
entertaining/serious **talk**
attractive/beautiful/breathtaking/delightful/pretty **view**
attractive/beautiful/delightful/funny/gifted/hard-working/pretty/talented **woman**

---

2 👥 Begin by asking the class to suggest yet more adjectives that could describe an animal and a book: e.g. a *tame/rare/fierce* animal and a/an *expensive/wonderful/dull* book.

In case of difficulty, suggest that the pairs try to think of opposites of some of the adjectives that collocated in **B1**.

SUGGESTED ANSWERS

amazing/incredible **adventure**
tame/rare/fierce **animal**
competitive/dedicated/trained/successful **athlete**
thrilling/boring/silly/old-fashioned/famous **book**
clever/silly/little **boy**
stupid/terrible **game**
enormous/huge **interest**
tasty/disgusting/dreadful **meal**
impressive/overrated/famous **painting**
famous/hopeless/brilliant **photographer**
fantastic/awful/dreary **place**
awkward/terrible/little **problem**
wonderful/nice/annoying **song**
incredible/improbable/long/short **story**
hard-up/lazy/diligent **student**
witty/stimulating/long-winded **talk**
fantastic/unforgettable/extensive/panoramic **view**
sensible/smart/intelligent/well-respected/successful **woman**

C There are many possible collocations in this exercise. It may be necessary to remind everyone to skip the ones they can't do easily, and come back to them later on – or ask another pair for their idea.

Ask the class to suggest other collocations for Question 1 before they do the rest of the exercise: e.g. a light **wind**   a pale **complexion**   a bright **light**   a colourless **city**

1.6 Tennis stars

READING

If possible, ask everyone to read the article before the lesson, to save time in class.

A **1** 👥 Doing this in pairs means that the students have to discuss the possible answers. We're dealing here with collocations again. There may be some disagreement about the best word or phrase – in some cases others are possible, but only one is 'the best'. (This exercise is similar to Part 1 of the Reading Paper.)

ANSWERS

1 B	2 C	3 A	4 B	5 D	6 B	7 C	8 A	9 B	10 D

2 👥 Again there may be some disagreement about the best word or phrase – in some cases others are possible, but only one is 'the best'. Allow time for everyone to justify their choices to each other. Highlighting or underlining quotations from the text helps when answering multiple-choice questions – and makes it easier to justify your answers to a partner. (This exercise is similar to Part 4 of the Reading Paper.)

Draw everyone's attention to the tip at the bottom of the page.

ANSWERS

1 C	2 C	3 A	4 D	5 B	6 C

B This can also be done in pairs. Even if it isn't, students should form pairs after doing the exercise and compare answers. (This exercise is similar to Part 3 of the Reading Paper – but in the exam there are more paragraphs missing, and one of the alternatives doesn't fit anywhere.)

ANSWERS

1 B	2 A	3 E	4 D	5 C

C 👥👥 This follow-up discussion raises many issues connected with this topic. The questions can be discussed in any order – but let everyone know how long they have for this.

At the end of the discussion, ask each group to report back to the class on the most interesting or controversial points which were made.

1.7 **Using participles**   ADVANCED GRAMMAR

See page 11 of the Introduction for more information on the **Advanced grammar** sections.

A   The contrasted sentences in this section illustrate some of the ways in which different structures are used to convey different meanings or a different emphasis.

SUGGESTED ANSWERS

1 Standing at the top of the hill, I could see my friends in the distance.
   – I was at the top of the hill and my friends were in the distance.
   I could see my friends in the distance standing at the top of the hill.
   – My friends were at the top of a distant hill, and I could see them there.

2 While preparing the meal, he listened to the radio.
   – The radio was an accompaniment to the main task of cooking.
   While listening to the radio, he prepared the meal.
   – Cooking was an accompaniment to his main interest: listening to the radio.

3 Finding the window broken, we realised someone had broken into the flat.
   – We saw the broken window and this made us realise that there had been a break-in.
   We realised someone had broken into the flat, finding the window broken.
   **– When the burglar found the broken window, he used it to make his entry. (This
     suggests that the window was already broken before he arrived and that made it
     easier for him to get in.)**

4 Before preparing the meal he consulted a recipe book.
   – He couldn't start cooking until he had found the recipe.
   After consulting a recipe book he prepared the meal.
   **– He looked for the recipe and then started cooking.
     (There is only a slight difference in emphasis between these two.)**

5 Crawling across the road, I saw a large green snake.
   **– (This sounds strange, and without a context could be understood to mean that the
     speaker was crawling across the road and came across a snake.)**
   I saw a large green snake crawling across the road.
   – The snake was crawling across the road when I saw it.

B It's probably best if everyone studies the examples in silence in class – or if possible, before the class, as homework.

C

ANSWERS

1 arranged   2 arriving   3 reaching   4 shaken   5 finished
6 required   7 completing   8 lifting

D

SUGGESTED ANSWERS

1 Not having a car, I usually travel by bus.
   Not having a car means that I usually travel by bus.
2 Chanting loudly, the demonstrators marched into the square.
3 Finding their way blocked by the police, they turned back.
4 Having heard that he collects butterflies, I asked him to tell me about it.
5 Finding none of her friends (waiting) outside the cinema, she went home.
6 Not knowing much about art, I can't comment on your painting.
7 Drunk too quickly, coffee can give you hiccups.
8 Feeling a bit under the weather, I went to bed early.

E

CORRECTIONS

1 Looking out of my window, I saw a crowd of people in the street.
2 We thought he looked ridiculous wearing bright yellow trousers.
3 His father treats him like an adult because he is rather tall for his age.
4 Having been given such a warm welcome he felt very pleased.
5 I saw three old men sitting together playing cards.
6 If washed in hot water this garment will shrink.

F **1** If you think this exercise might be too hard for your students as it stands, write up the 'missing verbs' on the board to help them:

face   go   hear   look   open   open   realise   shout   sit   think   wonder

SUGGESTED ANSWERS
1 opening   2 Thinking   3 realising/realizing   4 shouting/yelling/trying
5 Going/Walking   6 opening   7 looking/peering   8 Faced
9 wondering   10 sitting   11 hearing

2 Allow time for everyone to compare their continuations with each other.

1.8 'Golden rules'   WRITING SKILLS AND COMPOSITION

See page 19 of the Introduction for more information on the **Writing skills and Composition** sections. In future units, the sections on Writing skills and Composition are separate.

A **1** 👥 This is a discussion activity – these steps are not definitive, which is why the title is in inverted commas.

Some people say: *The only golden rule is that there are no golden rules* – but students should be encouraged to develop their own 'rules' and then be reminded to stick to them in future written work.

SUGGESTED SEQUENCE (open to discussion)
 1 **Look carefully at the instructions.**
 2 Discuss with someone else what you're going to write.
 3 Do any necessary research.
 4 **Think about what you're going to write.**
 5 **Jot down all the points you might make.**
 6 **Analyse your notes, deciding which points to emphasise and which to omit.**
 7 Use a dictionary to look up suitable words and expressions, and write them down.
 8 **Write a plan, rearranging the points in the order you intend to make them.**
 9 Write a first draft, perhaps in pencil.
10 Proof-read the first draft: eliminate errors in grammar, spelling and punctuation.
11 Show your first draft to someone else and get feedback from them.
12 Take a break.
13 **Look again at the instructions.**
14 Edit your first draft, noting any changes you want to make.
15 **Write your final version.**
16 **Proof-read your final version, eliminating any mistakes you spot.**
17 Have a rest.
18 Get feedback from other students on your final version (they are 'your readers').

2 Only the steps in **bold print** above might be feasible under exam conditions.

Draw everyone's attention to the advice box at the foot of the page before they start **B**.

B **1** ✒ Treat this and the next few compositions as a 'diagnosis' of each student's composition-writing. What are the major points each should concentrate on improving?

Make sure everyone understands your system of marking written work and the meaning of the symbols you use. At this level there's no point in your correcting every little mistake that students have made – it's better for them to locate and correct their own mistakes, with some guidance in the form of symbols in the margin – see **Mistakes: marking and correction** on page 15.

2 👥 Encourage everyone to read each other's work. The kind of feedback they give each other might include comments on and questions about:

- the content in general
- the style and how easy the piece was for them to read
- information or ideas that seemed particularly interesting or amusing
- information which was missing from the piece
- sentences which were less easy to follow

As this is probably the first composition that the class will have done for you, it's a good idea to **PHOTOCOPY** their work and keep it on file. Then, later in the course, you can compare their compositions with this earlier one and see how your students' written work has improved. The students themselves may find it reassuring to look at these early compositions again later, to see that they have made progress. Otherwise, at this level, it's often difficult for them to realise that their English actually is improving.

This model version can be photocopied and shown to the students if you think it would be helpful – but not if it might be disheartening at this early stage in their course.

1.8 Model version

You don't have to be rich to play squash: if you play at a public sports centre, rather than a private club, you soon discover that it's a game that everybody plays. Taking part in a league, you can meet people from all walks of life, and it's quite normal for men and women to play each other. However, unlike tennis, you can't play doubles, so it's not such a sociable game.

The reason why squash is such fun is that it's so easy to play. Beginners can have an enjoyable game right away and can get involved in the tactics and strategy of the game. With tennis, where it's a major achievement for a beginner even to hit the ball back over the net, you have to be quite proficient before you can do this. With squash, returning the ball is easy and you don't have to waste time retrieving all the balls that have been hit out. You only need one ball to play with and you can play at any time of the day or night and in all weathers. You don't even need to be strong to play: a soft, cunning service can be just as effective as a powerful, fast one. It does help to be fit and agile, though, because even though a game only lasts half an hour or so, during that time you're constantly using your energy and you don't have time for a rest while your opponent is off the court hunting for lost balls.

Perhaps it's because squash is such an energetic game that it's thought to be dangerous. Admittedly there is a risk of minor injuries like strains and sprains, or getting hit by your opponent's racket, because both players have to cover the whole court and sometimes get in each other's way. But if you're careful, and don't overdo it, it's no more dangerous than any other sport.

Leo Jones *New Progress to Proficiency*

Extra activity

This activity is particularly suitable for students who are keenly interested in the topic of this unit.

1 Choose one of your favourite sports or games (this could be a non-athletic game like chess, backgammon or Scrabble) – preferably one that the rest of the class don't know too much about.
2 Make notes on how it is played, using a dictionary and consulting a book of rules if necessary. Do this as homework.
3 Give a short talk to the class about your chosen sport or game, and answer their questions about it.

Finally . . .

Recommend to everyone that they should spend half an hour reading through the whole of this unit at home before moving on to Unit 2. This will help them to memorise the vocabulary and other points covered in the unit.

Flipping through earlier units in the book regularly, recalling previous lessons, is a simple yet surprisingly effective revision technique.

A sense of adventure

2

Background   The article is a review of one of Dervla Murphy's books. Most of her books concern travels she has made to exotic places, often in the company of her daughter Rachel. Among these are:

Full Tilt: Ireland to India with a Bicycle (1965)
On a Shoestring to Coorg: Experience of South India (1976)
Where the Indus is Young: A Winter in Baltistan (1977)
A Place Apart (1978) – a study of life in Northern Ireland
Eight Feet in the Andes: Travels on a Donkey from Ecuador to Cuzco (1985)
Muddling through in Madagascar (1985)
In Cameroon with Egbert (1989)

More recent journeys, not involving Rachel or any animals, have been in Africa on a bike:

The Ukimi Road (1993)
South From the Limpopo (1997)

A **1** 👥👥 This isn't just a warm-up discussion: it gives everyone the opportunity to consider some of the vocabulary related to the theme of this unit.

Among the qualities listed, the ones which are probably *least* important are:

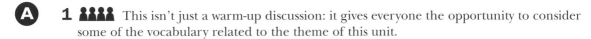

arrogance   charisma   compassion   dignity   humility   intelligence   knowledge   modesty

– but clearly this is a matter of opinion.

2 Ask the class to suggest adjectives to describe the mother and daughter.

B **ANSWERS**

1 Juana (4 legs), Dervla and Rachel (2 legs each)
2 In the Murphys' eyes: Juana, the mule
   In the reviewer's eyes: 9-year-old Rachel
3 Three months (¶ 5) – one week less than the *conquistadores* (¶ 12)
4 In a tent (¶ 11)

C **ANSWERS**

¶ 1   saunter = stroll
¶ 3   madcap schemes = crazy plans
¶ 4   frolic = amusing game   heartening = encouraging
¶ 6   overenthusiastically = without restraint   day one = the beginning
¶ 7   fretting = fussing and worrying   coveted = envied and wanted
¶ 9   homespun = unsophisticated
¶ 12   sticky moments = dangerous incidents
¶ 13   trusting soul = someone who believes other people are honest

D **ANSWERS**

1 She is sceptical and is sarcastic about their unadventurousness and greed
2 Five (when they went to South India)
3 Rachel was going to go to school
4 She lost patience
   She joined in with religious festivals too enthusiastically
   She wore unsuitable shoes which gave her blisters

5 It's pejorative – her views are considered to be unoriginal or naive by the reviewer
6 Potatoes, tinned sardines, noodles
   Juana ate alfalfa (a kind of grass)
7 She is stolen (and then presumably recovered because '*all ends happily*')
8 Worst: Juana is nearly killed falling over a cliff
   Best: the views and the kindnesses

E The ironic/sarcastic turns of phrase are <u>underlined</u> here. This may be open to discussion, and students needn't be expected to spot all of these:

<u>ONCE upon a time</u>, with travel writing, the rewards won related to the risks taken. No longer. Travel writers travel <u>by public transport</u>; often they just <u>hop in the car</u>. They travel round <u>British seaside resorts</u>; they <u>saunter</u> up <u>low</u> mountains <u>in the Lake District</u>. <u>Greatly daring</u>, they visit islands off the coast. There is no point in travelling hopefully; far better to arrive as quickly as possible and <u>collect your multinational publisher's advance.</u>

F After the discussion in groups, ask for a short report on the most interesting points that came up.

2.2 Articles and determiners

GRAMMAR REVIEW

Not all students have difficulties with articles in English. If these exercises present no problems for your students, this section can be omitted, or set for homework and discussed later in class.

A

ANSWERS

1 What was the mule like? ———— What is a mule like?
   What are mules like? ———— Could you describe their mule?

2 Do you like tea now? ———— Is the tea all right for you now?
   Do you like the tea now? ———— Have you overcome your dislike of tea?

3 Some of the difficulties were foreseen. ———— We expected a certain amount of difficulty.
   Some difficulty was foreseen. ———— We didn't expect any difficulty.
   No difficulty was foreseen. ———— Every difficulty was foreseen.
   The difficulty was foreseen. ———— We expected a particular difficulty.
   All the difficulties were foreseen. ———— Not all of the difficulties were foreseen.

4 Would you like some coffee now? ————Would you like a coffee now?
   Would you like your coffee now? ————Would you like the coffee now?

B Allow everyone a little time to study the examples in **B1** before they do the exercise in **2**.

SUGGESTED ANSWERS

COUNTABLE	UNCOUNTABLE
a piece of a hint a tip	advice
a round of	applause
an action	behaviour
an article of a coat a shirt	clothing
a game a joke	fun
a fact a piece of	information
a chuckle a laugh	laughter
an item of a suitcase	luggage
a song a tune a piece of	music
an item of a piece of an article a report	news
an improvement	progress
a drop of a fall of	rain

a piece of an analysis	....	research
a fall of a flake of	....	snow
a dish of a piece of	....	spaghetti
a class a lesson	....	teaching
a means of a car a train	....	transport
a journey a trip	....	travel
an asset a fortune a possession	....	wealth

C Again allow time for everyone to study the examples in **C1** before doing the exercise in **2**.

ANSWERS

1 knowledge   2 experience/adventure   3 success/experience   4 wood
5 adventure/experience/thought   6 pleasure   7 imagination   8 failure
9 butter/soup/cheese   10 cheese   11 love/knowledge   12 coffee

D After everyone has completed the exercise and compared their answers with paragraphs 7 and 11, they'll discover they have equally correct variations. Discuss these with the class.

SUGGESTED ANSWERS

The Murphys clearly see not Rachel but Juana, **their/the**[1] beautiful glossy mule, as **the**[2] heroine of **the/their**[3] story. She cost £130 and they fuss over her like **a**[4] film star, fretting about **her**[5] diet, **her**[6] looks, **her**[7] mood. Juana is coveted by all; as **the/their**[8] journey proceeds it is shadowed by **their**[9] parting from her. There is **a/the**[10] terrible moment when she falls over **a**[11] precipice to **Ø**[12] certain death but for **a**[13] divinely placed single eucalyptus tree in **her**[14] path.

She worries that **Ø**[15] religion is so little comfort to **the/a**[16] Peruvian Indian, that **the/their**[17] babies chew **Ø**[18] wads of **Ø**[19] coca, that **the**[20] boys Rachel plays **Ø**[21] football with on **Ø/the**[22] sloping pitches have no future, that she cannot repay **their/the**[23] kindnesses: **the/an**[24] ancient shepherdess who shared **her**[25] picnic lunch of **Ø**[26] cold potato stew on **a**[27] cabbage leaf, **the/an**[28] old man who set **his**[29] dog to guard **their**[30] tent at night.

E **CORRECTIONS**

1 Politics **doesn't** interest him, except when **an** election takes place.
2 **Grapefruit** is my favourite **fruit**, but I don't like **bananas**.
3 The news **is** depressing today: two **aircraft** have crashed.
4 There **is a** crossroads at **the** top of **the** hill.
5 Mathematics **was the** most difficult subject at ~~the~~ school for me.
6 **The** Hague is **the** capital of **the** Netherlands, but Amsterdam is **the** largest city.
7 ~~The~~ Women are usually safer drivers than ~~the~~ men.
8 We missed **the** bus and had to walk all the way home – it was quite **an** adventure!

F **ANSWERS**

1 Travel broadens **the** mind.
2 Love makes **the** world go round.
3 **The** greatest adventure of all is life itself.
4 **A** friend in need is **a** friend indeed.
5 Absences make **the** heart grow fonder.
6 While **the** cat's away, **the** mice will play.
7 Out of sight out of mind – as **the** saying goes.
8 **A** woman without **a** man is like **a** fish without **a** bicycle. (*feminist slogan*)

Extra information

Here are some nouns that tend to cause confusion, and which may lead students into making errors.

Nouns that are singular but look plural:

athletics   economics   maths   measles   mumps   news   physics   rabies
the Netherlands   the Philippines   the United States   the West Indies

Nouns that have irregular or unusual plurals:

analysis · analyses   crisis · crises   criterion · criteria   fungus · fungi   goose · geese
hypothesis · hypotheses   ox · oxen   phenomenon · phenomena

Nouns with identical singular and plural forms:

aircraft   crossroads   data   deer   fish   grapefruit   rendezvous   salmon   series
sheep   species   trout

Nouns that are always plural:

binoculars   clothes   glasses/spectacles   handcuffs   headphones/earphones   headquarters
jeans   knickers   pants   pliers   police   premises   pyjamas   scales   scissors   shorts
sunglasses   tights   trousers   tweezers

2.3   **Words easily confused**   VOCABULARY DEVELOPMENT

A useful source of words that particular nationalities tend to find confusing in English can be found in *Learner English* edited by Michael Swan and Bernard Smith (CUP, 1987). This book also covers grammatical and phonological difficulties that particular nationalities have in English.

Here, by way of example, are a few words that are 'false friends' for Greek speakers or which they sometimes mix up – some of these are covered in the exercises in this section:

agenda · notebook   agnostic · strange, foreign   air · wind   annoy · bother   cabaret · bar
ephemera · newspaper   fortune · storm   house · home   idiotic · private   pneumatic · witty
remember · remind   room · space   sympathise · like   trapeze · table, bank   woman · wife

(A)   👥 Consult a dictionary if you are in doubt about any of the meanings. (There isn't room to go into all the differences here.)

(B)   **1** 👥 | SUGGESTED ANSWERS
The words that do fit are given here, though some of the others might also fit if used humorously or imaginatively.

2 argument   fight   quarrel   row
3 sensitive   difficult   touchy   emotional   moody
4 attended
5 annoying   bothering   disturbing   harassing   pestering
6 notebook   exercise book   diary
7 absent-minded   forgetful
8 benefits   advantages   rewards
9 exclusive   private
10 eventual   possible   imminent
11 course   training
12 further   farther

2 Here, as in other multiple-choice vocabulary exercises in this book, the distractors (i.e. the wrong answers) contain useful vocabulary which can be used in different contexts. In the exam students can ignore the distractors, but in *New Progress to Proficiency* they're there as a source of extra vocabulary.

The following **Extra activity** focuses on the useful vocabulary among the distractors:

Extra activity

3 Write your own 'fill the gaps exercise' where the some of words that **DIDN'T** fit in **B CAN** be used.

For example:

1. *They have a savage dog, which neither of them can . . . . . . properly.*

   control ✓   check   restrain ✓   examine

2. *We had a long . . . . . . about the meaning of life.*

   discussion ✓   argument ✓   debate ✓   quarrel   row

Provided that you use the same sentence numbers, there's no need to write out the words in italics. Start with number 3.

4 Exchange exercises with another pair.

2.4 **Brazilian Adventure**   **READING**

Most students find writing summaries one of the hardest parts of the Proficiency exam, but with adequate preparation it can become much less formidable. The work in this section, and similar sections in later units, helps everyone to prepare progressively for the summary-writing they will have to do in the exam.

Background

Peter Fleming (1907–1971) was the brother of Ian Fleming, creator of James Bond. He is best remembered for his entertaining travel writing.

Brazilian Adventure (1933) describes his experiences of an expedition to Brazil, which he joined after seeing this advertisement in *The Times*:

> **EXPLORING** and sporting expedition, under experienced guidance, leaving England June, to explore rivers Central Brazil, if possible ascertain fate Colonel Fawcett; abundance game, big and small; exceptional fishing; ROOM TWO MORE GUNS; highest references expected and given. – Write Box X, *The Times* E.C.4.

(Colonel Fawcett disappeared on an expedition to find Eldorado and was never heard of again.)

His other books include *One's Company: A Journey in China* (1934) and *News from Tartary* (1936).

A

> **ANSWERS**
> 1 Four people were directly involved in the expedition:
>   the leader (Bob), the Organizer, Major Pingle, Captain John Holman
>   And peripherally: Major Pingle's German partner
> 2 Bob, the leader – the Organizer
> 3 Not very
> 4 Yes, but that wasn't his real name

B

 In Part 5 of the Use of English Paper, the passages are shorter and there are fewer questions to answer.

> **SUGGESTED ANSWERS**
> 2 Not a lot: at any rate, he had only shot one jaguar
> 3 To go by lorry instead of train **OR** To go by train instead of road
> 4 He was worried
> 5 A man who has had many adventurous experiences – or so he claimed
> 6 Major Pingle
> 7 At his headquarters in Sao Paulo, Brazil
> 8 By telegram
> 9 None
> 10 Buying provisions, employing guides and making all the necessary arrangements
> 11 An entertaining fiasco, but probably not a disaster

C

D 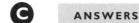 These are questions for discussion, but to settle any arguments students might like to know that the book was published in 1933.

The tone of the passage might be described as ironical, deadpan, humorous or amusing.

E ✎ This should be set as homework. The model summary may be photocopied.

2.4 Model summary

Although the Organizer was charming and had a beard, his vagueness didn't inspire confidence. He couldn't even commit himself on how they would get from Rio to Sao Paulo. He had given the responsibility for making the arrangements to someone called Major Pingle in Brazil, but it was unclear what arrangements he was making – if any – because only one message from Pingle had been received, and the Organizer had lost it.

Leo Jones   *New Progress to Proficiency*

This document may be photocopied.
© Cambridge University Press, 2002

Extra activity

1 👥 Work in pairs. Prepare a role-play of a radio or TV interview with the writer, the Organizer or Major Pingle.

2 👥 → 👥 Join another pair and role play your interview while the others act as the 'audience'.

2.5 **'If something goes wrong . . .'**   LISTENING

A 👥 These pre-questions, for discussion in pairs, will help everyone to approach the listening tasks more confidently.

B 🔊 **SUGGESTED ANSWERS**

1 a) physical exertion – he likes to be fit – mountaineering is a very good cardio-vascular exercise
   b) views (no reason given, but presumably because they are spectacular)
   c) danger – the thrill of being at the end of a rope and having to 'do it right'
   d) company – he has made good friends with fellow-climbers
2 rock-climbing: acute terror   mountaineering: worry, chronic anxiety
3 Alastair himself was unconscious – his partner had to save him
4 Because there was no evasive action they could take
5 Because there was a cable-car station at the top, where they knew they could shelter

TRANSCRIPT   *4 minutes 10 seconds*

NARRATOR: Listen to an interview with Alastair Miller. The interview is in two parts. Part One
PRESENTER: Alastair Miller was a member of a recent British Combined Services expedition to Everest. We talked to him about climbing mountains and asked what he enjoys about mountaineering.
ALASTAIR: I enjoy the sh...the sheer physical exertion because I enjoy being fit anyway and I do a lot of sport and running and that sort of thing and I like just to be physically fit, and I find mountaineering is a nice way of doing that and probably that's one of the best ways because you're not actually running and pounding your knees and Achilles tendons and things. But if you're walking hard at altitude and uphill then that's probably as good a cardio-vascular exercise as anything. So I enjoy that aspect of it.
   I enjoy the...the views, er...I enjoy the...the danger to a certain extent. I mean, I wouldn't go somewhere if I thought that I was going to kill myself, although I recognise that there is a risk of it. But I enjoy the...the thrill of being out on a...on the end of a rope knowing that if I don't do it right, then I am going to fall. Um...but hopefully that I'm going to get held and I'm not going to do a lot of damage, I...I wouldn't like to go climbing solo in a situation where if I fell I was going to kill myself. I enjoy the...the company, because I think you...you make tremendous friends on these expeditions and I've got friends that I've climbed with who are amongst my...my best friends ever really and I've climbed with them on... numerous other times now.

PRESENTER: As he admits, climbing mountains can be dangerous. Has he ever been frightened?
ALASTAIR: Oh yes, I'm sure I have. Er…it's difficult to define specific instances but again I think there's a distinction between rock-climbing and…and mountaineering where…and the…the mode of being frightened is…is slightly different. In…in rock-climbing it's much more acute, if something goes wrong, you know you're going to fall off. And in fact the worst…my worst accident was…I didn't really have time to be frightened in, because it happened all so quickly, and that was…we were climbing…we were rock-climbing in…in Yosemite Valley in California, and the thing that I was tied onto on the cliff just pulled out and I fell the whole rope-length between myself and my partner. And as I fell past him I remember shouting, 'Stop me!' and I do have a vague recollection of falling but then I obviously hit something on the way down and was unconscious at the end of the rope, and so it was probably a lot more frightening for him than it…it was for me. So that's the sort of acute terror that you get from rock-climbing.

In mountaineering I think it's more the worry that you're going to get lost, the weather's going to come in, er…you're going to get hit by an avalanche, so there's the sort of more a chronic anxiety level there and I'm aware of that all the time. The weather…it never seems to be absolutely perfect conditions wherever you are, whether it's Himalayas or Alps, you're always aware there's that little wisp of cloud on the horizon which in a couple of hours could build up into a major storm.

And the other frightening experience was climbing a route called the Frendeau spur on the Aiguille du Midi in the French Alps, we came to the top of that in a…in an enormous thunderstorm and as we were climbing the final snow-slopes there was lightning literally striking the snow behind us, and setting off mini-avalanches and that was very frightening. But you just had to be philosophical because there was nothing you could do to avoid this lightning and if it hit you, well, then that was it. The only comfort about that was that it's a mountain that has a…has a cable-car station at the top, so although we were climbing up towards the top of the mountain, we were actually climbing towards safety and were able to scurry into the…into the cable-car station and…and shelter from the storm overnight and…er…get the first cable-car down the next day and have a beer to celebrate still being alive!

C

ANSWERS

1 pyramid   36   2 or 4   supplies and equipment
2 North   (local) porters   the members of the expedition
3 Camp 2   fixed   safe
4 wash   change their clothes   teeth
5 cramped   comfortable   safe

D This follow-up discussion could be a whole-class activity if you prefer.

TRANSCRIPT   *3 minutes*

NARRATOR: Part Two
PRESENTER: What is it like taking part in an expedition to climb Everest?
ALASTAIR: A lot of it is boring, a lot of it's hard work, er…a little bit of it is frightening as we've discussed, and some of it is fantastically exciting and exhilarating and that's the bit that you remember and that makes up for everything else.

Then the major problem on any expedition, and certainly a large expedition climbed in the sort of style that we did, is…is the logistics of it. And to get all…it…as I'm sure people will know, it's what's called a 'pyramid effect': you've got 36 people at the bottom and you want to get two or four maybe at the top, so you slowly have to build up stores higher and higher up the mountain…er…to…to…in order to place your last four people on the summit. So you…there's an awful lot of carrying of stores and things. Now, on…on this particular side of Everest there are not a lot of local porters around, as there are on the south side, so on the south side you probably engage two hundred local porters who will carry your equipment up through the Khumbu Ice Fall into the area where you're going to be climbing from. On the north side you don't have that facility and you have to engage yaks. And so we had about 80 yaks loaded with kit, and they had to be looked after. The yaks would only go just a little bit above Camp One and from there on it was just expedition members doing all the carrying.

So that was how it worked. So you'd maybe do a week of carrying between One and Two, go down for a rest, and then come back up and find you'd be carrying between Camps Three and Four, or maybe eventually with luck, you'd actually get to be one of the lead teams and you'd be pushing the route out and of course that was when it became exciting and exhilarating to be places where nobody else had been. It was always exciting to…to…to be somewhere where you'd never been before, and I remember the first time I went up above Camp Two, I…it was absolutely brilliant: we were on fixed ropes which other people had put in so we were entirely safe, but for the first time we had crampons on and we were actually properly climbing rather than just walking.

A lot of it's uncomfortable, certainly above base camp, the facilities there . . . Camp One you might have, if you were feeling very brave, had a wash, but certainly above there you wouldn't do anything for a week or ten days, you would just not change your clothes, you'd only clean your teeth, but everything else was just in the same clothes crawling in and out of your tent and sleeping bag. Above Camp Two, which was at 20,000 feet [6,000 m] on the…on the very steep bit of the climb at Camps Three and Four we'd had to dig out ourselves and they were quite cramped and of course they…although they're comfortable and they're safe because if an avalanche falls across the top of a snow hole it might bury you in, you might have to dig yourself out, but it's less serious than being swept away if you're in a tent.

2.6 **Keeping the reader's interest**

A

1 The composition in the Student's Book is about 250 words long and seems to run out of steam after the first paragraph.

> **SUGGESTED ANSWERS**
>
> The more effective features are in **bold print**, the less effective ones are <u>underlined</u>. However, this sort of thing is debatable because different readers are interested in different things.
>
> It had been a long, tiring journey to S_____ . The ferry, which should have taken at most five hours, had had engine trouble and didn't arrive till 2 a.m. As the harbour itself was several miles from the main town – the only place where accommodation was available – and much too far to walk even by daylight, we **hoped against hope** that the local bus service would still be running. **Sure enough** one tiny, ancient blue bus was waiting on the quayside but **imagine our dismay** when we saw that **about 98** other passengers were also disembarking with the same destination. We **fought** our way onto the bus and waited for the driver to appear. A man **staggered** out of the bar nearby and **groped** his way into the driving seat – **presumably** he'd been drinking since early evening when the ship was supposed to arrive.
>
> We were <u>very frightened</u>. Most of the passengers hadn't seen the driver come out of the bar. The bus went <u>very slowly</u> up the steep road. On one side the cliffs **dropped vertically down to the sea hundreds of metres below**. We arrived in the town <u>at 3 a.m</u>, but there was no accommodation. We found a taxi to take us to the other side of the island. We slept on the beach.
>
> As it began to get light and the sun rose over the sea, **waking us from our dreams**, we realised that it had all really happened and that we were **lucky to be alive**.

2 Here is an improved version of the second half of the composition, making a total of about 350 words. This document may be photocopied for your students to see.

> **2.6 Improved version**
>
> We were absolutely petrified and we knew that most of the other passengers hadn't spotted the driver coming out of the bar and were blissfully unaware of what might be in store. It was a nightmare journey: the bus was so full that it could hardly get up the steep, narrow hill that led from the port to the main town. On one side of the road we could see the cliffs dropping vertically down to the sea hundreds of metres below us, and we were afraid that at any moment we would all go crashing down to our deaths.
>
> But we survived. We arrived in one piece, and although the whole journey seemed to have taken days, by the time we arrived in the town it was still only 3 o'clock. To our dismay, though, there was no accommodation to be had for love or money. Fortunately, we found a taxi which took us to the other side of the island where there was a beach we could sleep on under the stars.
>
> The next morning, as it began to get light and the sun rose over the sea, waking us from our dreams, we realised that it had all really happened and that we really were lucky to be alive.

Leo Jones *New Progress to Proficiency*

B

1 This is an open-ended task. The **Suggested answers** are intended just to give an idea of what might be produced.

> **SUGGESTED ANSWERS**
>
> 1 There was nothing I could do but **sit there and wait for my friends to return.**
> 2 It was only after **unlocking the door** that I **realised I didn't know how to disarm the burglar alarm.**
> 3 My big mistake was to **throw everything into the dustbin without checking first.**
> 4 All I could do was **sit there watching the rain fall.**
> 5 You can imagine how I felt when **I found out what a big mistake I'd made.**

6 It all started when **my friends said I could borrow their house**.
7 To my utter amazement **nobody had noticed what I'd done**.
8 To our surprise **a total stranger was sitting in the bath**.
9 Slowly opening the door, I **shone my torch into the cellar**.
10 After a while **we heard some strange noises coming from the refrigerator**.
11 Without thinking I **slammed the car door, trapping my fingers**.
12 I held my breath as **the dog sniffed me up and down**.

2 🖋 To save time in class, this can be done as homework.

3 Knowing that someone else is going to read the story helps to make the task more stimulating.

2.7 Position of adverbs   ADVANCED GRAMMAR

As will become clear from this section, it's impossible to lay down hard-and-fast rules about adverb position.

Make sure, however, that everyone is aware of the difference of emphasis achieved by placing adverbs in less usual positions, particularly at the very beginning or very end of a clause. Often, this is done using a comma (rather like a pause in speech) – or after a dash at the end of a sentence – as in these examples:

Adverb position usually causes students problems.
Usually, adverb position causes students problems.
Adverb position causes students problems – usually!

A

SUGGESTED ANSWERS

1 Tricia only wants to help. = **She's trying to be helpful, not interfere**
Only Peter wants to help. = **Nobody else wants to help, only Peter**
2 Pam doesn't really feel well. = **She's slightly unwell**
Anne doesn't feel really well. = **She's not totally well**
Jack really doesn't feel well. = **I assure you that he's not well**
3 Tony and Jane still aren't married. = **Contrary to our expectations they haven't got married yet**
Olivia and Paul aren't still married, are they? = **I know they used to be married, but I don't think/didn't think they are/were any more**
Still, Sue and Bob aren't married. = **Nevertheless, they aren't married**
4 I don't particularly want to see Lisa. = **I've no special desire to see her**
I particularly don't want to see Tim. = **He's the person I really don't want to see**
5 I enjoy eating normally. = **I like normal kinds of food, not unusual ones**
Normally, I enjoy eating. = **I usually like eating, but in this case maybe not**
I normally enjoy eating. = **I usually like eating**
I enjoy eating – normally! = **I usually like eating, but in this case I don't**
6 Carefully, I lifted the lid. – *dramatic and emphatic*
I carefully lifted the lid. – *not particularly dramatic*
I lifted the lid carefully. – *not particularly dramatic*
7 Paul just doesn't like flying . . . = **He simply hates it**
Olivia doesn't just like flying . . . = **She also likes lots of other things**

B Notice that, in formal style, *hardly ever, never, rarely* and *seldom* can be placed, for emphasis, at the beginning of a sentence, but that the word order changes:

Never have I been so insulted in my life.
Seldom have there been so many people at a concert before.

(This point is covered in **3.5 Using inversion for emphasis**.)

SUGGESTED ANSWERS

1 a We have **nearly/practically/virtually** finished our work.
  b I **utterly** disagree with what you said.
  c It is **hardly ever/rarely/seldom** as cold as this usually.

2 a I don't **altogether/entirely** agree with her.
  b Your work has **greatly** improved.
  c He isn't **exactly/altogether** brilliant.
  d I enjoyed the show **enormously/greatly**.

3 a The Olympic Games are held **once every four years**.
  b I don't have the information **at the moment**, so I'll call you back **in the evening/within the hour**.
  c **Most of the time** I agree with what she says, but **from time to time/once in a while** we don't see eye to eye.
  d Although she had washed her hair **the previous day/before breakfast**, she washed it again **in the evening**.

4 a I can't give you my answer **at once/immediately**, but I'll let you know **presently/eventually/later/shortly/soon**.
  b Let me know **later/afterwards** what you thought of the film.
  c It will **soon/presently** be time to go home, so you'll have to finish the work **afterwards/later**.

5 a She was behaving very **foolishly/oddly/strangely**.
  b He held up the prize **carefully/proudly** and thanked everyone **sincerely/warmly/thoughtfully**.
  c She took his hand **gently/lovingly/reassuringly** and looked **lovingly/apprehensively/gloomily** into his eyes.
  d I raised my hand **automatically/instinctively** to protect my face.

6 a **Luckily**, I found my wallet in the car.
  b **Strangely enough/Unfortunately**, she didn't get the job.
  c **Hopefully**, I'll have finished the work soon.
  d **Funnily enough/Amazingly**, they're getting married.

C More variations are possible.

CORRECTED SENTENCES

1 I have **seldom** seen him so furious and I was **absolutely** shocked by his reaction.
2 He loses his temper **from time to time** but **most of the time** he is in a good mood.
  or **From time to time** he loses his temper but he is in a good mood **most of the time**.
3 All enquiries will be handled **discreetly** and you may write to us **in confidence**.
4 'Don't worry,' she said **quietly**, taking my hand and squeezing it reassuringly.
5 She told them **many times** to take care but they **repeatedly** ignored her advice.
6 The door **suddenly** burst open and we all looked up **in surprise**.
  or The door burst open **suddenly** . . .
7 I do my homework **every day** and it **usually** takes me an hour.
8 He doesn't **just** like ice cream, he loves it so much that he eats it **every day**.

D **SUGGESTED ANSWERS**

1 After a while they replied to my letter.
2 I'm afraid that's a mistake I make again and again.
3 I often eat out in the evenings.
4 I've practically finished writing this report.
5 They reluctantly helped me. / They helped me reluctantly.
6 I particularly don't want to go for a walk.   (I don't particularly want to . . . *is less emphatic*)
7 Each branch of the company operates independently.
8 Presumably he will be feeling apprehensive.
9 You should always pay attention to your spelling.
10 She looked at me anxiously.

In this section the information and ideas given in the recording act as a basis for the composition.

A **1** Looking at the task before listening to the recording helps everyone to apply their previous knowledge and common sense to the task. Some of the answers could be very lightly pencilled in.

2

ANSWERS

PRECAUTIONS

DO	DON'T
1 four	
2 careful	trained
3 deteriorate/get worse	weather forecasts (especially in the newspaper)
4 time	darkness
5 speed/pace slowest	behind
6 stop walking	
7 somewhere to shelter	walk on/go on walking precipice
better/improved visibility	

EQUIPMENT

1 plan   route
2 compass   landmarks   how to use it   your nose   sense of direction
3 warm   waterproof
4 proper walking boots   sandals   trainers
5 rations   chocolate   raisins   sandwiches   (*and something to drink!*)
6 torch/flashlight
7 survival bag   survival blanket

And . . .

let someone know where you're going
what time you expect to be back
report your safe arrival

TRANSCRIPT   *5 minutes 50 seconds*

PRESENTER: OK, so…um…it's…um…it's a lovely sunny day and you feel like going for a walk maybe up into the mountains. And off you go, hoping for a good trip. So far so good but according to Denis Rosser, you could be asking for trouble. Now what's all this about, Denis?

DENIS: Well, yes of course, most of the time, the majority of the time you'll have a marvellous day, you'll get back safely, maybe you're feeling a bit stiff the next day, but there'd be no problem. But…er…you should bear in mind that there are risks…er…in going walking in the mountains because they can be very dangerous places. First of all, you should never ever head off into the mountains by yourself. That's very important. It's best to have at least four people actually in your party, and then if anything goes wrong, like someone breaks a leg, or sprains an ankle or something, one can stay with the injured person and two others can go off to get help. Er…so you should always be careful and not do anything you're not trained to do and take all the necessary precautions as well.

PRESENTER: What sort of precautions?

DENIS: Well, it's a good idea to expect weather conditions to deteriorate. You…you really mustn't rely on the accuracy of weather forecasts. But…er…but you should especially not…er…rely on ones in the paper, which are often at least twelve hours old before you…you read them. And mountains also have what we call their own micro-climate, which means that they have their own weather systems the…which can often differ considerably from…er…weather in the surrounding valleys or low-lying areas. I…in the mountains, the weather can change very very quickly as well, um…you can suddenly get thunderstorms developing and clouds come down quite suddenly.

So…um…*cough…* Excuse me. When you…when you set out, you should also allow yourself plenty of time, er…because you don't want to let darkness catch up with you while you're still out. It's…er…it's better to arrive in the valley low down when it's, you know, three thirty, four o'clock in the afternoon rather than having to scramble down…down some path at the last minute when darkness is coming down. Another important thing is…er…not to leave anyone in your group behind. I mean, this might sound a bit silly but…um…the pace of the party really should…should…should be the same as the slowest member of the group and not the quickest.

And if the…the visibility does worsen, if fog comes down or if you run into low-lying clouds or something, and you don't know where you are exactly, it's advisable to stop walking and find somewhere to shelter, and sit and wait for it to get better. Otherwise you might walk straight over a precipice or something, which wouldn't be too clever!

PRESENTER: Oh dear! But I suppose if you've got a map and a compass and things then, I mean, it's less likely to happen, isn't it?

DENIS: Er...well, yes I suppose so, but y...you must pr...you must plan your route first before you go really. I always mark my proposed route on the map with a...a yellow highlighter, which is a...a good tip, and you...you...then you know exactly where you are on the map all the time. And...er...and you must keep looking at your map, so...er...so you know while you're walking.

And you're quite right: you should...should be carrying a compass with you...um...it really is the only way of knowing which way you're going if you can't see the sun and...er...there aren't any landmarks or anything. And make sure you know how to use it properly. It's a...it's amazing how many people wouldn't like to admit to the fact that they can't use a compass. And the important thing is: don't just follow your nose and rely on your sense of direction because often that will mislead you.

PRESENTER: And what should you wear, I mean, what sort of clothes should you wear and do you need...do you need other equipment at all?

DENIS: Well, you...you ought to take a rucksack with you really. Er...and even if it's hot and sunny when you set out, you've got to be prepared for...for wet and colder conditions to develop. So...um...er...you need waterproof clothing with you and...er...you'll also need warm clothing. Um...and of course proper footwear: it's not...not...there's no point in wearing sandals or trainers or something like that, you've got to have proper walking boots. If it's very hot then it's OK to wear shorts, but do take some trousers with you in your rucksack...um...and not jeans, because...er...they don't keep out the cold and...er...they'll make you feel even colder if they get wet, and in fact you'd be better off not hav...you know, having bare legs than jeans, jeans are really not...not good at all.

Also in your rucksack you'll need some...er...rations, emergency rations for...er...if you get stuck: chocolates, raisins, sandwiches, something to drink, things like that. And...er...a small torch is good...um...if...er...if you do get caught in the dark. Er...and you should also pack a survival blanket or a survival bag...er... they're very lightwake...um...weight and...er...they take up...er...very little room. They're indispensible.

PRESENTER: Oh really? I mean, what...what exactly are they?

DENIS: Well...um...a survival bag is a large plastic bag which you can climb into to protect you from the cold and wet, and...um...the survival blanket is a...a large plastic sheet that reflects the heat back to you. Um...either...either...either of them will save your life if you...if you have to spend the night in the open. Er...and...er...they're very good...good...er...things to take with you.

PRESENTER: It doesn't exactly sound like a barrel of laughs, this trip, does it?

DENIS: No...it...actually I shouldn't...er...I shouldn't panic people. The thing is if you take the precautions and you've got all this equipment and you know what you're doing, you're better prepared and therefore...er...you can walk all day long feeling confident and...and you'll enjoy yourself more. And one...one more thing that's vital: before you set out, let someone know where you're going and what time you expect to be back...er...and in that way...um... When you do get back as well, you know, you...you must report your safe arrival to them, otherwise they'll be worried and they might send out a search party...er...when it's not necessary. But...er...er...if you do get into difficulties and people know, then there will be a rescue party there if you need it.

PRESENTER: Yes, you're right. Well, Denis, thank you very very much. I mean, I'm sure you're absolutely right, it's better to be safe than sorry – or maybe possibly to stay at home? Haha. Thank you very much, Denis.

DENIS: Haha. Thanks a lot.

3 👥 Two pieces of advice the speaker didn't mention:
Take plenty to drink – very important in hot weather
Take a mobile phone – a lifesaver if you get into difficulties

After this discussion the pairs should explain their ideas to the rest of the class – form larger groups ready for step **B**.

B 👥👥 Perhaps begin by brainstorming safety rules for one of the activities with the whole class before they try two more on their own.

C 🖊 The information given in the listening exercise, together with the discussions in **B**, now provides a basis for the composition which students are going to have to do. Insist that everyone makes notes (preferably in pencil) before they put pen to paper.

2.8 Model version

Dear Hilary

I must tell you about my exciting holiday in the Alps. I went with a group of people from the university sailing club and we were staying on Lake Thun. In spite of being there for sailing we thought we couldn't miss the chance of a ride on a mountain railway or a walk in the mountains and the spectacular views you get from high up. None of us is a fitness freak, but I suppose we're quite fit — except for Tim who's really overweight.

We set off a bit late but when we got to the top of the cable car it was clear and bright and only 3 pm. None of us had walking boots as we had come equipped to sail but we had pretty sturdy trainers. We didn't have a map either and anyway the footpaths are well signposted. We planned to walk for about two hours on a circular route and then get the last cable car down at 6 pm. That was supposed to allow us plenty of time to dawdle and deal with blisters!

Well, after about half an hour Tim really began to drag. He found the path too steep and was quite breathless. In the end, Jen said she'd stay with him and would meet us back at the cable car. That left me and Phoebe and Pete. We set off at a good pace and reached the point where we thought we'd turn back at about 4.30. But then a mist descended and we were quite nervous of missing our turning or slipping as it had become rather wet. However we carried on. Phoebe did slip and she twisted her ankle so badly she couldn't walk anymore. Unfortunately we didn't have a first aid kit. Phoebe persuaded Pete and me to go on and get help at the cable car. We didn't like leaving her but it seemed the only thing to do. Well, we just about made it to the cable car before it was due to leave and told them about Phoebe. The staff phoned down to the village and they sent a rescue party up to get Phoebe. We met up with Tim and Jen and finally arrived back at our hotel somewhat frazzled but relieved.

Leo Jones *New Progress to Proficiency*

2.9 *keep* and *hold*   VERBS, IDIOMS AND COLLOCATIONS

Units 2, 4, 6, 8, 10, 12, 15 and 16 have a page of exercises on collocations, idioms and phrasal verbs. There's no need actually to do this at the very end of the unit – it could be fitted in earlier if you have some spare time. Alternatively, it could be started off in class and finished for homework – or done for homework and discussed in class.

This section contains a selection of expressions that advanced students might find useful, but it is by no means comprehensive. For more information on phrasal verbs and prepositional verbs, consult the *Cambridge International Dictionary of Phrasal Verbs*, or an English–English dictionary.

This exercise covers collocations and some idiomatic phrases.

ANSWERS

KEEP   a diary   a promise   a straight face   in touch with someone   quiet
       someone company   someone in the dark   your eyes open
       your fingers crossed   your temper   yourself to yourself
HOLD   a meeting   hands with someone   someone responsible   your breath
       your head high

This exercise covers idiomatic phrases and some phrasal verbs.

ANSWERS

1 walk at the same speed as
2 compete with the neighbours in acquiring material possessions
3 maintain the same level of excellence/progress
4 Don't tell anyone – it's a secret
5 be thinking of you and hoping that you have good luck
6 bear a grudge against me for it
7 stand up to logical examination
8 not revealing the whole truth/all the facts
9 delayed
10 Wait   stay at the other end of the line (on the phone) and not ring off

This exercise covers phrasal verbs and some prepositional verbs.

ANSWERS

1 hold out
2 held out
3 keep off
4 keep   down
5 keep out of
6 holding   back
7 keep in with
8 hold   back
9 held out for
10 hold on

Extra activity

This activity, which could be done in pairs or as homework, gives everyone a chance to use some of the expressions in their own writing. A prize might be awarded to the student who uses the most expressions!

🖉 Write the first paragraph of a story, using as many of the verbs and idioms from page 33 as possible. Begin like this:

I didn't realise that I'd be held up for so long but . . .

Finally . . .

Recommend to everyone that they should spend half an hour reading through the whole of this unit at home before moving on to Unit 3. This will help them to memorise the vocabulary and other points covered in the unit.

Flipping through earlier units in the book regularly, recalling previous lessons, is a simple yet surprisingly effective revision technique.

Everyone's different!

3.1 **Getting away from it all**   READING

As the article is quite long it should, ideally, be prepared before the lesson. Any or all of the exercises in **B** and **C** can also be done as homework.

(A) **1** The reasons are obviously a matter of opinion, but some of the reasons why the writer might be envied are:

living in a beautiful landscape   being cut off from phones and work   seeing whales

and some of the reasons why she might be pitied are:

constant interruptions   no entertainments   no shops

2 👥 The discussion could take place before everyone has read the article, if this is more convenient.

(B) **1**

SUGGESTED ANSWERS		
NAMES	WHO THEY WERE	MEANS OF TRANSPORTATION
a (*not stated*)	depressed friend	float plane
b Dave, Diane & kids	her nearest neighbours	small boat
c Lise	lighthouse keeper's wife	Coast Guard helicopter
d Bob	lumberjack	on foot
e three men	Dept of Fisheries scientists	boat

2

SUGGESTED ANSWERS	
WHO THEY WERE	WHY MARGARET WAS RELIEVED
a Frank and his spouse	Frank was recovering from an operation and might have needed looking after
b A mother and her two sons	She couldn't have coped with the simple life and they were TV addicts who would have been bored, and annoying
c Guitar-playing friend	She wanted peace and quiet, not guitar music

3

SUGGESTED ANSWERS

a Local people she never met but who somehow knew she was alone and might need company, and who told Dave and Diane, Bob and the three men from the Department of Fisheries to visit her

b The writer is being ironic: she wants to show that she had been dreading the friend's visit and didn't want her to stay any longer

c There was so much that it's difficult to single out three aspects. But she certainly appreciated: watching the sea lions and whales   getting to know the people she met there   learning about solitude and loneliness

(C)

ANSWERS

foolproof · precarious   unassailable · vulnerable   outraged · unruffled
the bush · civilisation   unsolicited · invited   positively · not in the least
blissfully · unhappily   egged on · discouraged
abhors a vacuum · loves an empty space   came to nothing · did happen
flagged · continued   tentatively · confidently   bustle · calm

(D) 👥👥 If this follow-up discussion is absorbing it could become the basis for some written work, such as a short composition or paragraph. Or a fictional 'letter to a friend describing a stay in a small community', perhaps.

3.2 **Reporting – 1**

This section is far from comprehensive and some students may need more guidance and practice in this area of grammar. The transformation exercise in **C** can be treated as a 'test' of how confident and accurate your students are.

A Ask everyone to write sentences using any words they were unsure of.

> **ANSWERS**
>
> emphasise = stress   complain = grumble   confess = admit   disclose = reveal
> forecast = predict   infer = gather   insinuate = imply   order = tell
> promise = guarantee   reiterate = repeat   remember = recall   suppose = guess
> yell = shout

B **1** By stretching the imagination, alternatives are possible with each structure.

> **SUGGESTED ANSWERS**
>
> **They . . .**
>
> admitted   agreed   discovered   didn't expect   explained   hoped
> imagined   implied   didn't know   learned   mentioned   pretended
> never realised   reckoned   didn't remember   didn't reveal   didn't say
> shouted   suggested   wished   **. . . that we had done it.**
>
> advised   asked   explained   implied   mentioned   reckoned   didn't say
> shouted   suggested   **. . . that we should do it.**
>
> agreed   asked   couldn't decide   didn't expect   hoped   learned
> pretended   promised   refused   didn't remember   threatened   wanted
> wished   **. . . to do it.**
>
> advised   allowed   asked   didn't expect   forbade   persuaded   reminded
> didn't tell   wanted   wished   **. . . us to do it.**
>
> advised   agreed   asked   couldn't decide   discovered   explained
> didn't know   learned   mentioned   didn't remember   didn't reveal
> didn't say   suggested   wondered   **. . . when to do it.**
>
> advised   asked   couldn't decide   explained   implied   didn't know
> mentioned   didn't remember   didn't reveal   didn't say   shouted
> suggested   wondered   **. . . when we should do it.**
>
> asked   couldn't decide   discovered   didn't know   didn't remember
> didn't reveal   didn't say   wondered   **. . . if we had done it.**

2
> **ANSWERS**
>
> The six verbs that don't fit are:
>
> accused   apologised   blamed   dissuaded   forgave   warned
>
> You accuse someone . . .   of doing something wrong
> You apologise . . .   for doing something
> You blame someone . . .   for having done something wrong
> You dissuade someone . . .   from doing something
> You forgive someone . . .   for doing something
> You warn someone . . .   about something
>   *or* not to do something

SUGGESTED ANSWERS

2 He refused to help me and told me that I would have to do it by myself.
3 She advised me not to write it all out in longhand.
4 He blamed me for our missing the bus, accusing me of misreading the timetable.
5 He wondered if I knew when the performance started, not wishing to be late.
6 She suggested that I should telephone him to see if he was free that night.
   She persuaded me to telephone him . . .
7 She warned me not to start giggling during the interview.
8 He persuaded me to type the letter out for him, promising to buy me a drink to thank me.
9 She accused me of borrowing her dictionary.
10 He threatened to call the police if I didn't move my car.
11 She agreed to accompany me.
   I persuaded her to accompany me.
12 He forgave me for my rudeness, knowing that I was upset.
13 She implied that I should have finished writing the report.
14 She apologised for breaking my sunglasses by sitting on them.

This activity focuses on speaking, where we tend to report the gist of conversations, not the exact words.

1 The first part is done alone, but it may be necessary to brainstorm a few ideas with the whole class first.

2 👥 Make sure the questioners note down the answers they receive, rather than rely on their memories.

3 👥 Rearrange the pairs so that everyone has a new person to talk to. They should report their previous conversations. They should not only report the questions they asked and the answers they got back, but also the questions they were asked and the answers they gave.

9.8 Reporting – 2 is on page 103 of the Student's Book.

3.3 Punctuation and paragraphs   WRITING SKILLS

ANSWERS

; semi-colon   : colon   ! exclamation mark   . . . ellipsis/dot dot dot   - hyphen
– dash   " " inverted commas/quotation marks   • bullet (point)
¶ paragraph number   * asterisk   (brackets/parenthesis)   [square brackets]
/ stroke/slash   ' apostrophe   . full stop/period

Some further points

• *Quote . . . Unquote* is sometimes said instead of the cumbersome *Open inverted commas . . . Close inverted commas.*
• In handwriting it's more usual to use double quotes (" ") than single (' ').
• Dashes are more common in informal style than in formal writing – especially to add afterthoughts.
• Semi-colons are uncommon in informal style. Instead we tend to use a comma, or a full stop and a new sentence.
• Colons are used before explanations, and before a list, and also to introduce a quotation – but not to introduce direct speech, where a comma is more commonly used:
   He said, "Quotation marks are used to quote direct speech. Notice where the quotation marks and other punctuation marks are in relation to each other."
• Bullet points are also quite common these days – especially when listing ideas or points.

B Some variations are possible. Discuss these with the class if necessary.

SUGGESTED ANSWERS

A rabbit goes into a butcher's shop and asks, "Have you got any lettuce?"

The butcher says, "We don't sell lettuce here. You need the greengrocer's across the road."

The next day the rabbit comes into the shop and asks for some lettuce again.

The butcher tells him, "Look, I told you yesterday. We don't sell lettuce. You need the greengrocer."

The rabbit comes in the next day and asks the butcher again, "Have you got any lettuce?"

The butcher goes mad. He says, "Look, I'm sick of this! How many times do I have to tell you I don't sell lettuce! If you come in here again asking for lettuce, I'm going to nail your ears to the floor!"

The next day the rabbit comes in and asks the butcher, "Have you got any nails?"

"Nails? No."

"Right," the rabbit says, "Have you got any lettuce?"

C Several variations are possible.

CORRECTED VERSION

I have known Jan Hall, both professionally and personally, for several years.

Since 1998, when she first joined my department, she has been a reliable, resourceful and conscientious member of my staff with a thoroughly professional attitude to her work. She has cheerfully taken on extra responsibilities and can be relied on to take over when other staff are absent or unavailable.

She particularly enjoys dealing with members of the public, and has a knack of putting people at their ease. She is particularly adept at defusing delicate situations with an appropriate word and a smile.

As her portfolio shows, she is also a very creative and talented person, and her work shows great promise.

During her time with us her attendance has been excellent.

She is an intelligent, thoughtful and imaginative person. I have no hesitation in recommending her for the post.

D **CORRECTED SENTENCES** With comments.

1 **Sitting on the beach, we watched the windsurfers falling into the water.**
   – Participle phrases usually require a comma unless they are the complement of verbs like *watch, see, hear, find, notice,* etc.
2 **The aspect of punctuation which is most tricky is the use of commas.**
   – Commas are not used to separate identifying/defining relative clauses from the noun phrase. But commas ARE required before (and after) non-identifying relative clauses: *My best friend, who lives over the road, is rather shy.*
3 **Could you tell me when to use a semi-colon?**
   – Commas are not used in indirect speech after the reporting verb.
4 **Feeling completely baffled, we tried to solve the problem with which we were faced.**
   – Participle phrases usually require a comma. Commas are not used in identifying/defining relative clauses.
5 **He wouldn't dare say boo to a goose, he's so shy.**
   – A comma precedes a clause giving extra information.
6 **There were, surprisingly, no punctuation mistakes in his work.**
   – Adverbs which 'comment' on the whole sentence require commas. In this example, *Surprisingly, there were no . . .* might be more usual. And *There were surprisingly few punctuation mistakes . . .* would also be possible.

Extra activity

This is an open-ended follow-up activity. It may be necessary to collect all this work and check the punctuation. You may also need to settle any disagreements, remembering that the rules of punctuation in English are relatively FLEXIBLE!

1 ✏️ Write two short paragraphs describing two people that the rest of the class know, but without revealing their names or gender. Use *this person* instead of *he* or *she*.

2 👥👥 Join a group and read each other's descriptions. Can the others guess who is being described, whether the descriptions are accurate – and whether all the punctuation is correct!

3.4 Who's talking?

LISTENING

 🔊 The recording consists of five separate monologues. Pause the tape after each monologue for pairs to discuss their answers before they hear the next one. The answers given below are suggestions only. Plausible variations should be accepted if they can be justified.

SUGGESTED ANSWERS

FIRST SPEAKER

1 angry; at home
2 her husband (or older child?)
3 books or papers? (toys??)
4 the children (from school) or some people (from the station?)
5 indifferent – or defiant?
6 he wants to avoid conflict?

SECOND SPEAKER

7 a female stranger
8 he mistakes her for a well-known TV actress
9 TV stars or characters in TV programmes
10 doesn't want to get involved? aloof?

THIRD SPEAKER

11 a friend
12 the team captain, the organiser
13 sports kit and equipment
14 the sports field
15 the match

FOURTH SPEAKER

16 the manager of a factory or power station
17 reporters
18 an accident, causing pollution or a radioactive leak
19 . . . any accident of this kind ever happening again?

FIFTH SPEAKER

20 a busybody
21 a child (a little girl?)
22 flowers
23 intimidated?
24 . . . to make you cry

TRANSCRIPTS *4 minutes 20 seconds*

FIRST SPEAKER: . . . Oh, look at this! They're all over the place! I'm fed up with it, really I am. If I've told you once, I've told you a thousand times. Why should I have to do it for you? You're the one who put them there and they're yours not mine. Oh yes, I know, you're 'going to do it later'. I wish I had a pound for every time I'd heard that. Look, I've got better things to do, all right? Oh, don't look like that, of course it matters, it's symptomatic of your whole attitude, this. Oh God, it's almost time to pick them up now and I've got nothing done at all this afternoon, thanks to you. Yes, it is your fault and don't pretend it's not and they're just as bad. They think if you can get away with it, so can they. It's just not fair. Look, I'm warning you, if you don't make an effort to change . . .

★★★

SECOND SPEAKER: Excuse me, um…aren't you…er…? Oh…haha…no, course you're not, sorry. Silly of me. It's just that…er…in this light, but…er…now I can see I was wrong. Yeah. And you're quite a bit taller too. Sorry again. Has anyone mentioned the resemblance before, I wonder? No, no, I suppose not. Oh, don't you? Oh, you know, Jane…um…Jane . . . whatsername, can't remember her other name. She was in that sitcom: you know, she played the daughter and Geoffrey Palmer played the father. No, not Geoffrey Palmer the other one, um…the one who's in the coffee commercial. What's he called? Er…oh, you know, the mother was played by that blonde actress, the one who was in that accident recently. Miracle she wasn't killed, apparently. Anyway, she was the mother and this Jane was the daughter, and you look just like her, you know. So…er…can I . . .? Oh.

★★★

THIRD SPEAKER: . . . Well, I said I was no good at it and I told her not to include me but she insisted and said I was 'just being modest'. So I had no choice – well, I could have refused in *theory*, but I didn't want to let everyone down and she said it was too late to find anyone else. So I called off my other arrangements and got all the stuff you're supposed to have and got the bus all the way out there, and there I was all ready to go with all my things and just as it was about to start the heavens opened! Yes! So everyone took shelter and waited for it to stop, but it just got worse and worse. Anyway, after an hour or so of this, the ground was just . . . well, you can imagine, so they called it off and we all went to have a drink, which was fun, seeing everyone again after all that time. Still, I was a bit upset because she told me they wouldn't be needing me next time, and I'd taken the trouble to get all the stuff, not to mention the cost of it all, and now it looks as if I'm never going to have a chance to use it.

★★★

FOURTH SPEAKER: No, no. There's absolutely no truth in the rumour, none whatsoever. I've been assured by my staff, that every possible precaution is routinely taken and nothing like this could possibly have happened. The odds against it happening are literally thousands to one. So well you see it couldn't have happened. However, to set the public's mind to rest, the whole area is to be closed to visitors for a period of ten days while tests are made, I m…thorough scientific tests by our own team of experts. But, as I said, there's absolutely no danger to the public at this moment in time. Nor is there any likelihood in the future of any . . .

★★★

FIFTH SPEAKER: . . . no, no, no, I don't think s…no, you shouldn't. Look, I know there are lots of them but…but it's wrong. Now, what if everybody did it, there'd be none left, would there? And…and…y…you've got so many of them. It must have taken you ages . . . Look, no, stop…stop please, you can't put them back, not when…no, you can't put them back now. Look…it…it's just not possible. Please don't give them to me, I don't want them. Look, the important thing is that you don't do it again. They're…they're here for everybody to enjoy, you see? I mean, how would you like it if someone came into your garden and started taking yours? Quite honestly, you're a very, very . . . Oh, no, please, sorry, look don't get upset. I didn't…didn't mean to . . . Please don't. Look, I'm sorry, I didn't mean . . .

B 1 👥 These are open to discussion.

SUGGESTED ADJECTIVES	
FIRST SPEAKER:	irritable, short-tempered, excitable
SECOND SPEAKER:	diffident, nervous, introverted
THIRD SPEAKER:	reasonable, pleasant
FOURTH SPEAKER:	self-important, assertive – or possibly: shifty, deceitful, corrupt, untrustworthy?
FIFTH SPEAKER:	officious, interfering, bossy

2 👥→👥 Combine the pairs into groups of four. Point out that the descriptions shouldn't just be a list of adjectives. Maybe write up some useful gambits on the board:

It seems to me that . . .
I'd say that . . .
This person sounded as if . . .
I wasn't sure whether this person was . . . or . . .

C 1 ✎ This exercise gives more practice in reporting (see **3.2**). As it's quite time-consuming, it may be best set for homework. If so, play the recording again and ask everyone to make notes to help to remember what each speaker says.

2 👥 Encourage everyone to check that the other person's report uses reported speech correctly.

3.4C Model reports

FIRST SPEAKER:
She accused her husband of not tidying up the flat and reminded him that she didn't have time to do it herself. She suddenly realised that she had to leave to collect the children from school, but that didn't prevent her from warning him that he should mend his ways.

SECOND SPEAKER:
He had started talking to someone he thought was a well-known actress. When he realised he was mistaken he apologised, but he continued trying to make conversation with her. She ignored him and left him still talking.

THIRD SPEAKER:
She said she was upset because she had cancelled other arrangements and bought a lot of equipment in order to take part in a match of some kind. When the match was called off she was left with all the equipment, unused, and no prospect of being able to use it in the future. She had enjoyed meeting her friends again, though.

FOURTH SPEAKER:
He denied that there was any risk to the public, claiming that such an accident couldn't have arisen. However, he announced that the area would be closed to the public for the time being.

FIFTH SPEAKER:
The woman saw a little girl picking flowers and told her to stop. When she told the child not to do it again the girl started crying, which disconcerted the woman.

Leo Jones *New Progress to Proficiency*

3.5 ## Using inversion for emphasis ADVANCED GRAMMAR

 A

1 & **2** 👥 The emphatic phrases are <u>underlined</u>.

ANSWERS

1 <u>At no</u> level of society do women have equal rights with men.
  – *Emphasis on the word 'no' makes the sentence stand out and seem more dramatic.*
Women do not have equal rights with men at any level of society.
  – *Straightforward and unemphatic, unless read aloud like this:*
Women do not have equal rights with men at ANY level of society.

2 It occurred to me later that I had made a big mistake.
  – *Normal straightforward word order with the emphasis, as written, on the last phrase.*
<u>Not until later did</u> it occur to me that I had made a big mistake.
  – *Emphasis on the time and the delayed reaction to what had happened.*

3 <u>At the top of the hill</u> stood a solitary pine tree.
  – *By saving up the pine tree to the end, suspense is created. By changing the word order from what is 'normal', both parts of the sentence are emphasised.*
A solitary pine tree stood at the top of the hill.
  – *This is the 'normal' straightforward word order.*

4 <u>So lonely did</u> he feel that he went round to see his ex-wife for a chat.
  – *Emphasis on the depth of his loneliness.*
He felt so lonely that he went round to see his ex-wife for a chat.
  – *As written, no particular emphasis, but when speaking this sentence we could give the same emphasis as the first sentence by means of stress:*
  He felt *SO LONELY* that he went . . .

5 <u>Little did they know</u> that the sheriff was about to draw his revolver.
  – *Emphasis on their unawareness, more dramatic than the second sentence.*
They didn't know that the sheriff was about to draw his revolver.
  – *Unemphatic, matter-of-fact narrative.*

6 <u>Bang</u> went the door. <u>In</u> came Fred. <u>On</u> went all the lights. <u>Out</u> went the cat.
  – *The repeatedly 'unusual' word order makes this line more dramatic. However, this is rather overdone here and something like this might be preferable:*
The door went bang as Fred came in. On went all the lights and out went the cat like a rocket.
The door went bang. Fred came in. All the lights went on. The cat ran out.
  – *The sentences seem too short in this line, and it sounds rather lifeless.*

7 <u>Rarely are</u> shy people taken as seriously as assertive people.
  – *Emphasis on rarely. This sentence sounds very formal or literary, and might sound pompous if spoken rather than written.*
Shy people are rarely taken as seriously as assertive people.
  – *Straightforward and informal style.*

Note There are no inverted verbs in 5 and 6, but there is a change in word order, with the subject coming after the verb. Point out to everyone that there are restrictions on the use of inversion, as these 'counter-examples' show:

*Bang went it.   *In came he.   *On went they.   *Out ran it.   *Out went we.
*Down came it.   *Up they put their umbrellas.   *Back went we.   *Out I threw them.

B

SUGGESTED ANSWERS

1 Little **did she/anyone realise** that she would win the competition.
2 Not only **does she play** the piano brilliantly but she **sings well / is an accomplished violinist** too.
3 Never in my life **have/had I been** so humiliated!
4 No sooner **had I got into the bath** than the phone **started ringing**.
5 Under no circumstances **should/must** the fire doors **be locked/blocked**.
6 Not until **everyone had** finished **were the rest of us** allowed to leave the room. (*many variations possible*)
7 Only after **a long search/chase were** the police able to catch the thieves.
8 Not once during her entire **life has she been** in trouble with the law.
9 Not only **is he** rather naive but he **also seems to be** very sensitive.
10 No sooner **had we started** our picnic than **it started to rain**. (*many variations possible*)

C

SUGGESTED ANSWERS

2 Off drove the thieves with the police in hot pursuit.
3 Up went the umbrellas. Home we went, wet through.
4 Sitting beside her in the train was a tall dark stranger.
5 Lying under the table was a fat tabby cat, washing itself obliviously.
6 The edge of the cliff gave way and down she fell.
7 Behind the wall was a ferocious dog barking furiously.
8 Only/Not until then did I realise that I had made the biggest mistake of my life.

3.6 ## Long road to Utopia   **READING AND SPEAKING**

A

This exercise can be done by students in pairs. Or alone to start with, then in pairs later. This is similar to Part 3 of the Reading Paper.

ANSWERS

1 D   2 A   3 F   4 B   5 C   6 E

B

There's plenty to talk about here. However, some students in the class may feel uncomfortable with this topic, in which case you might have to skip it.

Ⓐ

SUGGESTED ANSWERS

1 sophisticated/worldly/crafty   2 cowardly/timid   3 unrepentant/unapologetic
4 accelerated/speeded up   5 innocent   6 hindered me/got in the way/
obstructed me   7 saved it/put it by   8 pushed it closed/pushed it to
9 made me more worried/upset me   10 stayed calm/kept his cool
11 synonym   12 closed it quietly

Ⓑ **1**

ANSWERS

		inadvisable	inappropriate	unaware
unbearable	unclearly	incompetent	inconsiderate	inconsistent
inconspicuous	unconventional	unconvincing	undecided	indecisive
undesirable	undignified	indiscreet	indistinct	inefficient
uneventful	unexpected	inexplicable	unfaithful	unforeseen
unforgettable	infrequent	ungrateful	ingratitude	unimaginative
unmanageable	unpredictable	unrewarding	insincere	insincerity
unsociable	unsophisticated	instability	unstable	insufficient
intolerant	untrustworthy	invisible	unwanted	unwelcome

2

ANSWERS

		disagreeable	disapprove	disarm
disconnect	discontented	disentangle	illegible	illegitimate
illogical	disloyal	immature	disorganised	impatient
impersonal	impossible	irrational	irregular	irrelevant
disrespectful	irresponsible	dissatisfied	dissimilar	

3

SUGGESTED ANSWERS

		clumsy · *careful*		fearless · *fearful/cowardly*
neat · *untidy/messy*	noisy · *quiet*	proud · *humble/modest*	rare · *common*	
restless · *calm*	tactful · *tactless*	talkative · *quiet/taciturn*	trivial · *significant/serious*	

Ⓒ

ANSWERS

conceited · *modest*   deceitful · *truthful/trustworthy/open/frank*
fussy · *easy-going/laid back*   lazy · *hard-working*   malicious · *kindhearted*
mean · *generous/kindhearted*   narrow-minded · *liberal*
neurotic · *nonchalant*   pretentious · *unassuming*   secretive · *open/frank*
solitary · *sociable/gregarious*   sullen · *cheerful*   touchy · *easy-going*

(*imaginative, perceptive* and *talkative* are distractors: they aren't antonyms of any words
listed)

3.8 Not waving ...

READING

Ⓐ

1 The two poems are recorded on the cassette (1 minute).

2 The answers given here are suggestions – your interpretation may differ slightly or
considerably.

SUGGESTED ANSWERS

1 He drowned, presumably
2 '*I was much further out than you thought and not waving but drowning.*'
  '*Oh, no no no, it was too cold always, I was much too far out all my life and not waving
  but drowning.*'
3 '*Poor chap, he always loved larking and now he's dead – it must have been too cold for him.
  His heart gave way.*'

4 Having fun, playing pranks
5 line 7: the water
   line 9: life
6 line 11: out of control, in despair
   line 12: unable to cope
7 Not having fun, enjoying himself
8 the man: *lonely   unappreciated   unhappy   solitary   unnoticed   doomed
            unlucky   desperate   sad   sorrowful   glum   pessimistic*
   the friends: *unappreciative   uncaring   laconic   unmoved   uninterested*

1 She is ambivalent: she wants a male friend but she is exasperated with men in general
2 They make it clear they are single, available and looking for a partner by making
   opening remarks and being friendly to her
3 She seems to be worried that time is running out: she may be 'left on the shelf'
4 Once you're committed to a relationship, breaking it off causes heartbreak
5 She's afraid she won't get another chance of finding a partner
6 All the other men she meets who aren't single, available or suitable as partners
7 *year · appear   ride · decide   gaze · days*   The rhyming adds humour to an
   otherwise pessimistic story
8 the poet: *lonely   desperate   witty   humorous   modest   self-deprecating*
   the men: *unreliable   exasperating   unpredictable   attractive   annoying
             desirable   scarce*

B 👥👥 Besides discussing the questions, if you or your students have any favourite poems
which you/they wish to share with the class, this might be an ideal time to do this.

3.9 It takes all sorts . . .   SPEAKING AND COMPOSITION

A 1 👥👥

SUGGESTED ADJECTIVES

sympathetic, considerate, warm-hearted, intelligent sensible, artistic	elderly, experienced, severe, sceptical, shrewd	sociable, sensitive, kind-hearted, blonde, stylish
solemn, serious, suspicious, miserable, shy, critical, reserved	funny, grey-haired, flamboyant, extrovert, energetic, lively, confident	amusing, humorous, affable, enthusiastic, genial, bald
	dark-haired, youthful, creative, charming, practical, boyish, unpretentious	sensitive, quiet, thoughtful, perceptive, modest, compassionate

2 👥👥 → 👥👥 Students may need some help with suitable descriptive phrases. If so, some of
the following vocabulary could be written on the board:

ANSWERS

Clothes:	dress, blouse, suit, flowery shirt, t-shirt, sweater, tie, hat
Age:	middle-aged, thirty-ish, in his/her sixties, in his/her early twenties
Face:	oval, round, dark-skinned, black, pale, suntanned, wearing glasses, clean-shaven, with a moustache, wrinkled, laugh lines
Hair:	curly, frizzy, straight, pulled back

B **1–5** Remind everyone to leave a wide margin on either side of their work and leave a line or two between each paragraph. This will leave them room to add extra ideas, and even to rewrite complete sentences later if necessary. There'll also be more space for you to add comments.

3.9 Model version

Dear Max,

I've written to Betty and Charlie to let them know when to expect you. They're both looking forward to seeing you and they've both offered to put you up for a few days. Just to prepare you, let me tell you something about them.

First of all: Betty. She's a single woman in her early forties and is passionate about music — she's a music teacher. Don't be deceived by her casual clothes into thinking she's easy-going — you should be aware that she is a tidiness fanatic. Everything in her flat has to be in exactly the right place and she's always cleaning. So make sure that you keep the guest room as tidy as possible and make your bed every morning. She has a quick temper, but she doesn't usually get cross with guests, only with her close friends! She's been a good friend of mine for a long time and you'll like her because she loves sitting up late at night talking about the world and telling funny stories. She has three cats, so try to be nice to them even if you aren't a cat-lover.

She'll meet you at the station, and you'll be able to recognise her because she's unusually tall and slim and has very curly red hair. She'll be tallest redhead at the station!

Charlie is a couple of years older than you and works for a firm of accountants. If he meets you on a weekday at the station, he'll be wearing a dark suit and he'll look like a typical businessman — but with no hair. He shaves his head and wears glasses, so look out for a skinhead businessman! (He's quite sensitive about losing his hair, so don't make any jokes about baldness!)

He has a small flat in the city centre, which he shares with a large black dog called Bruno, who looks very fierce but is actually a pussy-cat! If you offer to take him for walks while you're there, you'll be in Charlie's good books. There's a guest room which you'll be able to use for as long as you like. Charlie is pretty busy during the week but he and Bruno usually spend the weekend with friends in the country and he'll invite you to join them. They are a crazy bunch but really nice, so don't turn down this invitation!

Have a really good time and give Betty and Charlie all my love.
Send me a postcard!

Love,
Anna

P.S. Remember to phone them so they know when exactly you'll be arriving.

Leo Jones *New Progress to Proficiency*

4 Let's talk

4.1 Different ways of communicating   TOPIC VOCABULARY

A   1 & 2

SUGGESTED DESCRIPTIONS

He looks dangerous – intimidating and threatening.

Now look here, if you do that again you're going to regret it.

— Don't talk to me like that!

or *— I think you're overreacting.*

She looks delighted and triumphant – very pleased with herself.

I've done it! I've passed!

— Congratulations! Well done! I knew you'd do well.

He looks downhearted and depressed, very much down in the dumps.

Oh God, I don't know what I'm going to do.

— Cheer up! It's not as bad as all that. Try to look on the bright side.

B

ANSWERS

2 mumbling   muttering   whispering
3 jot   note   scribble
4 glance at   scan   skim
5 chuckling   grinning   sniggering
6 frown   scowl   sneer
7 scream   shriek   yell
8 imply   intimate   suggest
9 expression   phrase   idiom
10 attitude   expression   tone

4.2 Meanings and translations   LISTENING AND SPEAKING

A   1 Some reasons why one might be tempted to buy the product:

It fits easily into your pocket or bag
It translates between six languages
It might be a good substitute for a dictionary
You can hear words spoken, not just see them printed

2   **ANSWERS**

1 at the airport ✗   at the chemist's ✓   at the railway station ✗
at the bank ✗   business ✓   camping ✗   complaining ✓   emergencies ✓
in the post office ✗   making friends ✓   motoring ✓   restaurants ✓
shopping ✓   sightseeing ✓
2 Spanish, German, English, French, Italian
3 'How much does it cost to get in?'
'Please call the fire brigade.'
'Is that your best price?'
'We are still waiting to be served.'
4 'I have lost my voice.'
5 personal earphone (and the screen)
6 screen

TRANSCRIPT *6 minutes 15 seconds*

(The Voice was recorded from a real product: its intonation and stress patterns are sometimes rather eccentric!)

PRESENTER: As many of us who take our two weeks' holiday abroad will know, communication in a foreign language is often very difficult. Well, now there's a new gadget on the market for the tourist or businessperson, which can help to communicate in five different languages. It's called The Interpreter and it 'speaks' those languages. All you do is press the right buttons to find a word or phrase in, say, Spanish and it'll say aloud the same word or phrase in English or, if you prefer, German, French or Italian. Sarah Watts has been trying it out for us.

SARAH: The Interpreter has quite a wide vocabulary: over 13,000 words. It can say them all aloud and it can say them in phrases too. This means that all you have to do is press a button and either imitate what it says or just let The Interpreter speak to people on your behalf.

Voice: *Hello.*

SARAH: Oh, hello, how are you?

Voice: *I'm fine thank you.*

SARAH (*fast*): Good. Now there are many situations that a traveller, whether he or she is on business or travelling for pleasure, may find themselves . . .

Voice: *Excuse me.*

SARAH: Yes?

Voice: *Please speak more slowly. I do not understand. I'm sorry.*

SARAH: Oh dear. I'm sorry too. (*as herself again*) Well, let's take for example the situation of someone alone in a foreign city, wanting to strike up an acquaintance with someone in a bar, for example. Let's see what opening gambits The Interpreter can suggest.

Voice: *I am on holiday here.*

SARAH (*responding*): Oh really?

Voice: *Are you alone?*

SARAH: Yes . . .

Voice: *Would you like a drink?*

SARAH: Thanks, I'll have an orange juice please.

Voice: *Do you mind if I smoke?*

SARAH: No, go ahead.

Voice: *What is your name?*

SARAH: Sarah. What's yours?

Voice: *My name is . . .*

SARAH (*as herself again*): But then the conversation might start to get rather more personal –

Voice: *Are you married? Do you have any children? Are you busy tomorrow? Would you like to come out with me?*

SARAH (*responding*): Er…

Voice: *Please*

SARAH: No thanks. But, perhaps if you have a free afternoon you would like to do some sightseeing?

Voice: *What is there to see here?*

SARAH: Oh lots of things. There's a wonderful art gallery, and . . .

Voice: *How much does it cost to get in? Is there a guided tour? How long does the tour take? Is there a reduction for children?*

SARAH (*as herself again*): So much for culture. Of course the Interpreter's repertoire of phrases covers all eventualities, such as emergencies:

Voice: *Please help me. I have been robbed. Get the police. Where is the nearest hospital? My child is missing. Please call the fire brigade.*

SARAH: Very polite! And shopping. Let's suppose you want to buy something unusual . . .

Voice: *Where can I buy a bed?*

SARAH: Yes, that is unusual. Anyway, you go to a store and ask the assistant:

Voice: *Have you got a bed? Show me a bed.*

SARAH: Or you might ask, rather more politely:

Voice: *I would like a bed. I would like to see a bed. Which bed do you recommend?*

SARAH: So you select a particularly nice bed. And it might be worth checking if you can get a discount:

Voice: *Is that your best price?*

SARAH: There's no discount, but you still want to make your purchase:

Voice: *Can I buy this please? Do you take credit cards? May I have a receipt?*

SARAH: So your brand new bed is delivered to your . . . hotel? – no, you must have an apartment you want to furnish – But, oh dear, when you unwrap it:

Voice: *The bed is broken.*

SARAH: So you go back to the store and say:

Voice: *Can I exchange this bed?*

SARAH: This leads us on to the topic of Complaints. Let's suppose you're in a restaurant where the service is rather slow:

Voice: *We are still waiting to be served.*

SARAH: And after your meal:

Voice: *May I have the bill please? Is service included?*

SARAH: You examine the bill:

Voice: *I think you have made a mistake. You have overcharged me. I want to see the manager.*

SARAH: So, there we are, the Interpreter covers a wide range of social situations, as well as business situations:

Voice: *I am here on business. Where can I get some photocopying done? Can I send a fax from here?*

SARAH: And motoring:

Voice: *My car won't start. Can you repair the car? I have run out of petrol. Where is the nearest petrol station? I have a flat tyre. Can you tow me to a garage?*

SARAH: And, finally, at the chemist's:

Voice: *Have you anything for insect bites? Have you anything for sunburn? I want something for a headache. I want something for toothache. I have a cough.*

SARAH: Another useful one, which is not in the Interpreter's repertoire might be: (*hoarsely*) "I have lost my voice", perhaps!

The Interpreter comes with a personal earphone, and all the phrases appear on the screen as they are spoken, which is a great help in learning them and means that you can use it in complete privacy, without any of the people around you being able to hear it.

Voice: *Excuse me.*

SARAH (*responding*): Yes?

Voice: *Is it safe for children?*

SARAH: Oh, yes I think so. And you can use it anytime you want to.

Voice: *I am free tomorrow morning.*

SARAH: Oh good. Thank you for your help, by the way.

Voice: *You're welcome.*

B 👥👥👥👥 The follow-up discussion leads in to the Communication Activity in **C**.

C **1** 👥👥👥 As this is the first Communication Activity in the book, spend a few moments explaining the rationale behind it:

The Communication Activities involve an information gap, where each participant is given different information which has to be shared with a partner. Here each student has some information to study, which they have to tell their partner(s) about in their own words. They should not just read their definitions out loud to each other.

Student A looks at **Activity 14** on page 202, where there are extracts from the *Oxford Advanced Learner's Dictionary*, Student B at **24** on page 205 for extracts from the *Longman Dictionary of Contemporary English* and Student C at **31** on page 207 for extracts from the *Cambridge International Dictionary of English*.

This Activity may take some time to do justice to and complete – if necessary, postpone it till the next lesson. It's **NOT** a good idea to rush through it.

2 After the Communication Activity, everyone should compare all three sets of entries and decide on the merits of each dictionary.

4.3 **Attitudes to language** **READING AND SUMMARY-WRITING**

A 👥👥 If students are asked to prepare the text before the lesson, these questions could be 'points to think about' before reading the passage.

B This exercise is similar to Part 1 of the Use of English Paper.

> **ANSWERS**
>
> 1 C 2 A 3 D 4 B 5 A 6 D 7 C 8 B

C This exercise is rather similar to Part 2 of the Reading Paper.

> **ANSWERS**
>
> 1 B 2 C 3 D 4 C 5 D

D

> **ANSWERS**
>
> ¶ 1 *objective* = impartial *prejudice* = bias *instructive* = revealing
> ¶ 2 *exhilarating* = stimulating *euphoria* = happiness *mitigated* = moderated
> ¶ 3 *associations* = connotations *formulate* = devise *aesthetic* = artistic *pet* = favourite
> ¶ 4 *derisive* = contemptuous *badge* = emblem *intrinsic* = inherent
>   *the men* = workers *excite* = arouse

E 👥👥👥👥 Some of the points covered in this follow-up discussion will be taken up further in **4.7** The English-speaking world.

F ✎ This is similar to the kind of summary task that students will have to do in Part 5 of the Use of English Paper. The best way to approach this task is as follows:

1 First pick out the main points in the two halves of the text.
2 Make brief notes, attempting to rephrase some of the ideas in your own words.
3 For homework, write your summary.
4 Show your summary to a partner and ask for comments. Comment on your partner's summary.

4.3 Model version

Prejudices in favour of or against regional, rural or city accents or individual words reflect the standpoint of the listener and have no absolute validity; that is to say that 'pretty' or 'ugly' or 'admirable' in relation to a Birmingham or Dorset accent, for example, are words which only say something about the listener's background and attitude. The idea that the 'Queen's English' means wealth, position and education is also based on this subjective view and merely reflects the historical connection of a local dialect, East Midland English, with the location of Oxford, Cambridge and London.

Leo Jones *New Progress to Proficiency*

4.4 –*ing* and *to* . . . GRAMMAR REVISION

 A 👥 Continuations in **bold print** – meanings below *in italics*.

SUGGESTED ANSWERS

2 a We stopped to take photos but . . . **the light wasn't bright enough, so we went on walking.**
– *We were walking along and then stopped in order to take photos*
 b We stopped taking photos but . . . **we went on watching what was going on.**
– *We were taking photos and then we stopped taking them*

3 a Did you remember to send the fax or . . . **did you forget to send it?**
– *You were supposed to do it: did you in fact do it?*
 b Do you remember sending the fax or . . . **have you forgotten all about it now?**
– *Just think back for a moment: can you remember whether you did it or not?*

4 a I can't help you to feel better but . . . **I can sit by the bed to keep you company.**
– *I'm unable to assist you*
 b I can't help feeling better, but . . . **I realise I ought to stay in bed today.**
– *I'm unable to stop myself from feeling better*

5 a I'm not used to using a fountain pen but . . . **I'll try not to make a mess with it.**
– *I'm not accustomed to using one*
 b I used to use a fountain pen but . . . **now I use a computer all the time.**
– *I once used a fountain pen, but not now*

6 a She heard him scream, but . . . **she didn't take any notice.**
– *He screamed once*
 b She heard him screaming, but . . . **there was nothing she could do to help.**
– *He screamed repeatedly*

B **1**

COLLOCATIONS

to call	– someone on the phone
to contact	– someone by phone/by post
to drop	– someone a line
to get	– through to someone on the phone
to give	– someone a ring
to keep	– in touch with someone
to reply	– to a letter
to tell	– someone a story
to write	– someone a letter

2

SUGGESTED ANSWERS

2 in contacting them
3 telling   telling/giving it away to
4 to send them
5 tell the story
6 to reply to
7 keeping in touch with people/calling people
8 in getting through to her
9 giving me
10 to phone you
11 to leave a message on
12 to writing

C

SUGGESTED ANSWERS

1 taking a taxi/going by underground if you've got a lot of luggage
2 to go there some day
3 taking any exercise/doing anything strenuous
4 staying up late/going out for the evening/staying up all night
5 trying to read the book
6 listening   to listen to Mozart/listening to jazz
7 reading the book till I got to the end
8 walking in the hope that it might stop
9 working   having a good rest/going out tonight
10 crying/screaming   to listen/to stand by and do nothing
11 doing some extra homework/committing so much time to it
12 being/feeling   to feel much better/to recover
13 to get through/to make contact again
14 to buy/to have   to buy one
15 not to hear/to be deaf

4.5 **Paragraphs**

WRITING SKILLS

A This task is a lead-in to the theme of the section: analysing the reasons why paragraphs are used.

B This discussion is a lead-in to the theme of the article the students are going to analyse. If everyone has read the article beforehand this will save time in class.

C **1** After everyone has looked at the analysis, find out if there are any questions or disputes about the reasons given.

2 Now the students do the same with paragraphs 7 to 15. There are lots of other interpretations besides the ones suggested here:

SUGGESTED REASONS

7 A different example is going to be given
8 A general point is now going to be made, after the example
9 A solution to the problem is going to be suggested
10 A new character is introduced, who works for one of the companies
11 Now other companies are going to be mentioned
12 Now here's an example of one of those companies
13 Another new character or point of view is introduced
14 Another new point of view is coming up
15 The final points are coming (though this is still part of the previous character's quote) – the new paragraph gives them prominence

With the last part of the article, the students have to insert their own paragraph breaks. There may be variations from the answers below, which show the breaks in the original article:

> Mike Platt, commercial director of the business travel agency Hogg Robinson BTI, says: 'Our research among clients shows that they are increasingly using the train as an extension of the office, but they have two main concerns: one is the lack of privacy; the other is the poor signal they often get on their phone on the train.'
>
> Platt says he regards the ability to work for three hours as the second key advantage Eurostar has over the plane – the first being the ability to travel directly between city centres. Many companies take the opportunity to hold formal business meetings on Eurostar, calculating that if they book facing seats over a table, they can get away without their conversation being heard.
>
> But he adds: 'People are split down the middle about mobile phones. Half want to use them, and the other half regard them as noise pollution and say that they can't do their own work if they are next to somebody who is barking down the phone.'
>
> Last week saw the publication of yet another survey demonstrating that the British work longer hours than their European compatriots. Many of us clearly regard a train journey as an opportunity to do more work, rather than to relax and enjoy the journey. Maybe it is time we all let the train take the strain.

Extra activity

Ask everyone to look back at previous reading passages and remind themselves how many paragraphs there are in each of them:

Tinkling the ivories, jangling the nerves in 1.3 has 17 paragraphs
Hingis beaten by girl wonder from down under in 1.6 has 16 paragraphs
The ladies' man in 1.6 has 11 paragraphs
Eight Feet in the Andes in 2.1 has 13 paragraphs
Outlook Unsettled in 2.4 has 4 paragraphs
The great escape in 3.1 has 30 paragraphs
Attitudes to language in 4.3 has 4 paragraphs – each over 200 words long

In each case, why are there so many (or so few)? What is the effect of this?

Paragraphs in news articles tend to be very short, compared with books, perhaps because the typical reader's attention span is shorter. Also if there are longish quotes from people, each quote is usually a separate paragraph.

In the exam, where candidates have to squeeze a lot of different ideas into about 350 words, short paragraphs also seem better than long ones filled with complex sentences.

4.6 *Wh–* clauses   ADVANCED GRAMMAR

This section doesn't cover relative clauses, which are dealt with in **16.3**.

 1 Deal with any questions that arise and ask the class to suggest how each idea can be rephrased UNemphatically:

Intolerance annoys me.
I need a friend to lend a helping hand.
She always seems to succeed.
He may not get here in time, but it doesn't matter.

2
> **SUGGESTED CONTINUATIONS**
>
> 2 One thing I like is **sitting at home with my feet up.**
> 3 All I want is **something cool and refreshing to drink.**
> 4 What I feel like doing **now is having a rest.**
> 5 What we need now **is an expert's advice.**
> 6 There's nothing I enjoy more than **going for a long walk in the country.**
> 7 I just don't want **to upset him by raising the subject of work.**
> 8 Something that often surprises me is **the way some people find it hard to learn a foreign language.**
> 9 What I want to do right now is **have lunch.**

3

2 I really do like sitting at home with my feet up.
3 What I want to drink is something cool and refreshing.
4 All I want to do now is have a rest.
5 All we need now is an expert's advice.
6 I really enjoy going for a long walk in the country.
7 What I don't want to do is to upset him by raising the subject of work.
8 The way some people find it hard to learn a foreign language is very surprising.
9 The only thing I want to do now is to have lunch.

B

MATCHED SENTENCES

2 Say what you like. = Say whatever you want to.
   Talk to anyone you want to. = Speak to whoever you want.
3 Whoever did you give it to? = Who in the world did you give it to?
   To whom* did you give it? = Who did you give it to?
4 Why ever don't you phone him? = Why on earth don't you phone him?
   Why don't you ever phone him? = Why do you never phone him?
5 All the sentences in 5 mean the same as each other!

* *To whom . . . ?* in 3 would sound very old-fashioned in present-day English.

C

ANSWERS

1   Wherever **he goes, he takes a phrasebook with him.**
2   You can **arrive whenever you like.**
3   All **I did was stick out my tongue at her.**
4   What **you did was very rude.**
5   All **she needs is someone to tell her troubles to.**
6   I don't mind **where you put it.**
7   Whether **you write or phone doesn't really matter / is immaterial.**
8   Whenever **you arrive, get in touch.**
9   What **he said made a big impression on me/everyone.**
10 What **astonished me was her confidence.**

4.7   The English-speaking world

SPEAKING, LISTENING
AND COMPOSITION

A

  The diagram and the key are the basis of a discussion. There are many possible examples besides the ones given here, of course. Pool ideas at the end of this activity.

SUGGESTED ANSWERS

1 star   leader   butter
2 fat   happy   catch
3 hard   dark   drama
4 not · nought   nod · gnawed   sod · sawed   tot · taught
5 shirt   form   term
6 hot   want   soft · grass   laugh   palm
   kitten   bitter   utterly   attitude
   pass   glance   castle   laughter

B

◀)) Before playing the recording, maybe ask everyone which British and American accents they can recognise. Which do they find most pleasant to listen to, and hardest to understand? Can they recognise a Welsh and an Australian accent?

ANSWERS

1 AUS   2 USA   3 W   4 W   5 AUS   6 W   7 AUS   8 USA

TRANSCRIPT *8 minutes 20 seconds*

NARRATOR: Listen to three people discussing accents.

BILL: Well what do you think accents…the…the…our own accents can tell us about…er…the differences in the social class and education of…er…er…where we are?

RUTH: I was brought up in a kind of a well-to-do South Wales town. Um…and…er…there certainly were judgements made on people, that they…if they had a very…a strong Valleys accent, I mean, it's wrong but that's…that is the case, yeah.

SARAH: It happens, yeah. And what about education, were you taught better grammar in school then, or is that just . . . ?

RUTH: Well, you know, you hear…sometimes you hear someone say…um…like a classic way to talk i…in the Valleys would be, 'I do go down to town on a Tuesday and I do buy my bread.' Well, now that's not correct English, is it?

BILL: That's not grammatically correct.

SARAH: No. I mean, in Australia you…you…we don't have accents as such like over here. I couldn't believe it when I came to Europe and this diversity of accents from moving one mile to the next. You either have one or the other, so you can't have a class system, because you don't know where people are from. Which I really like, 'cause you again can't judge, like if I brought a boy home, my mum couldn't go, 'Ooh, he's not from a nice part of town!' you know, 'Don't go out with him!'

BILL: Well, I think i…it's interesting in America because, like Australia, we don't have the class thing so much, but we certainly have, in America a lot of different regional accents, I mean you've heard them in…in…on…in the movies and on television. But I think…er…this may be a silly generalisation, but I think, so far as I can tell, there is not a kind of value judgement that is levelled against the way people talk *per se*, it more depends on what they say.

SARAH: I mean, is there different accents from region to region?

BILL: Oh yeah. Sure. I mean, you…you…you've also heard…er…the New England accent, er…the Massachusetts accent of…er…J.F.K. remember, you heard the…you've heard the recordings of him, even though you weren't old enough to hear him yourself. And…er…real South, the Carolinas, and…and Georgia and that area, that kinda open…er…very soft Southern accent they have down there. And then there's the Mid-West, the kind of…er…I suppose the boring kind of long, nasal accent. And then there's New York and then there's West Coast where I come from. There's…I can't actually tell a lot of difference between Mid…Mid-West and my area of the West Coast, but there are lots of different ones.

RUTH: Yeah, it's interesting because, like, in Wales, it's a really tiny country, but there are such vast differences in accents, within kind of like miles, you know, apart.

SARAH: Yeah, and Australia's the same size as America and we've got two.

RUTH: Yeah, it's…it's incredible, I mean, it's like…um…in…in Cardiff, which is the capital of Wales, people talk like that and it's quite sort of nasal, you know and they says 'I go down the Arms Park, with my father and I has half a dark'. And then if you go, kind of just about ten miles away up to the Valleys, you've got, you know, people talking like that – oh I can't do it now, haha – 'I go down there…er… my…er…I've got a friend, you know, she says…um…I don't know, I…I'm finding it very difficult I am, you know'. And it's all…um…and then you go up to North Wales, which is…um…very 'sort of like that, you know, it's quite spiky, and…er…quite sort of…er…quite a difficult accent to understand'.

BILL: Well, this is very funny, that obviously there are certain areas that are funnier to listen to than others, now do people find them funnier? Inside Wales do they laugh at other people's accent?

RUTH: Defin…there's a…there is a North-South divide in Wales, I think, and it, you know, of course, we've got the added complication of the Welsh language, whereby people sort of in the North maybe will judge people in the South because the Southerners don't tend to speak Welsh as much as in the North or in the West…um…so they will, kind of, I've been called a half…a half Taff.

SARAH: See, it's the class system again, isn't it!

BILL: It is, yes.

RUTH: The Taff is the river that runs through . . .

SARAH: Like it's a bad thing.

BILL: Yeah.

SARAH: You know, it's amazing.

RUTH: But it's…it is. And then, you know, and we'll say, oh…um…there's a term in…in South Wales that refers to Welsh speakers as the 'Sharads'. *Sharad* is 'to speak' in Welsh. 'Oh yeah, he's a real Sharad, he's a real Welsh speaker.'

BILL: You mean he's pretentious about his speaking Welsh?

RUTH: Yeah, exactly.

SARAH: But do you know it's amazing, it's like when you…when I…when I first came over here, you sort of…you'd be scared of saying where people are from because you didn't want to insult them, because people take so much offence if you say they're wrong, you know, if you say they're from Bolton and they're from, you know, Denby, you know, 'Oooh!' You know, but, you can't tell that with Australia, and it's…a lot of people get confused between the New Zealand and Australian, I mean, I can't tell the difference between a Canadian and an American. Is there a difference?

BILL: Well, there is a slight difference, but you really have to be…you have to know the difference, I mean, Canadians…er…there's an 'ou' sound, when they say 'out', Americans say 'out' and the Canadians it's 'out', it's shorter, and 'about' and they also say 'Eh?' a lot. 'Eh?'

SARAH: Very, very similar like there's only a few little tiny things between New Zealand and Australia.

BILL: Very tiny little things.

SARAH: Like they say 'fush and chips' and we say 'fish and chips'.

BILL: Yeah, yeah.

SARAH: So it's only the close people that can…like we know the difference, but they don't. No one else do.

BILL: Now do you…do you find that some accents are easier on, and more pleasant on the ear than others?

SARAH: Oh, yeah.

RUTH: What, within Wales?

BILL: Within Wales and, well, and general of course as well.

RUTH: The…er…within…um…I…there is the classic Richard Burton, Port Talbot and Anthony Hopkins Welsh, which is beautiful . . .

SARAH: Which is lyrical isn't it?

RUTH: You know, and I would just…I would love to have that accent.

SARAH: But it's the same with American, isn't it? I mean, some of them, like you know, the Texas is sort of kind of cute to listen to, like everyone always says, 'Ooh, I'd love a Texas, you know, farmer guy!' As opposed to the New York, which is really crisp and sharp.

BILL: Yeah, yeah. When New York sounds like very nasal . . .

RUTH: Oh, but I love the New York!

SARAH: Yeah.

BILL: . . . and Texas is all very kind of round and slow everybody is different down there.

RUTH: But we went to New York last September and we just used to sit and listen. I mean, it was just fantastic listening to it.

SARAH: But the New York, it is a harsh, particularly the people, you know, the ones that are now native that are bringing accents in, that's what you find in Australia, there's actually only two accents, you've got the city accent and you've got the Outback, the Crocodile [Dundee]. Like, you know, 'G'day, mate!' Really slow, everything's like that. And then you've got the city one. But now, because we're a new country, we're getting so many immigrants, the second generations are now, think they've got an Australian accent, but it's mixed with their parents' accent.

BILL: Right yeah, you've got Greek-Australian, you got, you've got Irish-Australian . . .

★★★

SARAH: . . . and we realise we're all immigrants and you're pretty stupid if you start teasing someone else because you think, 'Well, where are you from originally?' It's only the Aboriginals who can really claim that they were there.

BILL: They were the originals.

RUTH: Do you think that…um…attitudes have…have changed towards accents over the years in the sense that, you know, were children encouraged when they were younger to lose their accents?

SARAH: I think the immigrants were and now they realise they don't have to, they're Australians and Australian is about being a multi-cultural society.

RUTH: Right. Yeah.

SARAH: But, yeah, I know my…I've got one very good friend who is Italian, and she used to get really teased because she sort of emphasised words differently and she really used to try but now she doesn't care.

RUTH: Doesn't care. I remember when I was growing up and I remember we had to…we were learning to sing…we were singing *Away in a Manger*, the Christmas carol, and I remember my teacher Mrs Sparks got really cross with us because we were singing…um…'Bless all the de-ar children' and it…and she used to say, 'It's not de-ar, it's dear' and we'd all be going 'Bless all the dear children' and it…and it was like, in some ways, if you had a strong accent it was discouraged, you know it was thought of as being common, whereas you know, now, it…if you…especially if you look at, you know, in broadcasting and things like that you get all sorts of accents from all over the country are encouraged.

SARAH: Yeah, well, what do you think of the Bri…you know when you hear a British P…you know, RP accent? I mean, I know if they came to Australia we'd go like 'Oooh, the Queen!' you know, we'd tease them. Is it the same in Wales, do you…are they looked upon as being . . .

BILL: Posh.

SARAH: . . . superior or posh?

RUTH: Yes, I mean, I think so. You'd get a posh Welsh accent, which would be somebody who'd speak sort of like that you know . . .

SARAH: Is that like English . . .?

RUTH: It's not, though, that's not RP.

SARAH: It's still not…it's still not RP.

RUTH: There's a posher version.

BILL: It's an equivalent.

RUTH: Yeah, an equivalent.

BILL: I think America has from the beginning . . . I mean, what Americans…when I was growing up, what people worried about was using incorrect grammar, it wasn't so much the accent you used, it was using, you know, using words that you shouldn't use or 'Don't say "ain't"' used to be something you'd hear.

RUTH: Oh right, yeah.

BILL: Er…but it…but actually the accent itself, no, I mean, we all…Americans consider they talk with an American accent and there's an end, so there was no conscious . . .

C **1** Allow plenty of time for this discussion, as some questions might be quite provocative. Any questions that are irrelevant for your students' language should be skipped.

2–4 These steps may be done by the same pairs, or alone. Make sure the students give each other feedback on their first sentences in Step 4.

5 ✒ Before you collect the completed reports, encourage everyone to show each other their work and give each other feedback.

Extra activity

In a multi-lingual class, the students could be asked to give a short oral presentation about their own country – they'd probably need to work in single-nationality groups to prepare this.

4.7 Model version

Throughout the world today there are an estimated 92 million German speakers, 76.5 million of whom live in Germany. The official German language, that is the one used in schools, academic institutions, in government and international dealings and above all in the written language, is called High German (Hochdeutsch) or standard German. This is the official language of Germany, Austria, Liechtenstein and one of the official languages of Switzerland. However there are quite a number of German dialects. These are generally spoken languages only and the people who use them are able to speak both dialect and High German but of course they write only in High German. The ability to function fluently and accurately in both written and spoken High German is vital to get a good job. There are also languages other than German and its dialects, spoken by minorities in certain areas.

There is a major historical language division between Northern and Southern Germany in terms of pronunciation and this is reflected in the dialects in those areas. Some of the dialects in Germany are the following: East Prussian spoken by migrants from the former East Prussia (now part of Poland) in the Ruhr area; Low German (Plattdeutsch) spoken in parts of North Germany; Fränkisch, Swabian in southern Bavaria, Bavarian, Mecklenburgisch, Badisch (Baden-Wurttemburg), Alemannisch (near Lake Constance), Saxon, the dialect of Berlin etc. In fact nearly every area has its own dialect. Although dialects are undergoing a surge in popularity as people seek their identity in local and regional culture, at the same time they are under threat from the growing influence of the media.

The minority languages are often the results of the redrawing of borders as is the case with the language of the 50,000 Danish speaking people in Schleswig-Holstein. They call their language Frisk. Another minority language is Sorbian spoken by about 30,000 people who live in Brandenburg near the Polish border. Their settlement in Germany goes back to 600 AD when they moved from Poland or Czechoslovakia. Frisian is spoken by people in the north western lowlands of Germany. There are also minority languages spoken by the many refugees and foreign workers in Germany.

Leo Jones *New Progress to Proficiency*

4.8 Forming adjectives

VOCABULARY DEVELOPMENT

The verbs that have two associated adjectives are in **bold print**.

ANSWERS

–able	acceptable admirable advisable breakable **describable** **forgivable** obtainable predictable **preventable** recommendable
–ing	astonishing convincing distressing disturbing **forgiving** inspiring overwhelming promising upsetting
–ive	communicative cooperative deceptive **descriptive** informative instructive possessive **preventive** productive

ANSWERS

–al	conventional educational **fictional** functional intentional musical personal professional proportional seasonal secretarial sensational
–ic	diplomatic enigmatic idealistic magnetic materialistic optimistic pessimistic realistic romantic
–ous	adventurous ambitious **fictitious** malicious religious spacious
–ly	fortnightly quarterly weekly yearly
–ed	curly-haired experienced long-legged pale-skinned

Notice also these suffixes:

–ed/–n   educated   finished   unknown   satisfied
–ical   alphabetical   historical
–ish   childish   stylish   boyish   snobbish
–y   draughty   funny   airy   brainy
–worthy   roadworthy   noteworthy   newsworthy   seaworthy   trustworthy

C

ANSWERS

1 poisonous   2 astonished   3 automatic   4 idealised   5 stylish
6 economical   7 heartbroken   8 satisfactory   9 legible   10 childish

Extra activity

Highlight the words in **A** and **B** that caused you difficulty. Then work in pairs and write a short exercise with gaps and give it to another pair to do, using words from **A** and **B**. For example:

I asked her about her trip but she wasn't very ... (communicative)

There is more on *–ing* and *-ed/-en* in **5.5 Adjectives & participles**.

4.9   *make* and *do*   VERBS AND IDIOMS

A

ANSWERS

MAKE: an agreement with someone   an appointment with someone
an arrangement   certain about something   a comment about something
an excuse   a good impression   friends with someone   a lot of money
love   a mistake   a profit or a loss   progress   a reservation
sure about something

DO: your best   business with someone   your duty   someone a favour
harm to someone   a good turn   the washing-up   wrong or right
your own thing

NOTE *make* often refers to creative or productive processes, while *do* often refers to the performance of a service or work

B

ANSWERS

1 manage to see
2 doomed
3 . . . how this concerns you
4 move up to allow me to sit there
5 invented
6 recompense/compensate
7 afford the necessities of life
8 repay you – I am very sorry and I can't compensate you
9 getting things out of proportion
10 have an embarrassing public argument
11 work harder/drive faster to catch up
12 show his good looks/personality well enough

C

ANSWERS

1 made off with
2 done   up
3 make up for
4 make up
5 made   up
6 doing up
7 done away with
8 making for
9 done out of
10 made off

Bon appetit!

5

5.1 To whet your appetite . . .   TOPIC VOCABULARY

In case the title of this unit is confusing, point out that it's only waiters and waitresses who say 'Enjoy your meal' in Britain. Many people don't say anything at the start of a meal, but some use the French expression: '*Bon appetit!*'

(A)   **1 & 2** 👥👥👥👥 Ask everyone to specify the location of the various places, and to justify their choices, rather than just name the establishments. Similarly, with the photos they should encourage each other to justify their reactions by asking, 'Why?'

(B)   **1** 👥

SUGGESTED ANSWERS	
Appetisers/starters	melon salad soup prawn cocktail
Fish/shellfish	oysters mussels lobster prawn shrimp scampi sole swordfish clams octopus squid eel
Poultry	chicken turkey duck goose
Game	venison pheasant wild boar rabbit
Herbs	parsley basil rosemary tarragon bay leaf marjoram oregano dill
Spices	cinnamon nutmeg allspice pepper ginger paprika cloves
Dairy products	cheese yogurt butter cream buttermilk
Nuts	hazelnuts walnuts chestnuts cashews pistachios almonds Brazil nuts pine nuts
Desserts	apple pie chocolate mousse profiteroles rice pudding pancakes trifle fruit sorbet
Cakes and pastries	Christmas cake Victoria sponge Danish pastry almond croissant chocolate éclair blueberry muffin

2 👥→👥 If your students are interested in cooking or eating, allow plenty of time for this discussion. They may need to be reminded of different ways of preparing and cooking food:

chop   slice   mix   weigh   knead   beat   whip
deep-fry   pan-fry   stir-fry   grill   roast   steam   parboil   sauté   microwave
bake   *etc.*

5.2 Everything all right, sir?   READING AND SPEAKING

The passage should not only provoke discussion, but is also the source of examples for **5.4 The passive – 1**.

(A)   This exercise is similar to Part 1 of the Reading Paper.

ANSWERS						
1 D	2 A	3 C	4 B	5 D	6 C	7 C

(B)   👥👥👥👥 Encourage everyone to think of personal experiences and share them. Maybe start the ball rolling by recounting one of your own horror stories.

(C)   **1** 🔊 On the recording, as a bonus and to set the scene for the role-play, there are some corny 'Waiter, waiter!' jokes to play to the class. Many of these depend on word-play.

TRANSCRIPT *1 minute*

PRESENTER: Listen to some 'Waiter, waiter!' jokes.

CUSTOMER: Waiter, there's a fly in my soup.
WAITER: Shh, don't talk too loudly, everyone will want one.

CUSTOMER: Waiter there's a dead fly in my soup.
WAITER: It must be the hot liquid that killed it, madam.

CUSTOMER: Waiter, there's a fly in my soup.
WAITER: Look, there's a spider on the bread, he'll catch it for you.

CUSTOMER: Waiter, what's this fly doing in my soup?
WAITER: I think it's doing the breast stroke, sir.

CUSTOMER: Waiter, there's a dead fly swimming in my soup.
WAITER: That's impossible, madam, dead flies can't swim.

CUSTOMER: Waiter, you've got your thumb in my soup.
WAITER: Don't worry, sir, it's not hot.

2 👥 Rather than being rude or superior, like the waiters in the recording, the students should try to be polite!

5.3 Running a restaurant   READING AND SPEAKING

A 👥👥 This is a warm-up discussion. Students with first-hand knowledge of work in the restaurant business should be encouraged to tell their partners about their experiences.

B
> **ANSWERS**
>
> 1 G   2 E   3 B   4 F   5 C   6 D   7 A

C 👥👥 Before starting this follow-up discussion, ask for the class's reactions to what they read in the article.

5.4 The passive – 1   GRAMMAR REVIEW

A
> **SUGGESTED ANSWERS**
>
> 1 I'm afraid all the cakes have been eaten.
> – *Someone ate them, but I'm not saying who did*
> I'm afraid I've eaten all the cakes.
> – *It was me that ate them, I confess*
>
> 2 Arsenal beat Chelsea in the final.
> – *We know both of the teams involved, no special emphasis*
> Spurs were beaten in the semi-finals.
> – *We only know about the losing team, emphasis on their defeat*
> Manchester United were beaten in the quarter-finals by Southampton.
> – *We know about both teams; the information about which side won is given emphasis when it is put at the end of the sentence*
>
> 3 He thinks people are plotting against him.
> He thinks he's being plotted against.
> – *There is no particular difference in emphasis, but the active sentence seems easier to read*
>
> 4 The dough was rolled out and then cut into teddybear shapes.
> – *This seems like a report in impersonal style. The focus is on the action, not on who made it happen*
> We rolled out the dough and then we cut it into teddybear shapes.
> – *Here it's us that did the work and it's more informal in style*
>
> 5 There was nothing to do.
> – *We were at a loose end, with nothing to occupy us*
> There was nothing to be done.
> – *There was no solution to the problem, no remedy for it*

6 My wallet has been stolen!
  I've had my wallet stolen!
  Someone has stolen my wallet!
  – *These three mean the same: My wallet is missing and I don't know who's responsible*
  That man stole my wallet!
  – *I accuse that man of stealing it*

B **Comments on the examples in the text** (<u>underlined</u> here)

> . . . more than 230 steak houses <u>owned by</u> Grand Metropolitan.
> – *This emphasises who the owners are: the active alternative* that Grand Metropolitan own *is a bit clumsy*
>
> Nowadays if you don't like what <u>is provided</u> in your meal
> – *The active alternative* what the restaurant provides in your meal *has to include the obvious information about who provides the meal*
>
> . . . diners who complain . . . have their bill <u>torn up</u>.
> – *The active alternative would take many words to explain:* they don't receive the bill because the manager or another member of the staff tears it up . . .
>
> A poll <u>conducted by</u> Berni
> – *Emphasis on who carried out the survey*
>
> . . . the scheme <u>was initiated by</u> a group of Berni managers and tried out in the north of England
> – *As the scheme is the subject of both verbs only one sentence is required and it is unnecessary to go into detail about exactly who tried out the scheme*
> Other branches of the chain tried out the scheme after a group of Berni managers had initiated . . . *is clumsy*
>
> <u>Armed</u> with this knowledge
> – *This can only be used in the passive with this meaning unless we say* I armed myself with this knowledge . . .
>
> Simon Smith, the manager, told me he <u>had been</u> pleasantly <u>pleased</u> at . . .
> – *The active alternative would be* The lack of unscrupulous diners had pleasantly pleased him *which sounds awful*
>
> Complaints <u>had</u> generally <u>been justified</u>.
> – There had generally been justification for the complaints *would sound very clumsy*
> . . . some people who did complain had to <u>be persuaded</u> to leave the bill to him.
> – *Focus on the persuasion, not on the manager who did the persuading*

C Many of the original sentences are inelegant and clumsy: the passive rewritten ones are better, and easier to understand.

> **SUGGESTED ANSWERS**
> 2 I was told by a friend that you have been awarded a scholarship.
> 3 Both cars were badly damaged in the crash, but no one was injured.
> 4 After the bather had been rescued, he was taken to hospital.
> 5 After he had been operated on, he was told to stay in bed for a week.
> 6 McDonald's hamburgers are sold all over the world.
> 7 Liverpool were held to a draw by Everton.
> 8 The square may be crowded with thousands of demonstrators tonight.
> 9 The plane was scheduled to land at noon, but it has been delayed.
> 10 The tennis match was rained off.
> 11 They were flooded with requests for free samples of the new product.
> 12 An escaped prisoner has been seen, who is believed to be dangerous.

(See also **12.5 The passive – 2**.)

A

SUGGESTED ANSWERS

1 She has a talking parrot. — *a parrot that can speak*
  Have you heard her parrot talking? — *Have you heard it speak?*
2 She is an old friend. — *a friend I have had for a long time*
  My friend is quite old. — *not young*
3 All the people concerned were there. — *the people involved or who were affected*
  All the concerned people were there. — *the worried people*
4 It wasn't a proper meeting. — *it was only an informal meeting, no formal or binding decisions could be made*

  The meeting proper began at 9. — *the main part of the meeting; there had been an informal gathering before that perhaps*

5 The members of staff present. — *who are/were there*
  The present members of staff. — *current*
6 Is he the person responsible? — *the person who did whatever has just been mentioned or the person who is in charge*

  Is he a responsible person? — *someone who can be trusted*
7 I have a friend living in London. — *who lives in London*
  She has no living relatives. — *all her relatives are now dead*
8 He is a complete idiot. — *an utter idiot*
  The complete meal cost a mere £5. — *the whole meal, including drinks*
9 She has an elder brother. — *older than her (his exact age depends on her age)*

  Her brother is elderly. — *old, at least 70 years old*
10 The film had a very involved plot. — *complicated*
  The actors involved were unconvincing. — *involved in the circumstances described in a previous sentence*

B Before they begin the exercise, perhaps remind everyone that adjectival expressions can come in three positions in a sentence:

Before a noun A very **interesting** story.
After a noun We need the best ingredients **available**.
After a verb She is fast **asleep**.

SUGGESTED COMPLETIONS

1 That was a really **tasty** meal.
  Those buns look absolutely **delicious**!
2 The journey was an **utter** disaster.
  The meal was a **complete** success.
3 The fire isn't **alight** yet.
  Don't leave the baby **alone** all night.
  Shh! The baby's **asleep** in its cot.
  Her two sisters look **alike**.
4 The president **elect** takes office next month.
5 That was the most disgusting meal **imaginable**!
6 Work expands to take up the time **available**.
  Work expands to take up the **available** time.
7 I love the smell of cakes (which are) **baking** in the kitchen.
  The houses (which were) **damaged** in the storm have been repaired.
  A survey **conducted** by Berni revealed some unexpected information.

C

SUGGESTED ANSWERS

1 Do you have all the **necessary** ingredients?
2 I object to his **downright** rudeness.
3 Don't forget to follow the **suggested** guidelines / the guidelines **suggested**.
4 The people **responsible** have all been arrested.
5 Never wake a **sleeping** baby.
6 In the sale there were bargains **galore**.

7 I'd love a **refreshing** glass of lemonade.
8 Can I try one of those **delicious-looking** cakes?
9 She is the nicest person **imaginable**.
10 It seems to me that he is an **utter** fool.
11 The meeting **proper** began promptly.
12 Some of the people **present** fell asleep.

5.6 Making notes

WRITING SKILLS

A **1–3** Each of the styles of note-making has its advantages. Pool ideas with the whole class when the pairs have compared their lists in step **3**.

The missing points are:
A
packaging: environmentally damaging – plastic bottles in landfill sites

B
distribution: transportation from overseas + water-short countries unnecessary + wasteful

C
Water Companies Association say: ' . . . '
British Soft Drinks Association say: ' . . . '

B **1** Pause the recording from time to time for the students to make notes. Some of the main points are in bold in the Transcript, but only the ones that are relevant to the topic of the article in **B2**.

2 👥 The idea is for the students to sift through their notes to find the relevant points to make in their article. This should be the main purpose of comparing notes.

✏ The article should be written as homework.

TRANSCRIPT *6 minutes 20 seconds*

LIZ (Presenter): Do you start your day with a cup of coffee? I know that I do. Or maybe a cup of tea? Or hot chocolate? Or perhaps you have some fruit juice and a banana. Now you may not know, but all these **products** come **from developing countries in the South**, and one of the problems is that these products are often produced by **farmers** who are **not earning enough to support themselves and their families decently**. Craig Thomas reports.

CRAIG: Yep, that's right. These products are freely traded around the world and because there's a plentiful supply of these crops, the **prices paid to the growers are low**. And they're often paid by **middlemen, who buy at the lowest price** and have to make their own profits. Now, to make matters worse the **world price fluctuates**, depending on harvests around the world. And this means farmers never know how much their crop is going to earn them. And, of course, they depend on selling their crops to buy food for their families and to pay for their children's education. Uh…to take an example, let's look at bananas, and we can see how this works. Er…Sally Anderson has recently visited the Caribbean island of St Vincent and she's…she's with us today. Um…Sally, you've talked to farmers there.

SALLY: Yes, I have, and the problem that banana growers in many small Caribbean islands face is that a farmer and his or her family runs a small farm of one or two hectares. And their livelihood depends on **bananas**, it's often their only crop, and they **can't compete on price** with the giant plantations of Ecuador and Colombia, where workers are paid as little as one dollar a day. The quality of their bananas is superior, but the price is higher.

CRAIG: Right, well, one solution to this problem is the Fairtrade scheme, which was set up in 1992 by development agencies including Oxfam and Christian Aid. How does this work exactly?

SALLY: Well, the **Fairtrade scheme guarantees a decent fixed price to growers** who belong to a cooperative. This is a **guaranteed minimum price**, and this means that they don't suffer when the market price is low and therefore they **can afford to feed their families and educate their children**. They sign a long-c…term contract, which covers the cost of production, a basic living wage and when world prices rise above the minimum they get a little bit extra: **10 per cent is added as a social premium** which goes into a **social fund** to help **improve their working and living conditions**. And in return they undertake to produce high quality bananas and **refrain from using child labour** and to s… to **sustain the environment**.

LIZ: But it's not only bananas is it, Craig? Wh…what other kinds of Fairtrade food are available?

CRAIG: Well, best-known and most widely available is coffee. After oil, **coffee** is the most highly-valued commodity in the world. It's a huge market. And coffee is grown mostly in developing countries. And unfortunately most of the coffee growers around the world don't make a good living. Er…they often have to sell to…er…unscrupulous middlemen at very low prices. **Even when the world price rises, they don't benefit**. Now, Fairtrade can help them to improve their lives enormously. Coffee is the most widely marketed product under the Fairtrade brand. Er…the…the…the label on each pack of coffee may even inform you which community the coffee comes from and how buying it will help the local growers to improve their lives. Er…this pack of Cafédirect that I have here has a nice picture of Mario Hernandez in Nicaragua saying, "We have seen achievements. Now I have **money to buy clothes for my children, to build my house**. Day by day things are improving, because of the better price." So, there you are, the buyer feels a personal connection with the farmer.

LIZ: Mm, that's excellent. And how many producers belong to this Fairtrade scheme?

SALLY: Well, there are over half a million farmers in about 13 countries, and they all belong to **cooperatives**, as I said earlier. So their **communities share the benefits**. Now, to make this work, consumers in the North are being persuaded to support the scheme by paying a little bit extra for their bananas. But in return they get a high quality product and, more importantly, they get the warm feeling that they are playing the part in helping poorer people in the South.

LIZ: Mm, important, absolutely. Now, apart from coffee and bananas, Craig, are there any other products that come under this Fairtrade scheme?

CRAIG: Oh, yes, you can buy tea, chocolate and cocoa, er…honey, sugar, orange juice – all with the Fairtrade logo on the pack. Er…in fact, there are over 70 different food and drink products available now in the UK. Some of these are organics, some are not, but the Fairtrade Foundation monitors the standards of production and the quality of the products, all products. And almost all these products are grown by small growers who belong to cooperatives. Er…because this is one way to keep costs down. There's no middleman involved if the products are bought directly…er…from the cooperative. Small farms are not as cost-effective as larger plantations. So, sadly, the price has to be higher.

LIZ: Mm, so would you say the problem for consumers is the price?

CRAIG: Well, that's right. Um…on average Fairtrade products cost around 30 per cent more than the equivalent non-Fairtrade product. So they are more likely to be bought by better off shoppers. But still the number of products is growing all the time, and their popularity is growing too. Um…manufacturers who use the Fairtrade logo pay 2 per cent of the wholesale price to the Fairtrade Foundation, which uses…er…that money to monitor the scheme, and to find new sources and…er…raise awareness among both suppliers and consumers.

LIZ: But the big question is: Can you taste the difference?

SALLY: Yes, you can! Windward Island bananas taste absolutely wonderful.

CRAIG: Yeah, and the coffee is great too. Well worth the extra few pence.

SALLY: But best of all you know you are making a worthwhile contribution to the welfare of farmers *and* their families.

5.6 Model version

The Fairtrade scheme was set up in 1992 by development agencies to try to make the life of the small producer in developing countries more secure. Most of the 70 products available in this scheme are grown by small farmers in the South who cannot compete with the big growers on price and, prior to the introduction of the scheme, were at the mercy of the world price and the middlemen for their survival. Usually they only produce one kind of crop and are thus more dependent on the vagaries of nature for success or failure. In many cases they do not earn enough to support their families or themselves and are never able to make long-term plans. Some cannot afford clothes for their children or the materials to build a house. The best known products in the scheme are coffee and bananas.

The Fairtrade scheme guarantees the farmers a minimum price however much the price fluctuates on the world market. When the world price goes above the minimum, the farmers receive extra. Fairtrade also cuts out the middleman who would always pay the lowest price possible even when the world price is high. In return the farmers organise themselves into collectives, agree to produce a high quality product, to sustain the environment and not to use child labour. In addition to the minimum price, they receive 10% extra when prices rise above the minimum and this goes into a social fund to benefit their whole community. The undertakings the farmers themselves make with regard to children and the environment also help to improve conditions in their community. Children are freed to go to school and their parents can provide them with books, and shoes for the walk to school. The scheme also raises awareness in the rich northern countries of the problems of the poorer south and gives them the opportunity to contribute effectively and to the long-term welfare of small farmers.

Leo Jones *New Progress to Proficiency*

CORRECT ANSWERS

1 **is** – sounds more definite
  be – more formal
  should be – less definite, formal: *should* would normally be unstressed here
2 **be given** – very formal
  should be given – quite formal
3 **should do** and **ought to do** – both mean the same here, asking for advice
  can do – asking for suggested alternative courses of action
4 **should arrive** – dramatic emphasis: cf . . . *when in walked Billy*
5 **feel** – normal, unmarked
  do feel – emphasising the verb
  should feel – more formal, less direct

Extra information

Students who have difficulty with using *be* + past participle, which is actually the **subjunctive**, should be reminded that its use is entirely optional. As long as they understand it and realise that it sounds rather formal, they may not actually need to use it.

In American English the subjunctive is used more frequently in informal language than it is in British English, where its use often sounds rather old-fashioned or pedantic.

The subjunctive in English

1 The subjunctive (i.e. the base form of the verb) is used in these examples:
  It is/was essential that every person **have** the same opportunities.
  I propose/proposed that everyone **sign** this petition.
  It's important that everyone **pay** their subscription.
  It was suggested that they **discuss** the issues.

2 The following verbs and phrases can be used with *be* + past participle or *should* (or the subjunctive):

  I was . . . alarmed   amazed   amused   annoyed   astonished   disappointed
  sad   shocked   worried   delighted   glad   happy   pleased
  overjoyed   thankful   **that . . .**

  It is . . . a disgrace   a mistake   a pity   a shame   a nuisance
  awful   disgraceful   terrible   wrong   **that . . .**

  alarm   bother   disappoint   interest   intrigue   puzzle   scare   shock
  upset   worry
  e.g. It **worried** me that they **should feel** so upset.
       It was **alarming** that he **should be** so critical.
       It **puzzles** me that she **should make** such silly mistakes.

3 And when making or reporting suggestions and recommendations:

  It is . . . essential   desirable   important   vital   necessary   **that . . .**
  and after these verbs:
    ask   demand   insist   prefer   propose   recommend   request   suggest
  e.g. It is **vital** that the results **should be posted** on the noticeboard.
       It is **vital** that the results **be posted** on the noticeboard.
       It is **vital** that the secretary **post** the results on the noticeboard.
       It is **vital** that the secretary **should post** the results on the noticeboard.
       I **suggested** that he **gave** a talk about his experiences.
       I **suggested** that he **should give** a talk about his experiences.
       I **suggested** that he **give** a talk about his experiences.

4 The verb *to be* has two subjunctive forms:
  I wish I **were** young and beautiful.   (past subjunctive)
  I insist that I **be** sent the results.   (present subjunctive)
  With all other verbs, there is no difference between the present and past subjunctive forms.

---

5 The subjunctive is also found in a number of fixed phrases and idioms:
Long **live** the President.
God **save** The Queen.
Be that as it may, . . .
Come what may . . .
Suffice it to say that . . .

Leo Jones *New Progress to Proficiency*

C Many variations are possible – and should be encouraged in questions 6 to 9.

> **SUGGESTED ANSWERS**
>
> 1 should make notes
> 2 should hand in
> 3 be done/should be done
> 4 should raise
> 5 should have to do
> 6 the environment should be protected
>
> 7 the weather should be so wet today
> 8 my friend should have lost her handbag
> 9 people should be so inconsiderate to each other
> 10 be elected/should be elected
> 11 should have any

(See also **13.4 Conditionals – 2**.)

5.8 Describing a process

LISTENING AND COMPOSITION

A 1 It might help students to separate the captions into stages in the process and the results of those stages, as well as guessing the likely sequence.

On the other hand, you may prefer to present it as a 'particularly challenging exercise' and see how they get on with it.

2 🔊 A difficult one! At least two playings are needed. You may need to point out that it's not necessary to understand any of the technical terms to do the exercise.

> **ANSWERS**
>
> | Top row: | 1 | 14 | 8 | 6 |
> |---|---|---|---|---|
> | 2nd row: | 11 | 4 | 3 | 12 |
> | 3rd row: | 2 | 5 | 13 | 10 |
> | 4th row: | 9 | 7 | 15 | |

And here are some questions for follow-up discussion:

• Which do you normally eat: butter or margarine? Give your reasons.
• What kinds of foods are thought to be 'bad for your health'? How much notice do you take of this knowledge in your own diet?
• What can you find out by reading the small print on food labels?

B 1 Arrange the class into groups of four. Students A and B look at **Activity 2** on page 199, C and D look at **15** on page 203. Each pair has different information about the processes of brewing beer and making wine.

If you don't actually have 12, 16 or 20 students in your class, form one or more groups of five with two students working together as 'Student A'.

2 👥 After studying the information together in pairs, and making notes, the pairs split up and then recombine, as explained in the Student's Book.

C 🖊 You may prefer to specify which of the two topics your students should choose, depending on their capabilities and interests. Perhaps don't worry about a word limit of 350 words for this exercise, and suggest that diagrams may be used in the article (though not in the exam, of course!).

The 'research' required may be no more than sitting down and thinking through a familiar process, such as writing an e-mail, or boiling an egg. Maybe brainstorm some suitably straightforward processes with the whole class.

TRANSCRIPT *2 minutes 30 seconds*

NARRATOR: You'll hear how margarine is manufactured.

JONATHAN: Everyone will tell you that margarine is natural and healthy.

JULIA: Yes.

JONATHAN: So it's made from vegetable oils like sunflower seed oil or corn oil, and vegetable fat is supposed to be better for you than animal fat. [Mhm.] Yes, it's supposed to contain less cholesterol, it's more healthy. [Mm.] And its sunny, natural taste seems attractive to people who care about their health, right? [Yeah.] But just how natural is it? Well, let me explain the process step by step. First of all, the sunflower or other plant seeds are heated and then crushed to release the oil. This is a sort of crude plant oil which still contains impurities like resins and gums. So, what they have to do next is to add caustic soda. [Oh!] Yeah, this removes waste products which form the basic ingredients of soap. [Oh, no.] Yes, it may surprise you to know that quite a lot of the soap we use actually comes from this process. [Right.] So the next step is to add fullers earth, which bleaches the oil. And then they have pure, refined oil. Now, next, the oil has to be reacted with hydrogen using a catalyst, in this case nickel, and this process hardens the oils. All right? [Mm.] Now, after that the oils have to be neutralised, then they're bleached, and filtered to remove any waste products. [Mm.] Now…haha…at this stage there's often a rather nasty smell! [Right.] And this is removed by heating the hardened oils until they melt again. [Mm.] Not finished yet! Then the oils are mixed with small quantities of fish and animal oils . . . [No!] Yep, to create the right kind of blended oils. But there are still more essential ingredients to be added. They have to add water, skimmed milk and some salt. And then they also have to put some flavour, artificial flavour, into this tasteless mixture and make it a nice yellow colour and put in some vitamins. [Ohh!] But even after this lengthy process the ingredients won't blend until they're emulsified. This is done by adding lecithin and monoglyceride to the mixture. Then the mixture is cooled and now, at last, it's ready to be extruded into a lovely plastic tub and a lid with pretty sunflowers is plonked on the top.

JULIA: Haha!

JONATHAN: So, that's how margarine is made. Butter, on the other hand, is simply made by churning cream. It's pure, it's natural and it tastes good too.

5.8 Model version

225g plain wholemeal flour

1 tablespoon ground cinnamon

1 teaspoon ground nutmeg

$\frac{1}{2}$ teaspoon baking powder

110g butter

110g honey

110g sugar

1 large egg

handful sultanas

handful walnuts, chopped

225g carrots, peeled and grated

This is a description of how to make a carrot cake. First of all you need a medium size saucepan in which you put the butter, honey and sugar. Put the pan on a low heat and allow the butter and honey to melt and the sugar to dissolve in the resultant syrup. Remove the pan from the heat and allow the mixture to cool slightly. Then stir in the measured flour, baking powder, spices, nuts, sultanas, beaten egg and grated carrots. When all the ingredients are well combined, turn them into a greased and lined loaf tin. Pre-heat the oven to 170 degrees C. Bake for about an hour or until the cake feels firm to the touch and a skewer inserted into the centre comes out clean. Leave the cake in the tin for 10 minutes and then turn it out on to a cooling rack. The cake is best eaten within 3 to 4 days.

Leo Jones *New Progress to Proficiency*

6

See the world!

6.1 Where would you like to go?   TOPIC VOCABULARY

A   👥 This is a warm-up discussion; the follow-up discussion in **D** covers place names and nationality words too.

B   If you think this might be a bit difficult, and want to save time, maybe read the whole passage aloud to the class (with pens down) – then ask them to fill the gaps.

> **ANSWERS**
>
> Soufrière is a small fishing port on the west **coast**[1] of the **island**[2] of St Lucia in the Caribbean. It lies at the centre of a sheltered **bay**[3] which forms a natural **harbour**[4]. The town is dominated by the Pitons: two mountain **peaks**[5] which were once **volcanoes**[6], covered in tropical **rainforest**[7]. If you travel **inland**[8] up the river **valley**[9] you come to a **plateau**[10] where there are plantations growing coconuts and tropical fruits, watered by little **streams**[11] flowing down from the hills. To the north there are impressive **cliffs**[12] plunging into the sea and around a **headland**[13] is a secluded hotel above a little **cove**[14], from where you can swim out to watch the fish around the coral **reef**[15]. The **view**[16] from the hotel is breathtaking.
>
> Despite its wonderful **setting**[17], warm **climate**[18], friendly people and delicious local **seafood**[19], Soufrière isn't a popular tourist destination, perhaps because it lacks the sandy **beaches**[20] tourists expect in a Caribbean **resort**[21].

Extra activity

🖎 When they've finished the exercise, ask everyone to write a similar description of their own region, using a dictionary to find suitable words.

C   After they've finished the exercise, get everyone to look at the words they *didn't* choose, and explain why they didn't choose them. What situations would they use those words in?

> **ANSWERS**
>
> 1 off the beaten track   out of the way   secluded
> 2 courteous   easygoing   hospitable
> 3 holidaymakers   pilgrims   travellers
> 4 drive   journey   trip
> 5 abroad   away from home   out of the country

D   👥 Although this section may look deceptively easy, even advanced students have difficulty in using English place names and nationality words, particularly when they are spelt similarly in their own language. Take the names of some of the principal cities in Italy, for example, in other languages:

Italian: Roma, Milano, Firenze, Venezia, Napoli, Genova
English: Rome, Milan, Florence, Venice, Naples, Genoa
German: Rom, Mailand, Florenz, Venedig, Neapel, Genua
French: Rome, Milan, Florence, Venise, Naples, Gênes

6.2 Learning the language   READING AND SPEAKING

Background   Rose Macaulay's best-known novel *The Towers of Trebizond* (1956) is an amusing account of a young woman's travels in Turkey accompanying an eccentric aunt. Her other novels include *Dangerous Ages* and *Keeping Up Appearances*.

These questions are similar to questions in Part 5 of the Use of English Paper. (In the exam, shorter answers than these are OK.) Finding the relevant information in the text is necessary in the Reading Paper too, of course.

To save time this section can be done for homework – then the students can compare their answers when they return to class.

SUGGESTED ANSWERS

1 They repeated things and spoke more loudly, believing that everyone can speak Turkish
2 Because she didn't expect them to ask questions when she said she didn't understand Turkish
3 Because a Mr Yorum was by then staying at the hotel
4 Because she had sent for him, he was saying 'I'm the person you sent for.'
5 She thought he might be offering to act as her interpreter
6 There was nothing to be done: there seemed to be so much confusion in Turkey that it didn't seem to matter

B & C After discussing how the story might continue, students read the continuation of the passage in **Activities 4** on page 200 and **16** on page 203. Encourage everyone to use their own words, and discourage them from reading the paragraphs aloud to each other.

6.3 The future   GRAMMAR REVIEW

A **SUGGESTED ANSWERS**

1 I think I'm going to scream.
   – *I won't be able to stop myself from screaming (if I don't get out of here soon)*
   I think I'll scream.
   – *It might be a good idea for me to scream (it might attract someone's attention)*

2 It's still raining in Scotland.
   – *According to the weather report, the rain is still falling there*
   It's still going to rain in Scotland.
   – *According to the forecast, rain is expected once again in Scotland*
   It will still be raining in Scotland.
   – *(When you get there) the rain won't have stopped*
   It still rains in Scotland.
   – *The Scottish climate hasn't changed, it still tends to be quite rainy there*

3 I'll phone him after work.
   – *Promise or offer: I undertake to phone him (maybe on your behalf, or because you want me to)*
   I'm phoning him after work.
   – *This is what I'm planning to do, I've set aside time to do it*
   I'm going to phone him after work.
   – *I intend to do it then – the normal 'uncoloured' future form*
   I'll be phoning him after work.
   – *Reassurance: I'm going to phone him (so don't worry)*
     OR (While something else is going on, at the same time) I'm going to phone him, and it may be a long call

4 When are we having lunch?
   & When are we going to have lunch?
   – *What time is lunch?*
   When do we have lunch?
   – *What is the planned, arranged time for lunch?*
   When shall we have lunch?
   – *When would you like to eat?*

5 What time shall I get to your house?
   – *What time would you like me to arrive?*
   What time will I get to your house?
   – *When will I arrive (if I leave town at ten)?*

> **6** I'll work hard tonight.
>   – *I promise to work hard*
> I'll be working hard tonight.
>   – *(Please don't phone me because) I'm planning to spend the evening working and I'll be busy*
> **7** Will you be going shopping today?
> & Are you going shopping today?
> & Are you going to go shopping today?
>   – *Is this one of the things you're planning to do today?*
> Will you go shopping today?
>   – *Request: I want you to go shopping*
> Do you go shopping today?
>   – *Is today your regular day for shopping?*

B Make sure everyone is aware of the possible variations, and that there is little difference in meaning between them.

> **SUGGESTED ANSWERS**
>
> **1** I'm going to   Will/Could/Can
> **2** Will you be   are in/go to/visit
> **3** Are you going to go   are you going to take/catch
> **4** breaks down   will you
>   *or* broke down   would you
> **5** to land   will be/is going to be/might be
> **6** lands   will have been
> **7** has in store for/will bring
> **8** is going to be/is likely to be
> **9** are away on   'll be/'m going to be   'll send
> **10** 'll have
> **11** get/receive   'll give you
> **12** decided/discussed   are going to do
> **13** phones/calls/needs/wants   'll   be having
> **14** will/is likely to   leave/have left
> **15** to reading   have

C **1 & 2** 👥👥 ✏ This section is crucial, especially the paragraph-writing task. It gives everyone a chance for some free practice and to find out the kinds of mistakes they make in using future forms.

6.4 One word – different meanings

VOCABULARY DEVELOPMENT

In Part 3 of the Use of English Paper, candidates have to choose one word that will fit into a gap in three unrelated sentences. The missing words may be homonyms or words used in different senses in different contexts. (See also **16.10** for more about Part 3.)

Allow everyone time to look at the examples at the top before they do the exercises.

A This is best done in pairs so that everyone can brainstorm the various possibilities. It's more fun too!

> **ANSWERS**
>
> **1** drive   **2** left   **3** show   **4** article   **5** second   **6** faint   **7** charge   **8** funny

B 👥 Again, doing it in pairs is more enjoyable than doing it alone.

> **ANSWERS**
> 1 pound   2 appreciate   3 firm   4 case   5 will   6 cover

Preparation   Before the next lesson, ask everyone to read the passage in **6.5 B** and do the tasks in **C** and **D**. Perhaps spend some time discussing the **questions** in **6.5 A** in class at the end of this lesson.

6.5   The friendly skies   READING

Background   Jonathan Raban's travel writing includes *Coasting*, an account of a journey by sea around the coast of Britain, *Old Glory* about a journey down the Mississippi River, and *Arabia through the Looking Glass* about a journey in the Arabian peninsula.

His novel *Foreign Land* is about an old man who returns to a much-changed Britain after a lifetime spent overseas. *Passage to Juneau* is a wonderful account of a solo journey in a yacht from Seattle through the Inside Passage to Juneau in Alaska.

In *Hunting Mister Heartbreak*, from which this passage comes, he tries to 'settle' in various parts of the United States, ending up in Seattle where he feels most at home.

A 👥👥 This discussion helps to set the scene for the theme of the passage.

B The passage should ideally be read at home before the lesson.

There are deliberately no laborious vocabulary exercises or tricky comprehension questions here. The emphasis is on enjoying the passage, and letting the sense carry the reader through despite the unfamiliar vocabulary and the 1200-odd words.

C 👤→👤
> **ANSWERS**
> 1 D   2 D   3 B   4 B   5 C
> 6 B *or possibly* D – *Oprah is Oprah Winfrey, the TV talk show host*   7 A

D The process of highlighting useful vocabulary in any reading passage should by now have become routine, but this should act as a reminder. If necessary, refer everyone back to the notes on vocabulary learning in **1.3 E**.

E 👥 Highlight some parts that amused **you**, so that you can compare these with the students' reactions.

6.6   Repetition   WRITING SKILLS

Make sure everyone appreciates the difference between deliberate repetition for effect, and the kind of unimaginative repetition of words, where the same words are repeated unimaginatively and not deliberately repeated for effect!

A **1 & 2** 👥 In case some students don't know where Saskatchewan (/sæsˈkætʃəwən/ or /səsˈkætʃəwən/) is, tell them it's right in the centre of Canada. The capital is Regina (/rɪˈjaɪnə/).

SUGGESTED ANSWERS (The repeated words and structures are underlined.)

10 Great Reasons to Visit Saskatchewan

Saskatchewan is a big province that constantly surprises. With its vast and changing landscapes, its colourful events and its rich heritage, it has a lot to offer. Covering it in a few words and photos is no easy task.

In the next 20 pages we present 10 great reasons why you should travel our province. Why Saskatchewan is special. Why it's a place where you belong.

We have thousands of reasons for you to see Saskatchewan – we're limited to 10 here. We're confident you'll find them reasons enough to visit. And that you'll find reasons more to return.

1. The Prairies

When people think Saskatchewan, they think prairies. They think fields of gold that stretch up against the horizon. They think bold, blue sky. They think vistas that seem flawlessly flat and that from the air resemble a patchwork quilt.

Prairie scenery can be breathtaking. Brilliant mustard and canola waving in the wind. Grain elevators standing like sentinels, signalling the approach of new towns. Sunsets offering their light shows of purple, orange and red.

The prairies are also rolling hills where you'd least expect them. Valleys full of wild flowers, prairie lilies and saskatoons. Plus plains and bush alive with prairie dogs, meadowlarks and white-tailed deer.

This year stop and smell the clover. See the images that have graced a thousand postcards. Visit the prairies.

2. The Parks

Hike a leafy aspen trail. Zip down a monster waterslide. Join a "wolf howl" under clear moonlight. Whatever your interests you can likely satisfy them in Saskatchewan's parks.

With nearly five million acres of Saskatchewan parkland, Mother Nature has plenty of places in which to work her spell on you. At our parks you can sink that championship putt, watch deer and elk by the roadside, relax at a four-season resort, or pitch your tent near a back country gurgling stream.

Waskesiu. Grasslands. Moose Mountain. Cypress Hills. Our parks are destinations, summer and winter. They put you in touch with a simpler, gentler world – a world where the sun shines bright and the deadlines and pressures of ordinary life are far, far away.

3. The Lakes

Get out your swimming trunks, unfurl those sails, dust off your water-skis, take the canoe and tackle box out of storage and book that cabin or resort. Saskatchewan's 100,000 – that's right 100,000! – lakes await you.

4. The Fishing

Picture a lazy day on a crystal clear lake. Morning mist comes off the water. An evergreen shoreline frames your horizon. A bald eagle circles overhead. Then suddenly your line tenses, and everything changes. Your battle with a monster of the deep has begun.

and

10. The People

If there are 10 great reasons to visit Saskatchewan, then there are a million reasons to come back. Our people. Superhearted. Lively. Famous for their hospitality.

With a mosaic of cultures, Saskatchewan is truly the world in one place. Native Indians and people with British, French and east-European roots. People who celebrate their uniqueness at annual celebrations like Vesna and Folkfest in Sasktatoon, or Mosaic in Regina. Where the food, fun and music of the homelands trail long into the night.

When all is said and done, it's the people you meet who make a vacation unforgettable. We invite you to meet ours. Through them discover the place where you belong.

B **1–3** 👥 ✏️ Begin by deciding, as a class, whether the pairs will be dealing with the whole of their country or just one region or city. It will add interest if the different pairs don't all discuss and then write about exactly the same place or attraction.

6.7 Revision and exam practice — ADVANCED GRAMMAR

This exercise revises some of the advanced grammar points introduced in Units 1 to 5. The questions reflect some of the HARDER questions of this type that come up in Part 4 of the Use of English Paper.

> **SUGGESTED ANSWERS**
>
> 2 We **were still waiting at midnight** for the plane to take off.
> 3 **Arriving at the airport, I was told** that my flight had been cancelled.
> 4 Never **having flown before**, I was very nervous.
> 5 The **only thing I want is to spend** the rest of my life with you.
>   or The **only thing I want to do is spend** the rest of my life with you.
> 6 Not **only do they go on holiday** in the winter but in the summer too.
> 7 Little **did we realise that** our hotel was right beside the airport.
> 8 I propose **that he be sent a letter** explaining the situation.
> 9 She **never fails to get the** right answers.
> 10 Only after writing several letters of complaint **did we manage to get** our money back.

6.8 The impact of tourism — LISTENING AND COMPOSITION

A

> **SUGGESTED ANSWERS**
>
> 1 200   2 about 75   3 off-limits   4 Europe (Germany, Italy, UK)
> 5a the underwater environment   5b the 'Robinson Crusoe' factor
> 6 imported   7 highly successful   8 get back home (unless they live in Malé)
> 9 beautiful/colourful   10 global warming

B This discussion helps to link the content of the recording to the composition the students have to write in **C**.

C Allow everyone time to read two other students' completed compositions before you collect them in and correct them.

TRANSCRIPT *5 minutes 30 seconds*

PRESENTER: The Maldives is a long chain of over a thousand tiny coral islands in the Indian Ocean. There are 26 atolls extending over 800 kilometres north-to-south and for 100 kilometres east-to-west. There are 300,000 Maldivians. Bob Allison has just returned from Malé, the capital. Bob, not all the islands are inhabited, are they?

BOB: No, Polly. Um…200 of the islands are inhabited and even these are very small. About 75 of these are developed as resorts and are off-limits to the general population. Likewise, *their* islands are generally off-limits to tourists so special permits or organised tours are the only way of visiting them. Tourism only came to the country in the 1970s. Until then the people lived from fishing and products of the coconut palm, as little else will grow in the poor soil.

PRESENTER: Right.

BOB: The people are all Muslims. A strict dress code applies and immodest dress is offensive to Maldivians. Maldivian staff are not allowed to serve alcohol, special staff from Sri Lanka or India have to do that.

PRESENTER: Right and what kind of people go there?

BOB: Well, the resorts in the Maldives attract tourists with promises of 'the last paradise on earth'. And if your idea of paradise is a pristine tropical island with swaying palm trees, pure white beaches and brilliant turquoise lagoons, then the Maldives will not disappoint. It's also a major destination for scuba divers, who come for the fabulous coral reefs and the wealth of marine life. Er…but it's not a place for low budget backpackers or for people who want to travel independently and live as the locals do. Most of the people who visit the Maldives are…are from Europe: mainly from Germany, Italy and the UK. It's a…a 12-hour flight from Europe and…er…500,000 tourists visit the Maldives each year.

PRESENTER: Mm, an…and what is unusual about tourism in the Maldives?

BOB: Well, the unique feature of tourism in the Maldives is that it is carefully managed. Er…the country's Tourism Master Plan identifies both the underwater environment and the 'Robinson Crusoe' factor as major attractions, but these are not seen as compatible with large-scale, low budget, mass tourism. The lack of local resources makes it necessary to import virtually everything a visitor needs, from furniture to fresh vegetables, so the Maldives cannot really compete on price. The strategy has been to develop a limited number of quality resorts, each on its own uninhabited island, free from traffic, crime and crass commercialism. The Maldivian tourism strategy also aims to minimise the adverse effects of tourism on traditional Muslim communities.

PRESENTER: Right.

BOB: Tourists can make short guided visits to local fishing villages, but must then return to their resort.

Er…most are satisfied with this glimpse of local life and culture. But to stay longer or to travel to atolls outside the tourist zone requires a good reason, um…a special permit, and a…a local person to sponsor the visitor. Most tourists come to understand the restrictions after a short visit to an accessible island. Er…it's difficult to imagine how isolated Maldivian communities would benefit from extended stays by uncontrolled numbers of tourists.

PRESENTER: Mm, a…and how successful has this strategy been?

BOB: Well, like it or not, this highly regulated tourist industry has been enormously successful. There are more and better resorts, a steady increase in visitor numbers, and a minimal impact on the natural and social environment. The Maldives is internationally recognised as a model for sustainable, environment-friendly tourist development.

PRESENTER: But the…there must be some disadvantages?

BOB: Yes, there are. Um…most of the resort staff have to live on the resort islands. Their homes are often on distant islands, difficult to reach from the resort islands, and they can only go back there from time to time for short breaks. It's easier for staff who live in Malé who can get back to the capital more easily. Still, the work they do is not unpleasant. And may be preferable to emigration.

PRESENTER: Sure.

BOB: The country is heavily dependent on tourism – there are also small clothing factories and fishing. Almost everything the tourist needs has to be imported apart from coconuts and fish. Each resort island has its own diesel generator for electricity. Water is produced from sea water in desalination plants on each resort island. And these costs are sure to rise in the future. And will tourists be willing to pay more for holidays in the Maldives? That's the question. And there are probably more serious problems . . .

PRESENTER: What are they?

BOB: Well, first of all, *El Niño*. Coral is vulnerable to changes in sea temperature. When the sea temperature rises above 22 degrees, the coral turns white because it expels a minute…the minute organisms that live within its hard limestone core. These organisms cannot tolerate a rise in sea temperature of over 1 to 2 degrees Centigrade for more than a few weeks. The beautiful colours of the coral are no longer there and divers are disappointed.

PRESENTER: Oh, right.

BOB: And this is happening all over the Pacific and Indian Oceans, not just in the Maldives. And the other problem is global warming. The average height of the islands above sea level is only 1.6 metres. Coral islands are vulnerable to a rise in sea level. A big wall has been built around Malé to protect it from the sea, but that may only be a temporary solution. As the sea level rises, by the end of the century some islands will be under the sea.

PRESENTER: So go there while you still can?

BOB: Haha, yes, I think so. Start saving up now!

6.8 Model version

Before tourism came to G__ it was truly a wild and beautiful place. Situated near a 10-kilometre stretch of sand on the northern coast of a Mediterranean island, with two rivers running clear and cold from the mountains, it was an obvious holiday destination. The scenery is breathtaking. The mountains which rise up in the centre of the island are snowcapped for most of the year and make a wonderful backdrop to the sparkling sea and the bamboo lined rivers. Fishing and small-holdings occupied the villagers before tourism. There was no natural harbour but a jetty had been built on rocks near the mouth of the larger river. Between the two rivers was a large area of marshland, home to many birds and mosquitoes! In the 19th century, when malaria was still a big problem, eucalyptus trees had been planted in an attempt to drain some of the water and reduce the number of mosquitoes. Those trees now tower majestically above the village square, providing shade from the hot sun. If you waded in the smaller river you could spot minuscule turtles, kingfishers darting along the water and herons and other water birds.

The first hotel was built about twenty years ago. It was small and seemed content not to be too busy. But in the last ten years tourism has really taken off here. A major trunk road was built from west to east along the northern coast which has made G__ accessible in an hour and a half from the nearest airport. Other hotels and self-catering apartments have popped up, some foolishly built very close to the marshes. There's a large and brash disco, a crop of chic souvenir shops and a wealth of simple restaurants. The village itself has improved in many ways and there's certainly enough work here between April and October to employ a good many locals and possibly incomers. The fishing fleet has been kept up and has impressive quays on both sides of the main river. The beach itself is so wide and long that it is quite possible to escape the cluster of sunbathers near the town and it could never be described as crowded.

The wild feel has gone, along with some of the wildlife, but the intrinsic beauty of the place still works its magic and has helped to keep the youngsters at home.

Leo Jones *New Progress to Proficiency*

SUGGESTED ANSWERS

1   accepted (with difficulty)
2   happen in the expected way   didn't succeed
3   made him too conceited   (*also*: made him drunk)
4   progressing   accompany
5   stopped liking   continue, complete
6   look at, discuss   occurs
7   Carry on, don't hesitate   be handy later
8   attacked
9   become independent   becomes successful   investigated, examined
10   was a great success   received a good reaction, was received gratefully

ANSWERS

1   came up with
2   coming out
3   gone up   go down   (*also*: come down)
4   come across
5   went on at   go in for
6   went down with   (*also*: came down with)
7   goes off/goes in for
8   came round
9   comes up
10   came apart

7

Spending your money

7.1 Shop till you drop!   TOPIC VOCABULARY AND LISTENING

A   The title of this section is a phrase used jokingly by people who love shopping. In the warm-up discussion encourage everyone to justify their choices, and not merely mention the names of each store.

B

ANSWERS

2 mall   shopping centre   precinct
3 articles   goods   merchandise
4 a bargain   good value   value for money
5 manufacturer   supplier   wholesaler
6 retailer   trader   vendor
7 purchase   sale   transaction
8 make a down payment   pay cash down   pay a deposit
9 guarantee   twelve months old   warranty
10 courteous   helpful   knowledgeable
   – obsequious *and* subservient *are also possible, but only if used lightheartedly*

C   **1 & 2** 🔊 The students should note down their answers to the questions and join a partner to compare their notes later.

SUGGESTED ANSWERS

1 responsibility   independence   constant challenge   dealing with people (i.e. the customers and her team)   unpredictability   being busy all the time
2 watching what's going on in the department   ensuring that stock is on display   supervising the staff   intervening when there is a problem
3 hard work   standing all day   working on Saturday (not a disadvantage for Amanda herself)   working one late night every week
4 to manage a department in a larger branch   to stay in the selling side

TRANSCRIPT *3 minutes 10 seconds*

PRESENTER: Amanda Hooper is twenty-six and is a department manager in a well-known department store. What does she enjoy about her job?

AMANDA: I think it's the responsibility that knowing that it's my department and that I can basically do what I like that, you know, that I think needs to be done to improve sales or to…um…have a more efficient team or to make my department look better and that's a constant challenge. Also you're always dealing with people, either customers or your own team, and people are very unpredictable, so one day is never the same as the next, it's always something different happening. And I like that, I like to be busy all the time.

PRESENTER: How much contact does she personally have with the customers?

AMANDA: Well, I mean I'm on the floor quite a lot because that's part of my job, to have a look at what's going on…um…see that stock's out, to see that everybody's doing what they should be. Um…but I don't actually serve customers as much as the sales assistants would do, I…I don't really go on the till and that's…sales assistants that's their job, and also to help and advise customers because they're the ones with the in-depth knowledge…um…you know, they know the ins and outs, what they can offer the customer, and they're better…perhaps better placed on a day-to-day basis to help a customer or choose something for them. Um…so…but I mean you do have to be on the floor, you have to hear what's going on, you have to check that they are being served correctly, that nobody's got a problem. So if you're about and there seems to be a situation developing, then you…you would go in and see everything was all right. But…um…my job isn't to stand around all day and help customers, that's…that's not what a manager's job is.

PRESENTER: What are the disadvantages of working in retailing?

AMANDA: It's hard work. You stand up all day, you don't sit down, as I've said. Um…it's hot, especially in this sort of weather. Sometimes some people would call the hours unsociable, I don't because I've never valued having a Saturday but I work a Tuesday to Saturday week and my days off are Sunday and Monday. So if I was a great sport fanatic like my husband, who likes to watch the rugby, um…I couldn't…I can't. Um…but that doesn't worry me because I hate sport anyway. Um…also we work a late night till half past seven on Wednesday…um…and that's…basically you should expect to work one every week.

PRESENTER: What are Amanda's ambitions?

AMANDA: Well, I've got one of the larger departments at the moment that…and that I look after and I'm responsible for, so really I'd probably be looking to move to a larger branch, still as a department manager…um…but perhaps with a more…bigger team and larger turnover…um…and also probably the extra pressures that working in a large branch brings. Um…but I think I always want to stay in the selling side…um…because that's, as far as I'm concerned, in retailing where it's at, retailing's all about selling…um…and without the selling side of it you can't do anything.

D Student A looks at **Activity 3** on page 200, B looks at **10** on page 201, C at **26** on page 206, and in a group of 4, D looks at **29** on page 207. Each Activity contains some information about dealing with people in shops and service industries and in other walks of life too. Allow a few moments for everyone to read through the information and absorb it, before they share it with each other.

7.2 Prepositions – 1   GRAMMAR REVIEW

This is the original article – some variations are possible.

> ### MONEY FIT TO LAUNDER
>
> Great inventions rarely work first time. **In**[1] 1990 the Reserve Bank of Australia, the country's central bank, shipped an order **of**[2] commemorative banknotes, **among**[3] the first to be made **from**[4] plastic film rather than paper, **to**[5] Western Samoa. The Pacific islanders' excitement **at**[6] their new two-tala notes soon turned **to**[7] anger. Ink rubbed off the surface and smudged the portrait **of**[8] Malietoa Tanumafali, the revered head of state, **in**[9] whose honour the notes had been issued.
>
> **In**[10] their early days, plastic banknotes shed ink, jammed **in**[11] note-counting machines and often refused to be refolded. But the Reserve Bank, which pioneered the technology, claims to have eradicated the sort of glitches that produced red (and smudged) faces **in**[12] Western Samoa. Australia issued its own plastic tender **for**[13] the first time in 1992. **By**[14] 1996, the country had taken the last **of**[15] its paper money **out of**[16] circulation. Now it is persuading other countries to follow its example.
>
> The Australians say plastic cash has two main advantages **over**[17] the paper variety. First, it is hard to forge. As well as fancy inks and watermarks, it has a transparent window that makes life difficult **for**[18] counterfeiters. The second advantage is economic. Plastic notes are hard to rip and even survive washing machines. Although each note costs **around**[19] twice as much as a paper one to make, it lasts up to four times as long. The advantage is even greater **in**[20] humid climates, where paper notes can survive as little as four months.
>
> Armed **with**[21] these selling points, the Reserve Bank's printing division is running a healthy export business. It makes plastic notes **for**[22] several countries, including Thailand, Brunei and a forgiving Western Samoa. DuraNote, an American company **with**[23] a plastic product, claims to be talking to central banks **in**[24] twenty-four countries. 'Until recently plastic cash was considered a novelty,' says Al McKay **of**[25] DuraNote. 'Now the central banks have become more cost-conscious they are taking it very seriously.'
>
> Such scrimping **on**[26] costs even extends **to**[27] recycling, it seems. Australia plans to turn worn-out plastic notes **into**[28] wheelbarrows, compost bins and plumbing fittings. There may be money **in**[29] such products, **in**[30] more ways than one.

7.3 Something for everyone   READING

West Edmonton Mall is now only the third biggest in the world – and may soon be fourth or fifth!

A **1**   Recommend that everyone concentrates on getting the gist of the passage and absorbing its atmosphere, rather than getting bogged down with unfamiliar words.

(This could be prepared before the lesson and then the students can compare notes in class.)

2 Discussion of reactions to the piece can take place before doing the questions, but you may prefer to postpone this till later if it suits the pace and tastes of your class better.

B 1

ANSWERS

¶ 2 *parlance* = jargon   ¶ 3 *avalanche* = plethora   ¶ 4 *barmy* = crazy   *mock-up* = replica
¶ 7 *meandered* = wandered   *critical faculties* = ability to judge objectively
¶ 8 *oasis* = refuge   ¶ 9 *blithely* = in a carefree manner   *coughing up* = spending
¶ 10 *state-of-the-art* = ultra-modern   *banal* = repetitive and dull
¶ 11 *proceeds* = profits   ¶ 12 *pleasure dome* * = palace of delights
¶ 13 *glorified* = seeming more important than in reality   ¶ 14 *gratifyingly* = agreeably

* This is a reference to Coleridge's marvellous poem *Kubla Khan*. Here are the opening lines:

Kubla Khan
by Samuel Taylor Coleridge (1798)

In Xanadu did Kubla Khan
A stately pleasure-dome decree:
Where Alph, the sacred river, ran
Through caverns measureless to man
Down to a sunless sea.
So twice five miles of fertile ground
With walls and towers were girdled round:
And here were gardens bright with sinuous rills
Where blossomed many an incense-bearing tree;
And here were forests ancient as the hills,
Enfolding sunny spots of greenery.

2

ANSWERS

1 oasis   2 proceeds   3 gratifyingly   banal   critical faculties
4 meandered   5 cough up   6 parlance   7 avalanche   glorified
8 mock-up   9 state-of-the-art   10 blithely   barmy

C

Some of these questions and the summary are similar to Part 5 of the Use of English Paper.

SUGGESTED ANSWERS

1 a tiepin, a woolly hat, a baseball pennant – and coffee and sandwiches
2 Albertan oil
3 pilgrims   shrine
4 sarcastic, humorous
5 admiring   scornful (i.e. ambivalent)
6 The model summary below shows just one person's personal reactions.

7.3 Model summary

There are two things I hate in our wonderful consumer-friendly world: one is shopping and the other is theme parks (Disney in particular). So being captive in a giant mall, even if it does have its own waterworld, golf course and endless eateries, does not appeal. Come to think of it, I also hate air conditioning, muzak and fluorescent light. The sheer size would be another turn-off. I'm afraid I can't find anything about this mall which attracts to me.

Leo Jones *New Progress to Proficiency*

SUGGESTED ANSWERS

1 I didn't have time to read the paper this morning.
  – *The morning is over, it's now afternoon or evening (maybe I read it later in the day, or could read it later)*
  I haven't had time to read the paper this morning.
  – *It's still morning, so theoretically there's still time to read it this morning*

2 I had tea when Pam came in.
  – *I waited for her to come before starting*
  I was having tea when Pam came in.
  – *I started before she turned up*

3 By the time we had had lunch it was 2:30.
  – *We finished lunch at half past two*
  By the time we had lunch it was 2:30.
  – *We started lunch at about two thirty*

4 Where has Steve gone for his holiday?
  – *He's on holiday now, which place has he gone to?*
  Where is Steve going for his holiday?
  – *Where does he plan to go (in the future)?*
  Where has Steve been going for his holiday?
  – *In recent years which place has he usually visited?*
  Where does Steve go for his holiday?
  – *Generally or usually, what is his holiday destination?*
  Where did Steve go for his holiday?
  – *His holiday is over now*
    or, possibly: *he's on holiday still*

5 I had hoped you would invite me.
  – *I'm disappointed because you haven't invited me*
  I did hope you would invite me.
  – *. . . but you didn't*
  I was hoping you would invite me.
  – *I was looking forward to the invitation you have now given me and I'm glad you have invited me at last*
    or *I'm disappointed because you haven't invited me*
  I hoped you would invite me.
  – *I was looking forward to the invitation you have now given me*
    or *. . . but you're not going to invite me/haven't invited me*

6 What are you doing?
  – *What are you up to at the moment?*
    or *What is your current job?*
  What have you done?
  – *I know/suspect you've done something wrong or foolish*
  What do you do?
  – *What is your profession or job?*
    or *What action do you take (in a situation already or about to be described)?*
  What have you been doing?
  – *What activities have you been engaged in recently (since we last met)?*
    or *I know/suspect you've done something wrong or foolish*

SUGGESTED ANSWERS

2 did you buy   suits
3 has been   has been/is
4 it had   started to   decided   wouldn't/might not   came out
5 has   been   touch   'll get
6 went   hasn't had   since
7 have been   since   have you been   didn't   would be/were going to be
  should have/could have   left   wouldn't have missed
8 was   used to/would   haven't got such a sweet tooth/don't eat sweets any more

C **1** 👥👥👥👥 This is an open-ended practice activity. Go round from group to group listening out for errors connected with the grammar in this section.

2 🖉 This written follow-up depends on having made notes in **C1**.

7.5 Enhancing customers' lives

LISTENING

A 👥👥 Perhaps ask the class to suggest other factors not mentioned, and other products they're interested in.

B 🔊 These multiple-choice questions are to be answered on the first listening.

ANSWERS
1 b   **2** c   **3** a   **4** d   **5** d   **6** d   **7** d   **8** b

C 🔊 These blank-filling questions are to be answered on the second listening.

ANSWERS

1 lunchbox
2 dream
3 counters   fresh fish   cream cakes
4 restaurants   (and snack bars, tea rooms, coffee shops, etc.)
5 beer garden   breeze   view
6 June 1   September 1
7 store directory
8 bow   welcome
9 10 am   7 pm
10 railway   platform   commuter train
11 service   pleasure   range
12 customer loyalty

D 👥👥👥👥 Encourage students who have experience of stores in other countries to describe them to their partners.

TRANSCRIPT *8 minutes 15 seconds*

NARRATOR: You'll hear a broadcast about Japanese department stores.

PRESENTER (Helen):   Every country has its own department stores. There are some which are luxurious and cater for the very rich, like Harrods in London or Bloomingdales in New York, while some are more downmarket. But there's one country whose stores are totally unique, and that is Japan. In Tokyo, for example, visiting a department store does not necessarily mean going shopping. You might go there to see an art exhibition, or to amuse the children, you might want to drink beer in the roof garden, to have a meal, or just to relax and hang out with your friends. A Japanese department store doesn't really aim to sell things you need every day, like a supermarket might. It sets out to 'find ways of enhancing customers' lives'. Richard Green reports on Mitsukoshi, the oldest department store in Japan.

RICHARD: That's right, indeed, Helen. Um…Mitsukoshi started out as a kimono outlet in 1673. This was the first store where people could come in, browse around, and pay on the spot with cash for kimono cloth, rather than paying in…er…interest-bearing instalments as was the norm in those days. The merchandise then quickly diversified to include daily necessities and gift items, and Mitsukoshi grew to become the best-stocked and most prestigious department store in Asia by the 1960s. The store's reputation made it *the* place to buy gifts, and the Mits…Mitsukoshi logo continues to stand for quality. Um…for examples of the very best in Japanese customer service, Mitsukoshi is *the* place to go. And their flagship store in Nihonbashi is wonderful!

PRESENTER: So you reckon that it's worth a visit if you're in Tokyo?

RICHARD: Absolutely, it's a must! The subway stops right beneath the store – er…the station, by the way, is Mitsukosh…Mitsukoshi-mae, which means 'in front of Mitsukoshi' – and the best way in is via the grand entrance, especially if you can make it for…er…10 o'clock opening time. Being bowed to by all the assistants as you walk into the magnificent entrance makes you feel like royalty, I can tell you! You could spend all day walking round…er…and there are plenty of places to rest if you get tired of walking. It has a theatre, a cinema, a museum and an art gallery – and classrooms. It offers concerts, lectures and, ooh, all kinds of classes. They have a Ladies' Club with lectures and lessons in traditional arts and crafts, painting, flower arranging, calligraphy, and languages. They have art exhibitions too and lunchtime theatrical performances. Er…and the ticket, believe it or not, includes a lunchbox with *sushi*, wine, sandwiches and a magazine.

PRESENTER: Well, that certainly is a nice way to spend a lunchtime!

RICHARD: Yes. And there's a 'dream room for resting babies', where you can leave your baby while you…while you do your shopping. They can even arrange your wedding: Western or Japanese style.

PRESENTER: Are there other department stores that…er…that offer the same sort of services?

RICHARD: Well, er…the fact is all the department stores offer very similar services. Er…they don't all have a theatre, but most of them have exhibition areas and run classes in a 'community culture centre', er…where people can go to…to learn languages, for example. And down in the basement of every store, you'll find an enormous food department – not a supermarket but a huge area with hundreds of counters selling everything from…er…fresh fish to cream cakes. And many of them give you a…a free taste of their wares. So it's a sort of high-class market. And…er…near the top of the building there are usually several floors with dozens of little restaurants. Er…all sorts: Japanese, Western, Indian, Chinese, tea rooms, coffee shops, fast food, you name it. Places where you can have a big meal or…or just a snack, if that's what you're after.

Er…in the summer you can go up to the…to the very top floor, where there's a roof area with a beer garden, er…a play area for children, and you can sit in the open air, enjoy the breeze and…er…enjoy the view of the city. One store even has a golf school on the roof, ha, believe it or not! But at the end of the summer on September 1st all this is closed, even if the weather's still hot, because that's the official end of the summer in Japan and people start wearing their winter clothes then…er…as well. So…er…you have to wait till the next Summer, which starts on June 1st.

PRESENTER: Mm. As a…as a non-Japanese speaker, how does one cope with these places?

RICHARD: Well, at the main…at the main entrance you can…you can pick up a store directory and a brochure in English. Anywhere in the store, if you ask one of the assistants…er, 'Do you speak English?', they'll smile and rush off to find someone who does. It really couldn't be easier. The other thing is, every store has staff whose only duty is to welcome customers. So you find many lifts have a young female operator in a uniform wearing white gloves, who bows to you as you enter the lift and welcomes you to her lift, and she announces what's on each floor as the doors open and bows to you again as you leave. A…and when the store opens in the morning at 10 am, the staff stand at the edge of their department welcoming you. And at the close of business at 7 pm they're there again saying goodbye to everyone.

PRESENTER: And are those the shop hours? It's always 10 to 7?

RICHARD: Yes, usually. Oh, and they're all open six days a week. Er…they're always open on Saturdays and Sundays and on national holidays. They do close one day during the week – but different stores in the same district all close on different days. The floors with all the restaurants are open later, er…usually till 10.30. Some stores have their own railways too.

PRESENTER: Their own railways?

RICHARD: Yes, the…these are stores owned by one of the private railway companies: um…Od…Odakyu, er…Keio, Seibu and Tobu in Tokyo, for example. Er…you take the lift or escalator from the store all the way down to the station, and you step out onto the platform, where your commuter train is waiting to take you home. Er…the main store is the terminus of the line. Um…and some of these companies own baseball teams too: the Seibu Lions are one of the top teams.

PRESENTER: It sounds like these stores are all quite similar to each other.

RICHARD: Mm.

PRESENTER: So how do they…how do they go about…um…creating a difference between them, making their own mark, if you like?

RICHARD: Yeah, well, at one store, the assistants wear badges showing their hobby, such as, well, it could be 'Flower Arranger' or…er…'Veteran Golfer', so that customers can relate to them on a personal level. At another store they might wear bright yellow shirts, so that customers can identify them easily. Department stores in Japan don't compete on price but on the quality of their service, and the…and the range of choice they offer. All the stores are full of the latest gadgets, fashions and accessories from all over the world. Um…so above all it's…it's really to do with how much of a pleasure it is to spend time there.

PRESENTER: And…er…can you only find these Japanese stores in Japan?

RICHARD: No, there are big Japanese department stores in Singapore, Hong Kong and other Asian cities. Er…there is a Mitsukoshi branch in London but it's quite small. Um…a large number of its customers are Japanese people. One of the things assistants at the London store have to do is to help worried Japanese tourists find their lost luggage or passports, or…er…get in touch with relations – it's all part of the service they offer. And of course it encourages customers to be loyal to Mitsukoshi when they get back home again. Customer loyalty is very important.

PRESENTER: Mm, absolutely, if your customers are happy, they'll keep coming back again.

RICHARD: That's exactly right.

PRESENTER: Well, Richard, thank you very much indeed.

RICHARD: Thank you.

7.6 Dear Sir, . . .

COMPOSITION

A 👥 Allow everyone a few minutes to prepare for the role-play before they actually start.

B Encourage everyone to read each other's work when they've written their letters, faxes or e-mails.

7.6 Model version

Dear Sir/Madam,

I am writing about the hi-fi system I purchased at your store six months ago. Since I bought the system I have moved house and am now living 150 kilometres away from your store. I have tried phoning you but the number has been constantly engaged or if I have been connected, I have been kept waiting in a queue and have not been able to continue hanging on. The last time I called, I waited for 35 minutes and still did not speak to anyone. So I have now resorted to writing.

Since I bought the system I have had nothing but trouble. First of all the CD player disc slot got stuck and wouldn't open or close. After three weeks you managed to provide me with a new system. Then the cassette player seized up and after a delay of six weeks you fixed it. Now the mini disk player will not function on record mode. One of my main reasons for buying this system was so that I could record my CDs on to MDs and listen to them on my car MD system. As I have a long drive to work it is important to me to have something entertaining to listen to instead of DJ chat.

Please can you suggest what I should do. As the system is under a year old you have a statutory obligation either to fix it or provide me with a satisfactory alternative. As I no longer live near your store I cannot deliver the system for repair in person. Nor am I willing to pay carriage on what would undoubtedly be an expensive delivery bill. I suggest that you arrange to collect it from my place of work (address enclosed) or nominate a store in my locality which will carry out the repairs on your behalf. Failing either of these options, I should like a refund of the full purchase price.

I enclose a copy of my original receipt with the details of the system on it.

I look forward to your early reply,

Yours faithfully,

Leo Jones *New Progress to Proficiency*

7.7 Further uses of –ing

ADVANCED GRAMMAR

SUGGESTED ANSWERS

1 receiving/dealing with/making   being/appearing
2 looking at/reading   discovering/finding out/seeing   buying
3 talking to/appealing to/speaking
4 reading
5 closing   (*This is really true.*)
6 taking/enrolling for/studying on/attending   doing   reading   keeping in touch   writing
7 to meeting
8 to being

ANSWERS

1 their/them coming   their/them watching   their/them being/getting   reading
2 doing/'s doing   his/him making
3 them/their smoking   them/their asking
4 Tony falling   Jane/me/my trying

SUGGESTED ANSWERS

1 It isn't worth travelling to London to do your shopping.
2 We were upset about his forgetting to inform us.
3 Instead of spending your money, it might be a better idea to save it.
4 Besides being a champion athlete, she speaks four languages fluently.

5 As well as having a job in an office, he works in a shop at weekends.
6 Without phoning them, you won't/can't find out if they're open.
7 Ever since first seeing her, he has been in love with her.
8 Your not consulting me beforehand was inconsiderate / Your failure to consult me beforehand . . .

 7.8 **Compound nouns** VOCABULARY DEVELOPMENT

A These are some of the compound nouns in the first six paragraphs. If your students have missed any of these, don't waste time pointing them *all* out. This is intended as a quick sensitising task, not a grammar test.

¶ 1 West Edmonton Mall   flatlands
¶ 2 fluorescent lights   indoor plants   service industries   department store
¶ 3 Empire State Building   jelly babies   cloakroom
¶ 4 consumer seductions   eating establishments   bingo hall
¶ 5 wave machine   undersea life   skating rink   golf course   financial service outlets
¶ 6 public relations   summer environment

B
SUGGESTED ANSWERS

air conditioning   burglar alarm   common sense   driving licence   fancy dress
estate agent   generation gap   greenhouse effect   hay fever   heart attack
hire purchase   income tax   junk food   mail order   mother tongue
nervous breakdown   package tour   paper clip   parking meter
pedestrian crossing   pocket money   shopping mall   show business
unemployment benefit   weather forecast   window shopping

C Many variations are possible.

SUGGESTED ANSWERS

one-parent family   current account/affairs   stainless steel   traveller's cheque
compact disc (player)   exclamation mark   swimming pool/costume/trunks
skating rink   delivery van/charge   chain store   clearance sale
travel agent/agency   wastepaper basket

D
SUGGESTED ANSWERS
1 shopping mall/shopping centre   window shopping/bargain hunting
2 current account/bank account   credit card
3 charity shop   clearance sale/discount store
4 mail order   delivery charge
5 bar code
6 estate agent/real estate agent   travel agent/travel agency/travel agent's
7 fancy dress   wastepaper basket
8 driving licence   traveller's cheques/pocket money

Preparation   Collect your own advertisements too, so that students who forget to do this will have some material to discuss in **7.9 C**.

 7.9 **Advertising: Sequencing your ideas** WRITING SKILLS AND COMPOSITION

A This is the sequence of paragraphs in the original article:
1   e   c   b   d   g   f   a   9

Variations may be possible.

B

SUGGESTED ANSWERS

¶ a	. . . *our* German branches . . .	Benetton's
¶ b	. . . payments to *the fashion chain* . . .	Benetton
	. . . saying *it* had no inclination . . .	Benetton
¶ c	. . . to sue *the company* . . .	Benetton
	. . . which *they* claim . . .	the group of German retailers
¶ d	. . . if *they* wore . . .	children of the parents who spoke to Mr Hartwich
¶ e	. . . protested against the *advertisements* . . .	the 'tasteless' ones mentioned in the headline
¶ f	Several *similar* cases . . .	similar to the proposed German lawsuits

C

👥👥 Hand out some of your own collection of ads to any groups whose own collection is meagre.

D

1–4 ✎ Discussion about which points to omit and possible sequences could take place in class – or these decisions could be made by students working alone at home.

Perhaps revoke the word limit suggested in the Student's Book if this is a topic that your students wish to write an extended essay about, particularly if they have a lot of examples up their sleeves.

7.9 Model version

Advertising comes in many forms. There are TV commercials which are often as entertaining as the TV programmes themselves. There are huge, colourful posters on hoardings in the streets and ads in newspapers and magazines, which undoubtedly brighten our lives. Then there is the endless stream of mail-order catalogues, and junk mail which attempts to personalise the advertising process, by addressing you by name in every line of the text. The lowest form of advertising is "cold calling" when companies phone numbers in the telephone directory and try to get you interested in their product.

The potency of advertising can be illustrated by two apparently unconnected facts: the huge budgets companies dedicate to funding their campaigns and the banning of tobacco advertising in Britain. Both underline the effectiveness of the process. But does it do us any good? Well, without advertising we wouldn't know about the many products on offer and the fact that we know there are several similar products means that competition flourishes and prices can be that bit cheaper. Advertising also provides a major source of income for newspapers and television companies. Without this income many newspapers would disappear.

On the downside, advertising has helped to encourage rampant consumerism where demand is created for totally unnecessary goods and in many cases for goods which the purchaser cannot afford. This creates discontent among those unable to buy, a temptation to live beyond one's means and maybe even crime among those who feel it is their right to own as much as the next man. This increase in materialism and the throwaway society also contributes towards damage to the environment. Some ads, e.g. those for alcohol, may have a negative influence on the young who may associate glamour, social success etc. with drinking and feel that they have to drink to achieve status with their peers. Although the effect of competition is to drive prices down, one cannot but wonder how much lower the prices would be without the costs of advertising.

Leo Jones *New Progress to Proficiency*

Have I got news for you!

8

A Part or all of this discusssion might be postponed until after **C**.
(*Have I got news for you!* is something people say when they have something surprising to tell someone.)

B

> **ANSWERS**
>
> *article* = report   *circulation* = number of copies sold   *editorial* = leader
> *issue* = number   *magazines* = monthlies & weeklies   *main story* = lead story
> *newsreader* = newscaster   *the papers* = the dailies   *reporter* = journalist
> *reviewer* = critic
>
> Further useful vocabulary: *columnist   correspondent   column   cover story   scoop*

C At the risk of seeming heavy-handed, here are brief explanations of the incongruities in each headline.

> **SUGGESTED ANSWERS**
> 1 Dogs normally attack cats
> 2 *Actual meaning:* The staff of the hospital are guarding the victim of the stabbing
>   *Funny meaning:* The guards at the hospital have stabbed a patient
> 3 *Actual meaning:* A drunk man was found by the police in a shop window
>   *Funny meaning:* Police officers were found intoxicated in a shop window
> 4 Teachers are normally considered to be wonderful – this one was atypical
> 5 Controversy over the price of butter is increasing, but you spread butter on bread
> 6 Lighter means less heavy, but also cigarette lighter
> 7 *Actual meaning:* A mine is a kind of bomb
>   *Funny meaning:* My . . . exploded . . .
> 8 *Actual meaning:* Negotiations about fish quotas . . .
>   *Funny meaning:* A talking fish . . .

See below for some more typical headline words and their 'translations' into normal English.

Extra activity 1

And here are some more genuine newspaper headlines. Write them on the board for the class to decipher:
a **Office death plunge probe** – There is to be an inquest after someone committed suicide by jumping from a window in an office block
b **Runaway couple vow to wed** – A young couple who have run away from their parents say that they intend to get married
c **Premier set to visit Britain** – The prime minister of somewhere is expected to make an official visit to Britain
d **More girls plump for new university** – More female students (than males, or than expected) have applied for places at a new university
e **Nurses sit in over cuts** – A group of nurses have protested about reductions in pay or government support by 'sitting in' (sitting down and refusing to move)
f **Shop hero saves tot** – A brave man saved a young child who was in danger in a shop

Extra activity 2

 Here are some words that are common in headlines – match them to the words you'd use in a normal conversation:

AXE   BACK   BAR, BAN   BID   BLOW   BOOST   CLASH   CURB   DRAMA   FLEE
FURY   KEY   OUST   QUIT   RAP   ROW   SCRAP   SHAKE-UP   SOAR   SPLIT
SWOOP   THREAT

anger   attempt   cancel   controversy   disagreement   division   encourage
escape   exclude   happening   lose your job   possibility   raid   reform   replace
reprove   resign   restrict   rise   setback   support   vital

Headline words

axe	= cancel	**outrage**	= annoyance
axed	= dismissed	**plan**	= proposal
bar, ban	= exclude	**pledge**	= promise
bid	= attempt	**quit**	= resign
blow	= setback	**quiz**	= question
boost	= encourage	**rap**	= reprove
call	= request	**riddle**	= mystery
clash	= disagreement	**row**	= controversy
crackdown	= tighter control	**scrap**	= cancel
curb	= restrict	**sex romps**	= sex
death plunge	= fatal fall	**shake-up**	= reform
drama	= happening	**shun**	= avoid
dumped	= dismissed	**snag**	= difficulty
feud	= quarrel	**snub**	= fail to attend
fury	= anger	**soar**	= rise
grab	= confiscate	**split**	= division
hurdle	= difficulty	**swoop**	= raid
key	= vital	**threat**	= possibility
oust	= replace	**turmoil**	= controversy

8.2 Modal verbs   GRAMMAR REVIEW

Ⓐ

SUGGESTED ANSWERS

1 Could you finish the article?
   – *Please finish reading or writing it*
   Were you able to finish the article?
   – *Did you manage to finish reading or writing it?*

2 Can you carry this box?
   – *Are you strong enough to carry it?*
     or *Please carry it for me*
   Could you carry this box?
   – *Please carry it for me*

3 You can't leave yet.
   – *You're not allowed to leave / I won't allow you to leave*
   You needn't leave yet.
   – *You're not obliged to leave (but you can if you want)*

4 I don't need to read the paper today.
   & I needn't read the paper today.
   & I don't have to read the paper today.
   & I haven't got to read the paper today.
   – *It isn't necessary for me to read it, I'm under no obligation to read it*
   I shouldn't read the paper today.
   – *It's wrong for me to read it, I'm not supposed to read it (but I may do so)*
   I haven't read the paper today.
   – *So far today I've had no chance to read it (but I may do later)*

5 There could be an election this year.
   – *It's possible that there will be one*
There has to be an election this year.
   – *This is the year when (by law) an election is held*
   or *The government are under a moral obligation to call an election*
There should be an election this year.
   – *It's likely that there will be one*
   or *There is supposed to be one, but it may not actually happen*
There will be an election this year.
   – *An election is going to be held this year, that's certain*

6 That could be Tony at the door.
& That might be Tony at the door.
   – *It's possible that it's him at the door*
That must be Tony at the door.
& That will be Tony at the door.
   – *I'm sure that he's at the door: no one else is expected*
That can't be Tony at the door.
   – *Someone is at the door but I'm sure that it's not Tony*
That should be Tony at the door.
   – *I'm fairly sure it's Tony*

B

SUGGESTED ANSWERS

2 They said that they might be able to help me.
They said that it was possible that they could help me.
3 He told me that I couldn't/mustn't use a dictionary in the exam.
He told me that I wasn't allowed/permitted to use a dictionary in the exam.
4 She asked me if I had to leave so soon.
She asked me if it was necessary for me to leave so soon.
5 He told us that we mustn't/shouldn't believe everything we read in the newspapers.
He told us that it was unwise to believe everything . . .
He told us not to believe everything . . .
6 She told us that she didn't dare to dive into the swimming pool.
She told us that she didn't have the courage to dive . . .
7 He told us that we needed to book a table.
He told us that it was necessary to book a table.
8 She wondered what time she had to arrive there.
She wondered what time it was necessary for her to arrive there.

C More variations are possible.

SUGGESTED ANSWERS

1 The minister for sports said that fewer people can swim than in the past.
The sports minister has said that more people are unable to swim than in the past.
2 People mustn't smoke in any cinema.
Smoking is not allowed/permitted in cinemas.
3 Passengers (will) have to wear a seat belt in the rear seat of a car.
The wearing of seat belts in rear seats is (going) to be compulsory.
4 Drivers will no longer have to keep to 70 miles an hour.
Drivers will be able/allowed to drive over 70 miles per hour.
5 Thousands of people had to leave their homes after the earthquake.
6 There may well be another recession.
A recession is likely in the near future.
7 The socialists should win the election.
The socialists are likely to win the election.
8 Many commuters couldn't get home because of a railway strike.
A railway strike has prevented many commuters from getting home.

D **1 & 2** 👥 🖉 If British customs and laws are very similar to your students' own customs
and laws, they might like to consider visitors from another more exotic country.

Extra information on *dare*

Some students find *dare* a tricky verb to use, as it can function both as a modal verb and a normal verb, as in these examples:

> I **daren't** jump.
> I didn't **dare** jump. / I didn't **dare to** jump.
> **Dare** you jump? / **Do** you **dare to** jump?
> **Don't** you **dare** speak to me like that again.

Notice also the use of *I daresay*:

> **I daresay** (that) the Liberal Democrats will win the by-election.

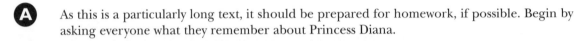 **8.3** ## *Goodbye, England's Rose . . .*   READING AND SPEAKING

The title of this section refers to the 1997 Elton John/Bernie Taupin song, which has sold more copies worldwide than any other record in history. It was based on their original song, *Candle in the Wind* (1973) – same music, different words, which was a tribute to Marilyn Monroe.

A As this is a particularly long text, it should be prepared for homework, if possible. Begin by asking everyone what they remember about Princess Diana.

B

> **ANSWERS**
>
> ¶ 1   *sideline* = unimportant event   *dignified* = shown respect
> ¶ 2   *reverberated* = echoed   *mythological status* = legendary position
> ¶ 3   *accelerated* = went faster   *unassailable* = invulnerable   *eroded* = damaged
>   *titillated and tantalised* = excited and fascinated   *spicy* = exciting
>   *alluring* = attractive
> ¶ 4   *gauche* = awkward   *chillingly* = frighteningly   *elusive* = mysterious
>   *alienation* = feeling of isolation
> ¶ 5   *unrelenting* = continuous   *causes* = charities
> ¶ 7   *hybrid* = mixed   *craved* = couldn't live without   *Establishment* = ruling classes
>   *dénouement* = ending

C This is a follow-up discussion.

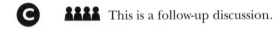 **8.4** ## '. . . that is part of the job'   LISTENING

A Before they listen to the recording, get the class to discuss these lead-in questions:

• What are the responsibilities of a news journalist?
• What is a typical day for a news journalist, do you think?
• What is it like to be a TV news anchor person?

> **ANSWERS**
>
> 1 off duty   **2a** ignore   **2b** calm   **3** distressing/upsetting   **4** part of the job
> 5 ridiculous   **6** goats ate/nibbled her clothes   **7** emergency   **8** accurate

TRANSCRIPT   *7 minutes*

JAYNE: My name's Jayne Evans, and I'm a news journalist, which is a broad term for what I've been doing for the last fifteen years. I've been news anchoring, I've been news presenting, I've been news writing, newspaper writing, and producing.

INTERVIEWER: And jobs like that always seem so glamorous and so exciting, and would you say they actually are?

JAYNE: Yes, of course they are. They are exciting, they are glamorous, but, and there is a big but, they are hard work as well. Now, when I say that to people they say, 'Oh surely not, no, you must be joking!' But they are hard work because you don't stop. You may have the most gorgeous, glamorous hotel room, you may be eating the most delicious meals, but you're still working, you're still thinking about what you're doing, and you're still thinking about the piece of television that you're making. So you're never really off duty, but, hey, I'm not complaining.

INTERVIEWER: No, fair enough, fair enough. What about when you were a news anchor person?

JAYNE: Um…I must admit that when I first started doing it, I didn't enjoy it very much, because I was so nervous. Of course you're going to be nervous, you've either…when you're doing the radio news presenting, you know that there are possibly thousands, millions of people listening to you. When you're on television, they're also looking at you, and s…looking at how you look, and looking at what you're wearing, and they're also listening to what you're saying. Everything, you think, everything has got to be perfect.

INTERVIEWER: And have you ever had to…um…present any really difficult news cases, or things that have…um…where the news changes all the time, where you have to think on your feet?

JAYNE: Well, that is part of the job. You're live on air, you've got a little earpiece in your ear and you've got the people in the gallery talking to you all the time, at the same time you're reading the words on the autocue and if things change, you have to ignore the words that are in front of you on that autocue and listen to what someone's telling you in your ear, and speak those words. So…but that is part of the job, that's what you're paid to do, you're paid to look calm on the in…outside, while, of course, on the inside things are all scrambling and you're in a panic, but your job is to present things calmly to the public.

INTERVIEWER: What do you think are the most sensitive stories you've had to deal with?

JAYNE: Well, there have been plenty over the fifteen years of my journalistic career so far. Some that really stick in my mind are having to go to the scene of accidents, for example, the Paddington rail crash. That's very hard, because you're dealing with something that is very shocking, you're seeing something that shocks you personally, but you've still got to remain calm, and you've got to deliver the news very calmly and very sensibly, and very informatively. Another experience that sticks in my mind very vividly, one that I haven't been able to forget, is when I went to Romania, shortly after the overthrow of Ceaucescu, and I went to some of the hospitals there, and I saw cots with babies in them, all of whom had AIDS or hepatitis, and I knew those babies were going to die. So those stories that…that stick with me, they're…sometimes I think about them in the middle of the night, they're perhaps the downside of this profession, that sort of story, but even then, when you are covering that sort of story, there's a satisfaction in knowing that by covering it you're…you're telling the world what's going on, and what you're doing does actually matter.

INTERVIEWER: Yes, definitely. So do you have to develop a…a way of detaching yourself?

JAYNE: Ideally, you should. I think all of us are human, and I have to be honest that after covering stories like those stories, like…er…disasters, when you're dealing with bereaved people, I find it difficult to sleep for a few nights, and I'm only human, every journalist is only human, but in the end you have to try and put it to the back of your mind, because it is important that you tell the story properly and tell the story fairly, and do justice to the people who are bereaved or the people who are suffering. That's the most important thing. But yes, it does affect me, it does affect every journalist who covers stories like that, but that is part of the job.

INTERVIEWER: That's the darker side certainly, what are the funny bits?

JAYNE: Oh, there are so many funny bits, that's the great thing about this career. And I think what you have to develop is…um…a sense of the ridiculous, and enjoy the ridiculous, there are times when I've thought, 'What a silly way to make a living!' Times when I've been surrounded by herds of goats that are nibbling at my clothes, or times when I've been asked to deliver a piece to camera while hanging off the side of a boat, or I've been asked to jump out of an aeroplane and do a parachute jump for a report, and you think, 'Why am I doing this? I'm scared, or I'm dirty or I'm cold or I've got animals eating my clothes, why am I doing it?' But then you laugh and you think, 'Well, what a great…great way to make a living. And, hey, someone's paying me to do this'. It's ridiculous, but it's fun.

INTERVIEWER: Is there a typical day for a news journalist?

JAYNE: Well, no, there isn't and that is one of the most pleasing things about this profession, because you never know what's going to happen. If you're a news journalist, and you're sitting in the office, reading the newspaper, drinking coffee, you're waiting for something to happen, you're almost like another emergency service, in that when something does happen, you drop your newspaper, you drop your coffee, and you run out of the door with your notebook and your coat over your arm to the scene of whatever's happening. For example, I was sitting in Television Centre working for the BBC a couple of years ago, when the news came through that there was possibly a bomb planted at a race course, they said, 'Quick get out there'. So I got straight into a taxi, went to the…went to the race course and reported on what was happening, reported on the evacuation of the people coming out and filed my reports, my…mine was the first report to go on to the radio to say what was happening. It was a very exciting time. Another story I remember, again I was sitting there reading the newspaper, drinking coffee, and my news editor…editor said, 'Quickly get out there, apparently there's been a murder'. And I had to rush to the scene of a murder, where it was a very sad story, where…um…three children had been murdered, and again you get there first, you have to think on your feet, you have to broadcast almost immediately with the information that you have to hand, and then once you've done one broadcast, you gather some more information and you update your broadcast, and so the day goes on. It's very very busy, there's lots of adrenalin pumping, and while that adrenalin is pumping it's very important that also whatever you broadcast is accurate, so it's a very difficult combination of things. Your…inside your…your mind is racing, but you have to make sure that the words that come out of your mouth, or that come out of the end of your pen are accurate.

B 👥👥 Encourage everyone to talk about the positive and negative aspects of journalism, including TV news coverage. Can they think of recent stories that have been handled badly? How much credence do they give to information that's reported in the papers?

A ANSWERS
1 B   2 F   3 A   4 E   5 C   6 D

B 👥👥 People who are powerful, pompous and self-important are the most suitable targets. Tell the students who you'd like to attack.

C **1 & 2** 👥 🖊 Making notes helps to bridge the gap between finding the relevant information in the text and writing a summary. The notes should be short. If time is short, though, and in the exam, it's probably OK to underline the relevant information in the text in pencil, or to highlight it.

The equivalent summary-writing task in the exam (Use of English Part 5) is based on two shorter texts, not a long one like this.

8.5 Model summary

Noël Godin believes that certain famous people who are full of their own self-importance and who lack humour should be deflated by a good dose of custard pie thrown in the face. His targets include big bosses and those who abuse their power. The pompous and those who restrict the freedom of others are also in line for a cream attack. He sees himself as a slightly mad terrorist who is making a political statement but who wounds only the self-esteem of his victims.

Leo Jones *New Progress to Proficiency*

The use of hyphens with prefixes is very hard to lay down rules about. The prefixes in **A** usually have a hyphen, the ones in **B** don't usually have one.

A The words with ? are possible but unusual.

ANSWERS

anti-	anti-American anti-democracy? anti-federal anti-feminist anti-monarchy anti-test? anti-union
pro-	pro-American pro-democracy pro-federal pro-feminist pro-monarchy pro-union
pre-	pre-cooked pre-packed pre-test
super-	super-intelligent superstar superstore
half-	half-American? half-asleep half-brother half-cooked half-expect half-packed? half-time half-truth half-way

B The words with ? are possible but unusual.

ANSWERS

re	reappear rebuild recapture refasten refillable regrow? reload renumber reprint reunited reusable revalue? rework?
un	unblock unfasten unload unusable
over	overbuild? overestimate overload oversimplify overvalue overwork (+ overgrown)
under	underestimate undervalue
out	outgrow outnumber outvote

Point out that prefixes can also be used creatively or 'actively', as in these examples:
Once something is printed you can't **unprint** it.
This area has been **overbuilt**. (= there has been too much building)

C **ANSWERS**

self-	self-defeating self-educated self-employed self-explanatory
	self-governing self-preservation self-sufficient
co-	co-director co-exist co-owner
counter-	counter-measure
ex-	ex-director ex-official ex-owner ex-policeman ex-president
semi-	semi-automatic semi-circular semi-educated semi-employed?
	semi-official semi-productive?
sub-	subheading substandard subtitle

D **ANSWERS**

1 oversimplification
2 overestimating
3 pro-strike   outvoted
4 counter-productive   over-react
5 subtitles
6 super-rich   superstars   outsell
7 self-explanatory
8 half-expected   ex-wife
9 counter-attack   pre-arranged
10 reappeared   half-frozen

And here are some more prefixes which you might like to remind your students about:

ante-	(= before)	ante-natal anteroom
auto-	(= by itself)	auto-reverse auto-record auto-timer
fore	(= before)	forewarned is forearmed foretaste
post-	(= after)	post-war postgraduate
mega	(= large/great)	megastar megadollars
mono	(= one/single)	monosyllabic monochrome
bi	(= two/double)	bilateral bilingual bisexual bicentenary bi-annual
tri	(= three/triple)	trilateral trilogy triplet

8.7 *There . . .*   **ADVANCED GRAMMAR**

A **1 & 2**

SUGGESTED ANSWERS

1 There's somebody waiting to see you.
   – more informal
2 There are no easy answers to most political problems.
   – more informal
3 There's no point in trying to explain the problem to them.
   – no special difference in emphasis
4 There is more coverage given to sport in some papers than others.
   – less emphasis on some papers
5 Luckily for us there was a telephone box nearby.
   – no special difference
6 There's no need to shout, I can hear you perfectly well.
   – more informal
7 There are 14 branches of Mitsukoshi in Japan – and (there are) 14 associate stores too.
   – slightly more emphasis on the number
8 Come quickly! There has been an accident! There may be some people hurt!
   – more informal
9 There he stood with a sheepish grin on his face.
   – more amusing, narrative technique
10 There were fifteen of us waiting in the lecture hall.
   – more emphasis on the number.

B SUGGESTED ANSWERS

1 will be/to be   2 must be no   3 comes   4 is a lot of   5 is just one
6 denying   7 being   8 seems

C SUGGESTED ANSWERS

1 The police say **that there were fewer than 5,000 people in the peace demonstration.**
2 The forecasters say **that there will be more sunshine next week.**
3 The England soccer manager says **that there is no doubt that his team will win tonight's international match.**
4 Environmentalists say **that there are too many cars causing pollution and accidents.**
5 According to the newspaper **there could/might be a general election this year.**
6 There **have been attempts to reconcile both sides in the teachers' strike/dispute.**
7 There **have been fewer road accidents this year.**
8 There **were no casualties when the ferry sank.**

Some students confuse *There . . .* with *It . . .* in sentences like these:

It's a shame/pity you couldn't come.
It's difficult to know who is in the right.
It gets dark earlier in the winter.
It's Peter who is responsible.
It was a good thing you warned me.

D 👥👥👥 Student A looks at **Activity 8** on page 201, B at **17** on page 203, and C at **27** on page 206. There's a short news item for each student to tell their partners about in their own words, using *There . . .* They should retell the stories in their own words – there's no point in reading them aloud to each other.

8.8   Hitting the headlines   LISTENING AND SPEAKING

A 🔊 ANSWERS

1 Japan   2 USA   3 Italy   4 Italy   5 Japan   6 USA   7 Italy   8 Italy

B 👥👥👥👥 Write the continents on the board to help everyone to think of different stories:

Africa   Asia   Australasia   Europe   North America   South America   (Antarctica?)

Maybe add some important individual countries too.

C 👥👥👥👥 If possible, record the radio news in English from the BBC World Service and play it to the class. Better still, video the TV news from CNN or BBC World and show the video.

TRANSCRIPT   *5 minutes 30 seconds*

ANNOUNCER: And now it's time for 'Strange But True', introduced by Joanne Thomas.
JOANNE: Hello, and welcome to this week's collection of unusual stories which really happened this week, but did not hit the headlines. Today we hear about a Japanese boat made out of old beer cans, an office worker who pretended to be blind, and some very unsuccessful robbers in the USA. But first Sally Vincent in Rome, with news of an over-enthusiastic lifeguard. Sally?
SALLY: Thank you, Joanne. Well, for holidaymakers the sea can be a dangerous place, what with sharks and jellyfish and pollution and strong currents. But at the Italian resort of Ravenna these perils paled into insignificance alongside lifeguard Lorenzo Trippi, who was recently sacked for accidentally killing three people with lifebelts. Mr Trippi, a former discus-thrower, had been employed by Ravenna municipal council on account of his 'excellent physique and willingness to do good'. Things started to go wrong from the word go, however. A fellow lifeguard told reporters: 'Whenever he heard a cry he would rush into the sea and scream, "Don't panic!" And then he'd throw the life preserver at them.' Unfortunately, Mr Trippi couldn't shake off the habits of his discus-throwing days and would launch his lifebelts with just a little too much force and accuracy. Each time he hit his target square on the forehead and knocked them out – and they drowned. On several occasions he also threw lifebelts at people who were merely waving to relatives. One holidaymaker said: 'I was signalling my wife to get me an ice-cream with nuts, and the next thing I knew a lifebelt hit me in the face and broke my jaw.' So Mr Trippi is now looking for another job better suited to his talents!
JOANNE: Thank you, Sally. William Cosgrove in Tokyo was at the quayside to welcome home a Japanese folk hero.

WILLIAM: Four and a half months ago the Japanese adventurer Kenichi Horie set out from Salinas in Ecuador in a solar-powered boat with a difference – it's a cigar-shaped vessel made out of 27,000 recycled aluminium beer cans and driven by an electric motor. This week he sailed into Tokyo Bay after making the world's first solar-powered crossing of the Pacific Ocean. The nine and a half metre *Malt's Mermaid* has 12 square metres of solar cells that can generate one and a half kilowatts of electricity to recharge its two nickel-hydrogen batteries. One battery drives the boat's motor, the other the fridge, a radio, the lighting and a video recorder. He started out with 120 cans of Malt's beer, planning to enjoy one can of beer each evening while he was at sea, but one of his water purifiers broke so he had to conserve his stocks of liquid in case the other water purifier broke.

Mr Horie is a folk hero in Japan. He was the first person to sail solo across the Pacific – that was back in 1962. Since then he's made 7 more solo voyages, including crossing the Pacific in the world's shortest ocean-going sailing vessel, measuring just 2.8 metres – and sailing round the world both latitudinally (which is the normal way) and longitudinally (via the Arctic and Antarctic).

JOANNE: Amazing. Well, they do say that crime doesn't pay. This is what four men in the USA found out recently. Here's Philip Miller.

PHILIP: Henry Norton and his brother Billy were sent to prison yesterday in Oklahoma after being convicted of bank robbery. They broke into a bank in the middle of the night, emptied the safe of $100,000 and also stole the bank's video camera, which was recording their crime. Unfortunately for them the video recorder was located in another part of the bank, so they didn't get the videotape of them stealing the camera. The police were able to watch the video at their leisure and use it as evidence in their trial.

And in Kentucky last week two men tried to pull the front off a cash machine by running a chain to the bumper of their pick-up truck. But instead of pulling the front panel off the machine, they pulled the bumper off their truck, with the chain still attached to the machine. Also attached to the bumper was . . . their license plate! So the police had no difficulty in finding them early the next morning.

JOANNE: Duh! And finally here's Sally Vincent again from Rome.

SALLY: Some people will do anything to keep hold of their job. But there aren't many who can match the dedication of Claudio Ferro from Rovigo in Northern Italy. For 20 years he persuaded his fellow office workers he was blind. It all began when Mr Ferro applied for a job as a switchboard operator. This is what he said in an interview last week: 'I thought they'd be more sympathetic if I was blind, so I went to the interview with a white stick and dark glasses. They were extremely kind, especially when I pretended to fall down the stairs on my way out.' The ruse evidently worked because Mr Ferro landed the job, and spent the next two decades bumping into doors, knocking things off tables, and accidentally rubbing up against attractive women. He had no regrets and still says: 'It was wonderful. People got my shopping for me, and took me on holidays, and I always got a huge Christmas bonus.' His subterfuge was eventually discovered when fellow workers spotted his photo in a paper after he won a national cross-country roller-skating competition.

JOANNE: And with that from Sally Vincent, it's goodbye from us at 'Strange But True'. Join us again next week at the same time.

8.9 Freedom

SPEAKING

Students from countries with less democratic regimes may find some aspects of this section too controversial. You may need to be aware of this and be prepared to skip some parts.

A This could be done in pairs, or with the whole class as a warm-up.

B Arrange the class into an even number of pairs so that they can join forces as groups of four or five in **C**.

C There's plenty of scope for discussion here. Find out what the consensus of the class is after the groups have discussed the eight topics.

8.10 Long and short sentences

WRITING SKILLS

A

SUGGESTED ANSWERS

1 shortest sentence: These are bad times for talking.
  – an abrupt, intriguing opening, making you want to read more.

2 longest sentence: [1]Early in the Seventies [2]Mr Weeds did break his silence [3]to ask his wife [4]if she wanted to go to Thailand, [5]and she broke hers [6]to say no, [7]but otherwise all has been mutual muteness, [8]a fact which, insists Mrs Weeds, in no way affects their love for each other.
  – the sentence contains eight different ideas (numbered in the quote above).

> Giving a lot of information in a single sentence is economical, but it's harder for the reader to take it all in, especially at the end of the sentence.
> 3 Direct speech is used three times by the writer (plus once by Mrs Weeds). This makes the whole article seem more immediate and authentic than if reported speech had been used, as it is in the longest sentence.

B   👥 Here are the relevant sentences from the other articles. Discuss with the class what the effects are.

Flying too close to the sun

1 She was 36.
2 As with Kennedy and with James Dean, John Lennon and Marilyn Monroe, she was a superstar who died young in violent circumstances, and as with them, it will guarantee her a mythological status.
3 'Unthinkable,' people said . . .

Cream and punishment

1 Gloup.
2 Meanwhile, 30 pie-throwers, who have been standing in groups of three, suddenly come together, and, in a whirlwind of cakes, they strike their target.
3 Lots – it's an interview.

Extra activity

Ask everyone to look at their own most recent compositions and discuss these questions:

• If any sentence is over-long, can you suggest a suitable place to break it?
• Where should any over-short sentences be joined into single sentences?
• Where could direct speech have been used more?

C   **1–3** This model version is the original article.

8.10 Model version

Possibly the worst day in the history of organised – or rather disorganised – crime was experienced by Miami thief Natron Fubble, 35, surely a prime candidate for the title of 'World's Most Inept Robber'. The day started with an early morning raid on a delicatessen which was cut short after the shop owner hit Mr Fubble in the face with a giant salami, breaking his nose. An attempted bank robbery ended before it had even begun when he met his mother in the same bank and was sent to do some shopping for her. The climax, however, came late in the afternoon, when pursued by irate customers after another failed hold-up, he took refuge in the boot of an empty car. Unbeknown to the clueless criminal, however, the car was in fact a police surveillance vehicle whose owners, returning from a cup of coffee, drove for five days across America tailing a suspicious lorry. His whimpers were eventually heard just south of Seattle where he was removed at gunpoint and arrested. He was sentenced to two years in prison, despite claiming he was on a top-secret undercover mission for the FBI.

Leo Jones *New Progress to Proficiency*

8.11 ## Points of view   SPEAKING AND COMPOSITION

A   **1** 👥 Form an even number of pairs – and give everyone enough time to come up with plausible stories for their protagonist. Different pairs should prepare different stories.

2 👥➜👥 Combine the pairs into groups of four (or five).

B   **1–3** ✎ The first two parts of this could be done in class by students working in pairs.

8.11 Model version

<u>Before the incident</u>
I was at Elements nightclub in town, having a night out with my friends and my brother. We danced a lot and I had had a few drinks. I don't mean I was drunk, just chilled, you know. Anyway, these guys started hassling us, making comments on our clothes, our hairstyles, our dancing. In fact they were being pretty rude about us altogether. In the end, I'd had enough and threw a punch at the one with the loudest mouth. One of the bouncers came up and warned us both. They backed off after that. They were out of their heads on something. I think it was booze. Anyway we stayed until the club shut. It was about 2.30 when we left.

<u>The attack</u>
Max and I started to walk back home. We had gone about 200 metres from the club when we were jumped on. We managed to throw them off and started running. We ran through the shopping precinct and car park and headed for home along the river. They seemed to be pretty fit and soon caught us. They threw me to the ground and Max ran off. There were three of them. They were extremely drunk and were yelling all kinds of abuse at me. The one I'd hit in the club started kicking me all over my body. I was trying to protect my head with my arms when another one pulled my arms away. The loudmouth then laid into my head. He kicked me on the left side of my head and cut my eye. My ear was very painful too. After that I lost consciousness. I was dimly aware of them talking; they sounded scared and I think they thought they might have gone too far.

<u>After the attack</u>
The next thing I remember is Max calling me. He was trying to make me stand up but I couldn't. The pain in my head and left ear was terrible. I kept fainting. I came to again in Casualty where a nurse and a policeman were asking me questions. I made a statement 3 days after I was attacked. I had to stay in hospital for 6 weeks. My hearing in my left ear is impaired and I'm terrified to go out.

Leo Jones *New Progress to Proficiency*

8.12 *bring* and *get*

VERBS AND IDIOMS

SUGGESTED ANSWERS

1 made me realise   raise   go unpunished for
2 caused   find a way round/find a way to manage in spite of
3 find a way of dealing with/recover from   asking for advice or help from
4 reveals/shows everyone my worst characteristics   be friendly with
   making me feel depressed
5 made the whole audience laugh   understand the point of
6 criticising/poking fun at him   recovers from
7 get revenge   have my revenge on
8 nearly run out   come to the end of
9 make them understand
10 trying to communicate
11 make him less shy
12 fall asleep   not making enough progress with   got out of bed   started
   completed/accomplished

ANSWERS

1 get on with   2 get out of   3 got off with   got at (bribed or threatened)
4 get down   5 brought about   6 get on   get in with   7 get on to/bring up
8 get round   9 get round to   10 get up   11 bring up   12 getting up to

9 A learning curve

Happy days?

LISTENING AND TOPIC VOCABULARY

Begin by asking the class what they understand by 'the three Rs'. (The 'three Rs' are **R**eading, w**R**iting and a**R**ithmetic.) Perhaps they'll be surprised to know that this term is used even in serious discussions about education.

A (steep) learning curve describes a skill that is hard for someone to master, particularly if they are being trained to do something or have to learn what to do in a new job. Some people also say that one's school days are *the happiest days of your life*!

A   Pause the recording at the places marked with ★★★, to give students a chance to 'catch up' and write their answers.

> **ANSWERS**
> 1 geography   hate children   chemistry   beauty
> 2 Latin   subject   enjoyed her pupils/what her pupils did
> 3 **a** good fun/interesting
>   **b** beneath contempt
>   **c** utterly contemptible
>   **d** relationships and friendships
> 4 bully   victimised   English   heard   disapproved

TRANSCRIPTS   *6 minutes 40 seconds*

PRESENTER: Ruth, you went to school in Wales. What kind of school did you go to?

RUTH: I went to a comprehensive school, um…which…er…was just around the corner from me, so it was really near. It took me five minutes to get to school every morning. I'd wake up at ten to…ten to nine and be in assembly at nine o'clock!

What I didn't like about…er…our school…um…really, well it was one particular subject and that was geography. And I think the only reason I didn't like it was because of the teacher I had. And…er…his name was…um…Mr James, and he just seemed to really hate children. He…I don't even know why he was a teacher. He had no time at all for us, and he used to look at us with such scorn. And I can remember dreading his lessons so much because he was so nasty. I remember once going into the lesson and I just thought, 'I can't stick it here any longer!' So I pretended to faint, and even though I did a really good job, I think I was quite convincing, he…er…still had no sympathy for me whatsoever, and just said, 'Oh, get out of the classroom, Ruth Jones!' and was just really horrible.

Er…I really really didn't like chemistry. Um…all those symbols and…and formula [formulae] and things like that, and I know some people…I remember one teacher saying, 'But chemistry is beautiful.' And I just thought he was mad. I mean, now that I'm older I can kind of see the beauty of science and all that, but…haha…when I was like fourteen I couldn't stand it. It used to make me physically ill to have to go to a chemistry lesson.
★★★

PRESENTER: Sarah, you went to school in England, is there one particular teacher that you remember from your school days?

SARAH: Well, my Latin teacher. I mean, I undoubtedly did Latin because of Mrs Marston, hahaha, who was a completely chaotic teacher. She…her passion for the subject overrode any lesson plan, so we were constantly taken off at tangents, and grammar was flung up on the blackboard, so I never understood Latin grammar. But I just adored it because of her complete passion for the subject. And also, she really enjoyed what we did, and that was…that was another hugely important element. Um…she wasn't…if she…if we'd done little Latin plays or something, she would roar with laughter at the back of the classroom, so there was a sense that she took genuine pleasure from what we did, as well as communicating something herself.
★★★

PRESENTER: Christine, you went to school in Scotland, what kind of school did you go to?

CHRISTINE: Well, it was a school which you went to at five and you stayed, all being well, until you were eighteen. And there were boys and girls, and it meant that you developed a really interesting…er…view of boys, which changed as you got older. So when I was very little the boys were good fun…um…and because I was a bit of a tomboy, they had…they did things and played with things in the classroom that I thought were much more interesting than the things the girls played with. And then we went through a phase of ignoring the boys strenuously because they were completely beneath contempt, and I suppose that was between the ages of about $10\frac{1}{2}$ and about 14 or 15. And then discovering that boys were awfully interesting but not the boys in your own year group which were…who were utterly contemptible…um…because girls and boys are so different in their development, aren't they? And a

14-year-old girl can see no merits whatsoever in a 14-year-old boy. And all the girls are…are gazing at the 16, 17 and 18-year-old 'big boys', who are much more interesting.

And then as we got to the end of our schooling…er…what in Scotland would be the fifth and the sixth year, in England would be the lower and the upper sixth years, the last two years. Of course things…the boys had caught up really and we became very good friends again all of us and so our last two years at school, um…I think we…we had lovely relationships and lovely friendships. And…er…we did lots of things together. And when we left school we had an amazingly tearful last evening, er…of…of…nearly fifty of us who'd been in the year group, of whom about thirty had grown up together since they were five. And leaving school was actually quite hard for us because having established good relationships with the boys around us in our last two years we all had long memories.
★★★

PRESENTER: What are your strongest memories of school?

CHRISTINE: Of hating some of it. My strongest memories are negative ones, of a period in my two last years in primary, as it would be, 11 and 12 where our class teacher . . . I just loathed her and so did almost everybody else in the class and she was a bully and she taught very traditionally and it was very much 'the three Rs' [*reading, writing and arithmetic*] and we were…we just had tests all the time, we were drilled in grammar.

And she also had an uncertain temper and was a great shouter, and her…the tip of her nose would go white when she was really angry and her whole face would go scarlet. And she also used the belt very freely, and I didn't approve of that, I thought it was wrong. And she used to belt people [*beat them with a leather belt on the hand*] for spelling mistakes. And I'll never forget, Anne Black and Alan Davidson who couldn't spell, and they used to make spelling mistakes and if by Friday you had twenty mistakes out of the hundred, twenty a day, you got the belt in front of the class and I just thought that was so wrong. And it never improved their spelling, I mean years later as sixth-formers they still couldn't spell. And Anne Black used to get it particularly badly because she was English, because her mother was English, and she used to spell as she sounded and she used to make…create the most awful offence by spelling *saw* S O R rather than S A W: *I sor it* because that's how she heard it. And she used to be victimised by Miss Rae, for her English spelling and so I…I really didn't like her. I just thought that the way she treated people was wrong, it wasn't with respect, it was…um…I don't quite know what she was doing when she bullied people, but she was a big bully. And I grew up very s…firmly disapproving of that way of treating children.

B 👥👥👥👥 This discussion draws on some of the themes raised by the speakers.

C 👥👥 Make sure everyone knows what they're supposed to do: that this is intended to be an activity where students discuss the vocabulary and the relationships between the words. This is not an exam-style test and there are no 'right answers'.

A few words of justification about the examples:

1 award · grant · scholarship   (all money that is given to finance someone's education)
  grant · loan   (the two most common ways of financing higher education)
  trophy · prize · award   (all honours that may be given for outstanding achievement)
  award · scholarship   is another possible combination: both are only given to the brightest or luckiest students, unlike a grant which all students are entitled to
  ✗ reward   isn't connected with education, unless discussing its rewards or pleasures. Unlike a *prize* or *trophy* it is simply cash to pay someone back for doing something, like finding something that has been lost.

In the suggested answers below, the words with similar meanings are connected with a dot: · . The odd one out is at the end, after the cross: ✗ . Other combinations may be possible.

> **SUGGESTED ANSWERS**
> 2 certificate · degree · diploma · doctorate   certificate · diploma   recommendation · reference · testimonial
>   ✗ licence (connected more with driving than with education, though it has something in common with a *certificate*)
> 3 assignment · composition · essay · paper · report   dissertation · thesis
>   ✗ article   (not usually written by a student, but by a journalist or an academic)
> 4 comprehensive school · grammar school · secondary school
>   junior school · primary school   kindergarten · nursery school
>   ✗ gymnasium   (= hall where pupils do PE: physical education)
> 5 BA · BSc · first degree   MA · master's · MSc   BSc · MSc   MA · BA   doctorate · PhD
>   ✗ bachelor   (unmarried man)
> 6 grades · marks · scores · credits
>   ✗ numbers   (the other words have something to do with assessment)
> 7 continuous assessment · evaluation   examination · test   study
>   ✗ questionnaire   (not a way of assessing, but a way of gathering information)
> 8 class · seminar · study group   seminar · lecture
>   ✗ conference (a gathering of people who attend a series of lectures and seminars)

9 apprentice · trainee · participant   freshman · student · undergraduate   graduate · post-graduate   pupil · schoolchild
   ✗ contestant   (someone who enters a competition or game show)
10 academic year · half-term · holiday · vacation   semester · term
   ✗ financial year   (a term used in business)
11 correspondence course · distance learning course   evening course · part-time course · sandwich course   degree course
   ✗ race course   (where horse races are held)
12 associate professor · lecturer · don   coach · trainer   instructor · trainer professor · teacher · tutor
   ✗ business associate   (no connection with education)

D Perhaps also ask everyone to come up with some more questions that might be asked (in the exam Speaking Paper) about the two photographs.

9.2 Writing an application   COMPOSITION

This composition task comes early in this unit, while the discussion in **9.1 D** is still fresh in everyone's mind. There's another essay-writing assignment in **9.9**, later.

A 👥 Make sure both partners have time to take their turn as interviewer.

B **1–3** 👥 ✒ If any of your students ARE Japanese, draw their attention to the alternative suggestion.

It may be necessary to remind students how a formal letter should be laid out. This is best done on the board in class, in collaboration with the students :

```
                                                  your address,
                                                  but not your name
                                                  at the top


the title, name
and address of the person
you're writing to
                                                  Date on the right

Dear . . . ,

   Main body of letter starts


   Yours sincerely,
   Your Signature
      your name
```

In the exam, the instructions usually say: 'Do not write any postal addresses.' This means exam letters should begin 'Dear . . . ,'

9.2 Model version

My name is ___ and I am __ years old. I was born in ___ and am a ___ citizen. I live with my parents in a small village called ___.

I attended my local elementary school before going to high school in ___, the regional capital. I finished my studies at high school two years ago. My favourite subjects at school were languages and history. Now I am studying English and Spanish at ___ University. When I finish my studies, I hope to take up a career in the travel industry, perhaps as an airline flight attendant or in a travel company. I love meeting new people from different countries, finding out about different cultures and sharing experiences with them.

During the vacations I have a temporary job as tour guide and I have accompanied many groups of tourists from different countries around my city, showing them the sights. I particularly enjoy groups of Japanese people, because they are so interested in learning more about foreign cultures and ask such interesting questions. Although I can communicate with some of the younger Japanese visitors in English, the older ones find it hard to speak and understand me. I find it so disappointing and frustrating that we cannot communicate with each other.

At my university, I have got to know a number of Japanese students. Talking to them has taught me a lot about Japan and its culture and history. I would really love to visit Japan and learn Japanese. But these are just dreams for me now because flights to Japan are more expensive than I can afford, and living where I do, it's not possible to attend any Japanese language courses.

I know that Japanese is a difficult language to learn, but I enjoy challenges. Living in Japan for three months might be a difficult experience for some people, but I have heard so much about Kyoto from Japanese people, that I know I would instantly feel at home there. It would be the most marvellous place to be when learning Japanese.

Being awarded a Sakura Scholarship would be a golden opportunity for me. It would make my dreams come true!

Leo Jones *New Progress to Proficiency*

Extra activity   Write your own CV, giving details of your education and including any vocational training and work experience. Compare this with a partner's and ask for suggestions on how it could be improved.

9.3   My lessons in the classroom

READING AND WRITING SKILLS

Begin by asking everyone this lead-in question:

- How would you expect a group of 13-year-olds to behave in class?

A **1–3**

SUGGESTED ANSWERS
1 They had had no inkling that she was about to decide to give up teaching
2 She had become increasingly terrified and nervous at the prospect of teaching
3 Not particularly well
4 They became bossy, noisy and they had empty heads, thanks to the pressure of their peers
5 She would have had to stay behind after school herself (supervising detention)
6 The teaching staff of the school
7 They greet her and then carry on messing about
8 Having the stamina and a liking for teaching

B

ANSWERS
beating loudly = pounding   incomplete = patchy   hungry = breakfast-less
tell off = remonstrate with   laughing disrespectfully = sniggering
way of putting things right = redress   unable to take action = incapacitated
exercise control = assert myself   laughing shrilly = cackling

C   Follow the procedure suggested in the Student's Book.

9.3 Model summary
She believes that children have changed for the worse over the years and behave badly. Nowadays they are under pressure from advertising and from each other: the disruptive pupils dominate the hard-working pupils, which disturbs the whole class. Parents must also take their share of the blame, allowing their children to stay up late watching videos and not feeding them properly, so that when they come to school they are tired and hungry, and unable to concentrate on their work.

Leo Jones *New Progress to Proficiency*

9.4 'It's just the most wonderful thing'

LISTENING

A 🔊 Begin by discussing this question with the class:

- What would you say are the advantages and disadvantages of teaching as a profession?

ANSWERS

1 the long holidays ✓   helping students to manage their work ✓
  a good lesson ✓   working with people ✓
  helping students to pass exams   making a contribution to students' lives ✓
  the funny things that happen ✓   finding quick solutions to students' problems ✓
  communicating her passion for English literature

2 remember

3a subject   **3b** person

4a subject   **4b** people

5a law   **5b** gap year

6a friends   **6b** support

7a extra-curricular   **7b** workload

8a distractions   **8b** focus

TRANSCRIPTS   *5 minutes 20 seconds*

NARRATOR: You'll hear interviews with Sarah Wilson, a teacher at St Mary's School in Cambridge, and Claudine Kouzel, a sixth-former. First Sarah.

SARAH: My name's Sarah Wilson, and I work in a girls' school in Cambridge, and I'm a teacher of English. And I'm also Head of Sixth Form, which means I look after the Sixth Form girls and look after all of their interests.

INTERVIEWER: And how big is the school?

SARAH: Um…there's about 500 girls in the school…um…and the Sixth Form's a relatively small one, there's about 80 girls.

INTERVIEWER: And…um…what do you most enjoy about your work?

SARAH: There's a whole range of things. Some things are really satisfying, because you can solve them quickly, so if somebody's upset because they can't, you know, their world seems to be caving in, you can usually take the pressure off them, and that's hugely gratifying. Um…another th…other times, you work with somebody for a long, long time, it might take them eighteen months to get round to being able to manage their work, or whatever. And that's also hugely gratifying, working with somebody over a long time. But also, I…when…when a lesson goes really well, it's just the most wonderful thing.

INTERVIEWER: I mean, did you imagine that you'd have endlessly long holidays when you went into teaching, which I'm sure is not the case at all?

SARAH: Oh, no, it is! Hahaha! I mean, the holidays are undoubtedly the most wonderful aspect of it, because when you…there's a curious thing, as the term progresses…um…you disappear into the school life…um…completely, and you need the holidays to remember who you are. Um…but I…but they are, and…and I would never dispute that, they are a great bonus, they…they're wonderful.

INTERVIEWER: So, besides the long holidays, what would you say you find most rewarding about teaching?

SARAH: Um…I think, working with people and the hilarity of things that can happen, just because human beings being what they are. And…and also the sense that you…you are contributing very profoundly to somebody's life.

INTERVIEWER: And…um…what do you not enjoy about your work?

SARAH: Um…I find…sometimes I find it very difficult coming from a pastoral point of view, so I very much see the girls as human beings, and sometimes…um…academic staff see the needs of their subject, and I find, sometimes balancing that quite hard, and I find that quite distressing.

INTERVIEWER: And is it a job you'd recommend to people?

SARAH: Yes, definitely. If you love your subject, and you enjoy people, then…um…teaching would…would be an excellent profession. Um…but I think, people who go into it because they don't know what else to do, and don't like people, it is a disaster.

★★★

NARRATOR: Now Claudine.

CLAUDINE: My name is Claudine Kouzel. I'm sixteen years old, and I'm a student at St Mary's School, here in Cambridge.

INTERVIEWER: And what sort of subjects are you studying?

CLAUDINE: I'm studying Spanish, English Literature, Biology and Chemistry.

INTERVIEWER: And this is for C . . .

CLAUDINE: For AS Level.

INTERVIEWER: A…yeah, AS level. And where do you…what do you think you'd like to study at university?

CLAUDINE: At this stage, I'm thinking of law, but I'm not entirely sure about that.

INTERVIEWER: And do you think you'll do a gap year?

CLAUDINE: Um…I don't think so. I think I'd just like to get started and…I mean, it depends. If I get a place that I can defer my entry and actually go to South America or something like that, but, you know, that's not really guaranteed so . . .

INTERVIEWER: No.

CLAUDINE: …I'm not sure.

INTERVIEWER: And what do you enjoy most about school?
CLAUDINE: It's mainly the people here. It's all…having all the friends around you, and I think the support of the teachers as well.
INTERVIEWER: What do you not enjoy so much about school?
CLAUDINE: I think, undoubtedly when you get into the Sixth Form, there is a lot of pressure. So…you've always got to think of the future, and try and balance…um…extra-curricular activities with, you know, the heavy workload that you've got on.
INTERVIEWER: And I suppose it could be…um…quite easy to just try and do too much?
CLAUDINE: Definitely. I think you can actually be pulled in so many directions, that you've got to be careful that your work doesn't slip as a result.
INTERVIEWER: And, what do you think you'll be doing in ten years' time? What would you like to be doing in ten years' time?
CLAUDINE: That's quite a hard question. Um…ten years' time? OK, I'm sixteen now, I'll be twenty-six. Um…I would like to have…have a successful career, I would like to travel as well. Um…I'm not actually thinking of having a family too early on. I'd like to kind of enjoy life and do all the things I want to do and then settle down, I think, and then have a family.
INTERVIEWER: This is a single sex school, so only girls. Do you think that's good?
CLAUDINE: I do actually, because I went to…um…a co-ed school before. Um…and I think, when you're doing your GCSEs and A Levels, you can have a lot of distractions, especially from boys, and I think having all girls really focuses you into what you want to do. So I mean, if I had kids I would definitely send them to a single sex school.
INTERVIEWER: They say it's better for girls to be at a single sex school than for boys, don't they?
CLAUDINE: Yeah.
INTERVIEWER: How do you sort of relax or forget about school? What do you do in . . .
CLAUDINE: My spare time?
INTERVIEWER: Yes.
CLAUDINE: Well, I haven't got much spare time, to be honest…um…but I like to read, watch some television. I like going to the theatre as well.
INTERVIEWER: Yeah, well you keep pretty busy at school, don't you?
CLAUDINE: Oh, definitely, yeah.
INTERVIEWER: Thank you very, very much.
CLAUDINE: Thank you.

B This discussion deals with issues raised in both **9.3** and **9.4**.

9.5 Question tags and negative questions GRAMMAR REVIEW

A

SUGGESTED ANSWERS

1 He didn't use to play squash, **did he?**
   – *but now he does, and I'm a little surprised about it*
   Didn't he use to play squash?
   & He used to play squash, **didn't he?**
   – *I'm fairly sure he did in the past*
   He used to play squash, **did he?**
   – *You told me he played once, but are you quite sure about that?*
   Did he use to play squash?
   – *I'd just like to know if he played once*

2 **Isn't** this a great party!
   & This is a great party, **isn't it?**
   & What a great party!
   – *these mean the same and would be used in similar situations*
   This is a great party!
   – *This one seems a little lukewarm in comparison, but it means the same.*

3 So you enjoyed my talk, **did you?**
   – *I know you enjoyed it, but I'd like you to say it again or tell me more*
   So **you didn't** enjoy my talk?
   – *I know you didn't like it, but I'd like you to tell me why*
   So **didn't you** enjoy my talk?
   – *I suspect you didn't like it, but I'd like you to confirm it or tell me I'm wrong*
   So **did you** enjoy my talk?
   – *I don't know if you liked it*

4 **Isn't** it strange that everyone thinks they are experts on education?
  – *Don't you agree that it's strange (I'm encouraging you to agree)*
  It's strange that everyone thinks they are experts on education.
  – *I'm telling you this (you may or may not have an opinion on this matter)*

5 **Didn't** she do well in her exam!
  – *this is an exclamation – she really did well!!*
  She **did** very well in her exam.
  – *I'm telling you: she got good marks*
  Didn't she do well in her exam?
  – *This is a question: I'd be rather surprised if she did badly, which is what I have just heard, but you seem to know more than I do*
  Did she do well in her exam?
  & **How did** she do in her exam?
  – *both mean: Tell me what you know about her success*

B **ANSWERS**

1 hadn't we?
  Hadn't we better stop work soon?
2 aren't I?
  Aren't I right about this?
3 wouldn't you?
  Wouldn't you rather stay in bed than get up early?
4 can't they?
  Can't anyone apply for the scholarship?
5 will there?
6 shall we?
7 did they?
8 won't you/will you?
9 did he?
10 oughtn't they?

C **ANSWERS**

sure:	1	3	7	8	10
unsure:	2	4	5	6	9

TRANSCRIPTS *2 minutes*

PRESENTER: Listen to the examples and then do the exercise in 9.5 C.

WOMAN: This is a great party, isn't it? ↘ (*falling*)
WOMAN (*aside*): I'm sure, but I want you to agree.
MAN: He used to play squash, didn't he? ↗ (*rising*)
MAN (*aside*): I'm unsure, but I think you know.

1 MAN: We arranged to meet at 7:30, didn't we? ↘ (*falling*)

2 WOMAN: Mm. But the film doesn't start till 8:30, does it? ↗ (*rising*)

3 MAN: Yes, but there'll be time for us to have a drink beforehand, won't there? ↘ (*falling*)

4 WOMAN: OK. You remember that film we saw last month, don't you? ↗ (*rising*)
  MAN: Yes.

5 WOMAN: It *was* Al Pacino, not Robert de Niro, in that film, wasn't it? ↗ (*rising*)

6 MAN: I always get Al Pacino and Robert de Niro confused, don't you? ↗ (*rising*)

7 WOMAN: Mm. You don't like Robert de Niro, do you? ↘ (*falling*)

8 MAN: Not really . . . I think we both prefer Al Pacino, don't we? ↘ (*falling*)

9 WOMAN: Mm, you *do* know it's Robert de Niro who's in tonight's film, don't you? ↗ (*rising*)

10 MAN: Oh. In that case it might be better if we went to see something else, mightn't it? ↘ (*falling*)
  WOMAN: Don't be so silly – you'll enjoy it!

D 1 & 2

SUGGESTED ANSWERS

2 All our work **will be done for us by robots and computers one day, won't it?**
   Won't all our work be done for us by robots and computers one day?
3 Computers **couldn't be installed in every classroom, could they?**
   Couldn't computers be installed in every classroom?
4 No robot teachers **have been invented yet, have they?**
   Haven't any robot teachers been invented yet?
5 Teachers **should be paid on results, shouldn't they?**
   Shouldn't teachers be paid on results?
6 Students **are often supported by their parents, aren't they?**
   Aren't students often supported by their parents?
7 The school-leaving age **might be raised to 19, mightn't it?**
   Mightn't the school-leaving age be raised to 19?
8 More **teachers would have to be employed, wouldn't they?**
   Wouldn't more teachers have to be employed?

9.6 Abstract nouns

VOCABULARY DEVELOPMENT

A 1

ANSWERS

-ation	cooperate administrate
-ion	destroy satisfy suspect
-ment	astonish enjoy punish

2 Make sure everyone gets their spelling right.

ANSWERS

-ation	application concentration explanation isolation justification negotiation pronunciation (pronouncement = solemn announcement) recommendation representation variation
-ion	contribution description invention objection opposition reception
-ment	achievement acknowledgement amusement embarrassment encouragement management

B 1

ANSWERS

-ty	humble senior
-ance	insignificant intolerant
-ence	absent present intelligent refer
-ism	real absent national/nationalistic/nation optimistic
-ness	clumsy fair happy rude
-ship	apprentice relate scholar sponsor

2

ANSWERS

-ty	authenticity availability creativity equality familiarity generosity honesty loyalty productivity reliability stability
-ance	extravagance relevance
-ence	diffidence incompetence inconvenience independence insolence self-confidence
-ism	favouritism professionalism symbolism
-ness	carelessness half-heartedness mischievousness (or mischief) narrow-mindedness selfishness
-ship	companionship friendship leadership

C

SOME SUGGESTIONS

-ation	imagination	organisation	realisation
-ion	alienation	creation	direction	protection
-ment	replacement	requirement	retirement

-ty	informality	normality	instability	eligibility
-ance	disappearance	resemblance	disturbance
-ence	reminiscence	persistence	disobedience
-ism	plagiarism	journalism	sexism	extremism
-ness	helplessness	aggressiveness	mildness
-ship	membership	ownership	comradeship	craftsmanship

D

ANSWERS

-dom bored free

-th broad filthy healthy long stealthy strong warm wealthy wide

-cy democratic bureaucratic delicate efficient fluent frequent inadequate inefficient redundant urgent

and enthusiastic hysterical hungry proud sarcastic successful

E

SUGGESTED ANSWERS

1 inconvenience
2 reliability/relevance/adequacy
3 enthusiasm description
4 bureaucracy inefficiency
5 favouritism fairness cooperation
6 relevance justification explanation
7 qualifications negotiation
8 references leadership
9 intolerance incompetence unreliability extravagance stubbornness *etc.*
10 loyalty professionalism self-assurance generosity reliability *etc.*

9.7 Managing your study time

A

ANSWERS

1 c 2 b 3 a 4 b 5 d 6 d

B

Rather than providing synonyms to choose between, this task gets the students to do the work. English–English dictionaries should be used.

ANSWERS

bluffing	= deceiving by pretending to be cleverer than he really was
assiduously	= painstakingly
blotted out	= made an effort not to think about
at sea	= confused
segments	= sections
strategically	= in a well-planned manner
dribble away	= gradually be lost
dipping into	= reading short passages, not the complete book
glazed over	= unfocused
prime	= best times for concentration, when you're on top form
swamp	= overcome, inundate

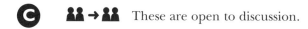 **C** These are open to discussion.

> **SUGGESTED KEY PHRASES**
>
> ¶ 4   organisation of time   time management
> ¶ 9   dividing big jobs into smaller sub-tasks
> ¶ 10 'investing' time
> ¶ 12 take control

9.8 / Reporting – 2   ADVANCED GRAMMAR

Before starting this section, ask everyone to look again at **3.2 Reporting – 1**.

 A

> **SUGGESTED INTERPRETATIONS**
>
> **1** He told me that he would be arriving **tomorrow**.
> – *His expected day of arrival is tomorrow (he may have said this yesterday or on a previous day)*
> He told me that he would be arriving **the next day**.
> – *His expected day of arrival was the day after he spoke to me (he didn't say this yesterday)*
>
> **2** She **advised** me to spend more time reading.
> – *This is the gist of what she said and gives no special emphasis to the report*
> She **urged** me to spend more time reading.
> – *This gives special emphasis to the speaker's insistence*
>
> **3** He **dismissed** my plan as unrealistic.
> – *He rejected my plan*
> He **had doubts about** the effectiveness of my plan.
> – *This is more tactful: he disagreed with my plan, but didn't reject it completely*
>
> **4** He **promised** to make the call soon.
> – *Clearly a promise*
> He **said** that he would make the call soon.
> – *This might be a promise, or just a statement of what he was going to do*
>
> **5** She **agreed**.
> – *She expressed her agreement*
> She **assured me** that I was right.
> – *This emphasises her wish to make me feel good*

 B   The answers are in **bold print** below. Some of the interpretations are open to discussion.

TRANSCRIPTS WITH ANSWERS   *3 minutes*

PRESENTER: Listen carefully to each speaker and select an appropriate adjective to describe their attitudes. ONE

1ST SPEAKER: Could I have a word with you? Yes. Well, you see, I've been looking at *your* work and comparing it with…with what the others have been doing and well, you know what I think about *everyone else's* work, don't you? I mean, it's improved a lot. Anyway, looking at yours in comparison I must say that you really are…I mean, yours is far and away the most . . .   **– angry**

PRESENTER: TWO

2ND SPEAKER: Could I have a word? Ah . . . yes, well . . . Look…um…I've been…I've been watching your work and I've been comparing it with…er…with [what] the others have been doing and well, er…I mean you know what I think about everyone else's work, I mean that's…that's improved quite a bit. But…uh…looking at yours, I…I have to say, I mean, you've… you've really…you've just not…um…well, I mean, yours is just…it's just . . .   **– disappointed** or **diffident**?

PRESENTER: THREE

3RD SPEAKER: Could I have a word? Yes. Well, you see, I…I've been looking at your work and comparing it with…er…with what the others have been doing and…er…well, you know what I think about everyone else's work, don't you? I mean, w…it has improved a lot but . . . Anyway looking at yours in comparison I must say that you've really…I mean, yours is far and away the . . .   **– impressed**

PRESENTER: FOUR

4TH SPEAKER: Could I have a word? Yes. Well, you see, I've been looking at your work and comparing it with…er…with what the others have been doing and…er…well, er…you know what I think about everyone else's work, don't you? I mean, *it* has improved a lot. Anyway looking at *yours* in comparison I must say that you've really, I…I mean, yours is far and away . . .   **– sarcastic**

PRESENTER: FIVE
5TH SPEAKER: Could I have a word? Yes, yes. Well…um…you see, I've…I…I've been looking at your work and…um…comparing it with…er…with…er…with what the others have been doing and…um…well, um…you know…you know what I think about everyone else's work, er…I… I know you do. I mean, er…th…that's improved quite a bit, hasn't it? Well…er…anyway, looking at yours in comparison I…I…I must say I…that you've really…er…I mean…er…yours is far and away the most . . . **– diffident** or **disappointed**?

2 **SUGGESTED SUMMARIES**

2 The second speaker regretted that my work hadn't improved in comparison with the others' work.

3 The third speaker congratulated me on my work and commented that it was much better than everyone else's.

4 The fourth speaker was unimpressed by my work and thought that everyone else's work had improved considerably.

5 The fifth speaker was unwilling to commit himself, but thought that my work had improved less than everyone else's.

C **SUGGESTED ANSWERS**

2 He promised to tell me when they arrived.

3 She reminded me to hand in my work (that evening).

4 He regretted that I couldn't make it to the party (the night before).

5 She congratulated me on passing.

6 He assured me that I would manage if I remained calm.

7 She insisted that I (should) visit them at the weekend.

8 He disagreed with me (politely).

9 She warned me not to park on the/that double yellow line.

10 He reproached me for behaving in that way / for my behaviour.

11 She claimed that she'd have helped me with my work if she'd had more time.

12 He suggested that we (should) organise our time more efficiently.
He suggested organising our time more efficiently.

9.9 **Progressive v. traditional methods** **LISTENING AND COMPOSITION**

A **1** We'll hear more about the school in **A2**.

2 The questions are similar to Part 2 of the Listening Paper.

ANSWERS

1 B	2 C	3 A	4 C	5 B	6 C	7 A	8 C

TRANSCRIPTS *7 minutes 40 seconds*

NARRATOR: Listen to the interviews with a pupil and a teacher at Summerhill School. First Beth Titchener.
BETH: My name's Beth Titchener, I'm fifteen years old and I'm a pupil at Summerhill School.
INTERVIEWER: Tell me, what is…what…tell me about Summerhill School. How does it differ from other schools?
BETH: Well, the main difference is that the pupils don't have to go to lessons. And Summerhill's a democratic school, so everybody's equal and every…we have meetings, and everybody in the meeting has an equal say, where…in the meetings we discuss things like, oh, daily goings-on in…in the school and if someone's been making trouble or something, we discuss that in the meeting. And everybody has an equal vote, whether you're, you know, one of the youngest pupils or the Headteacher.
I can make my own choices about what I do, whereas in another school I'd be told what I have to do every day, and here I have much more responsibility over my own life. In a normal school you wouldn't be…you wouldn't be given any responsibilities. I think in most places children aren't seen as responsible enough, they don't think children are, you know, capable of holding any responsibilities.
INTERVIEWER: What made your family decide that this was the right school for you? Or you and presumably your family decide it was the right school?
BETH: Um…I don't know. I think it's because every…or quite often when I'd come home from my last school, because I went to a normal skate…state school before, when I was about nine or something, and every time when I'd come home I'd be like, 'Why do I have to do what the teachers say all the time? Why do I have to always do what they say?' I'd have screaming fits on the way home, saying, 'I don't want to go back to school tomorrow, I don't want to go back!' And then my parents took me

out of school for a while, but I just got really bored because I had no, you know, no people to socialise with or anything. And so, we came to look around at Summerhill and I really enjoyed visiting here, so I decided I wanted to be here, but I didn't fully understand the philosophy of the school or anything when I first came because I was only about ten or eleven, so . . .

INTERVIEWER: I think from the outside a lot of people I imagine, you know, think, 'Oh, pupils don't have to go to lessons, that probably means no one would choose to go to lessons.'

BETH: I think when people are…when people don't go to lessons, I mean, because if you don't have to go to lessons, I mean, quite a lot of people when they first come to Summerhill, they've had to go to lessons for such a long time that as soon as they think, 'Oh, I don't have to go to lessons' they don't go to any lessons for ages, they just play, and after a while you start finding interests, like you discover what you're actually interested in, not what you're just made…been made to do, so like I had quite a lot of Japanese friends before and they'd be all talking in Japanese and I'd be like, 'Hang on a minute, I want to learn to understand them as well because this is really annoying me. I can't understand what these people are doing or what they're talking about and stuff.' So I decided, 'Yeah, I want to go to Japanese lessons.' And I went to every Japanese lesson I had, as much as possible until I could…had a kind of rough understanding of what they were talking about.

INTERVIEWER: If you had children would you send them here?

BETH: If they wanted to come here, yeah. I'd definitely, I'd ask them.

INTERVIEWER: And have you got brothers and sisters at home?

BETH: Yeah, I've got a younger brother, who came here for a while and then he…didn't really suit him and so.

INTERVIEWER: And what about friends…um…if you've been here five years, some of the…some of your friends must have left, I mean, do you still keep in touch with them?

BETH: Some…most of them, yeah. I mean, sometimes it's quite hard to keep in touch because most of them are from foreign countries and they, like, quite…some of my really good friends have gone off to school in Japan or New Zealand or somewhere, but we keep in touch a bit, yeah.

INTERVIEWER: I think that's wonderful. I mean, they're always going to be there wherever you travel, you'll be able to…um…touch base with them or you'll have a whole network of friends all over the world.

BETH: Yeah. There's so many people here from different cultures and different countries, you get to learn about lots of different…different peoples, different ways of living and stuff. It's what I also think is really good is there's hardly any racism in Summerhill, because there's so many foreign people that you kind of…everybody has to learn to live with people from other countries, and a person speak…coming from a strange country which you're not used to, speaking a strange language, generally in Summerhill people are more interested in them rather than…because they're used to everyone being different.

★★★

NARRATOR: Now Michael Newman.

MICHAEL: My name's Michael Newman, I've worked at Summerhill for six years, and at the moment I'm teaching English, but…er…when…for my first four and a half years I taught Science here, and then for another year I've been a House Parent, so I've been very lucky, I've moved from one job to another within the school.

INTERVIEWER: And what do you really enjoy about your job?

MICHAEL: Um…I enjoy it…it's the only teaching job I've ever done where I can be myself, where I don't have to pretend or act, to have authority or to tell children what to do. You've kind of…you can be at the same level, you can have friends with the children and if you make a mistake or if you have a joke, you don't have to worry about losing control of the class, so you can just relax and be yourself.

INTERVIEWER: Do you think your teaching methods are different within this environment?

MICHAEL: It's very different in the sense that the children control what I do, so a child can interrupt me and say, 'No, I don't want to learn this!' and then I have to change it. So the very act of teaching becomes one of negotiation…um…if you were to see me, you wouldn't know that, unless you see…the children interrupted, if you were to see one of my lessons you'd think, 'No, this is a normal lesson,' because I…I, you know, I…I do lessons, GCSE [General Certificate of Secondary Education] English lessons, and the children will come and they have an expectation, they know it's a GCSE lesson, they'll probably have confidence because they've seen me teach already, that I'll be teaching them things that are relevant and that are interesting. But there will be moments in any of those lessons where someone could s…put their hand up and say, 'Well, I don't want to do this!' and…and we'd have to re-negotiate what's…what I was teaching and what they didn't like.

INTERVIEWER: But presumably if the rest of the group do want to do it, it's… they are outvoted.

MICHAEL: Oh yeah, yeah.

INTERVIEWER: Had you heard about Summerhill before…I mean, did you set out to teach here?

MICHAEL: No, I mean, um…i…if I look back, I mean, my whole life focuses on this place, but it was by chance that I worked here. I was in Italy teaching English as a foreign language for a year and a half and…er…and my mother was sending me the Guardian adverts, and I just saw it advertised, you know community school, democratic school. And I've always been interested in chil…how children learn ethics and values, and I just thought if I worked here I could see…see that happening, and actually…and see it happening without the authority of a parent or without the authority of a teacher. And I'm very interested in what happens in the meetings, and how the children here…they talk about what's right and wrong, they talk about, you know, 'Should we vote that way or not?' and 'Is it wrong to punish?', you know, 'What if you do fine someone, what should it be?' I mean, you have all these wonderful moral dilemmas, and there's a lot of discussion at the moment, in the meeting now in fact, about smoking and should you be allowed to smoke, what age should you be allowed to smoke, what should be the fines if you…you smoke? And you sh…you know, and you're not allowed to smoke, you know. Should the school be able to control your…your personal behaviour, should it…should the school show concern for the health of all its members? All those issues will be discussed by six-year-olds to sixteen and all the staff.

INTERVIEWER: That's fantastic!
MICHAEL: It is, yeah and it's affecting, and they're discussing it not as a role-play or as a debate, but actually, what they vote in the end's going to control the way they live.

3 👪 In this follow-up discussion it may be necessary to brainstorm some further educational practices and teaching methods that students consider to be 'progressive' or 'reactionary' before starting the discussion. Perhaps refer back to what Christine said in **9.1** or Sarah in **9.4**.

B **1–3** 🖉 These steps should not be rushed. It takes time to analyse and discuss notes. As preparation for the exam, it's important for students to know how long it takes them to make notes – and probably try to speed up the process.

9.9 Model version

Most pupils in most countries don't have a choice of the kind of education they receive: they go to their local school and follow the courses that school provides, which is probably fairly traditional.

In a traditional school, the assumption is that the teacher has knowledge which he or she shares with the pupils. This may involve 'chalk and talk' methods where the pupils sit in rows facing the teacher, who stands at the blackboard and lectures the pupils. A textbook is used, which contains all the information that the pupils require. Discipline is strict and misbehaviour is punished with detention or other sanctions. Examination success is the main purpose of this style of education.

In a progressive school, the classes are often smaller, and the pupils work together in pairs or in groups under the guidance of the teacher, discovering information for themselves as they work together. Discipline is self-imposed, and in very progressive schools (such as Summerhill) pupils can choose to miss lessons and do nothing. Becoming a good person is the purpose of this style of education.

Both methods have their critics and supporters. Supporters of traditional methods maintain that pupils need to be motivated by exams and are not mature enough to decide when to attend classes. Of course the teacher has more knowledge of the subject than the pupils and so it is his or her job to give them that knowledge, and to encourage them to learn and work hard and pass their exams.

Supporters of progressive methods claim that each child is different, and may not be ready to learn at the same time. If they do choose to attend a particular class they are much more highly motivated than if they attend unwillingly. Self-imposed discipline is more effective than discipline imposed from above. Examinations are a curse, not a blessing.

Different methods may suit different children. It is hard to reconcile the two sides to this argument, except by answering these questions: 'Which kinds of methods would I like to learn by?' and 'Would I send my child to a progressive school, or a traditional one?'

Leo Jones *New Progress to Proficiency*

Mother nature

10

10.1 Animals and plants

TOPIC VOCABULARY

(A) **1** After the discussion, allow time for students to note down ten vocabulary items, and for them to compare them with each other.

People tend to refer to *mother nature* in a gently ironic way. The word *nature* is sometimes a feminine noun: 'Nature has her own way of maintaining a balance'.

2 This is a very open-ended brainstorming activity. Perhaps ask each group to announce two or three less familiar words that someone in their group came up with. Here, for example, are some suggested vocabulary items:

bird-watching botany budgerigar cages endangered evolution foliage guard dog
habitat hamster kitten pollution puppy recycling roots

(B) **1**

> **ANSWERS**
>
> 1 endangered   2 breeding   3 accepted   4 naturalist   5 worked up
> 6 wither   7 recycled   8 species   9 rodents   10 reptiles   11 prey
> 12 domesticated   13 vermin   14 claws   15 plumage   16 feelers
> 17 flock   18 endearing

2 Make sure there's enough time to consider the unused words – this kind of exercise isn't a test, it's a way of learning new words.

And here are some follow-up discussion questions, which provide a link to the next section:

- What is the strangest thing you've ever eaten (or seen someone else eat)?
- Could you kill an animal if you wanted to eat it?
- What are the different reasons that people have for being vegetarian?
- What other animals are useful to humans in other ways than just being eaten?

10.2 'Our cousins in the ocean'

LISTENING

(A)   This preliminary discussion encourages students to pool their previous knowledge and ideas.

(B) **1** 🔊 Pause the tape at the place marked with ★★★ in the Transcript, which is the end of **B1**.

> **ANSWERS**
> 1 c   2 b   3 b (*or* a?)   4 a   5 c

2 🔊 Ticks beside the following reasons:

he feels an inexplicable affinity with them ✓
their brains are large ✓
they can move in spectacular ways ✓
some whales are impressively large ✓
they are perfectly suited to living in the sea ✓

TRANSCRIPT   *6 minutes 30 seconds*

PRESENTER: This week, we hear from zoologist, Ray Gamble.
RAY: My name is Ray Gamble, and I'm the Secretary of the International Whaling Commission. That's the body made up of 43 member governments who have responsibility for the management of the whaling industry, the regulation of that industry, and the conservation of the whale stocks throughout the world.
PRESENTER: Why isn't there a total world-wide ban on killing whales ? Why can't whales be totally protected from being hunted?

RAY: We've had many problems in terms of management of whale stocks…er…because certain, particularly Arctic communities are very heavily dependent on the natural resources of a very severe environment. And so the…um…the Inuit people, the Eskimo peoples of Greenland and…er…northern Canada and Alaska, have argued that they, in spite of a…a ban on commercial whaling, should be permitted to carry on catching for subsistence purposes. And so we have developed over the course of years, and…and with a great deal of…of heart-searching, a…a specific management regime for aboriginal subsistence whaling, which is much more heavily dependent, not on the number of whales in the ocean, but on the perceived need of the indigenous peoples who are hunting the animals. They need them for subsistence, for cultural purposes, er…social purposes. Um…many of these communities…um…feel bound together by the fact that they are hunters together. And so this has been a very important factor to build in on top of the…the basic biology of how many whales there are in the ocean.

And so I've had the chance of going out to…um…Alaska with the Eskimo whalers, standing on the frozen Arctic Ocean, and watching the bow-head whales swimming along the…the leads, the cracks in the ice that open up in the spring, and…and the hunters go out in their seal-skin boats and…and harpoon – hand harpoon, using the…the old…er…traditional techniques. Er…er…and that's a…a very interesting experience.

PRESENTER: But this may not be what enlightened people in Europe and North America want to hear, as Ray explains.

RAY: And of course many people now in the comfortable Western world…er…have a very different view of what a whale is…is there for. The aboriginal subsistence hunter sees it as part of his total environment: he's dependent on the animal and he feels a special relationship to the animal because it does sustain his life. But to the…the Western communities…er…which are not dependent on…on flesh for food now – there's a…a general movement against eating red meat – um…there's a…a preference to see the whale as a…a beautiful animal, as a…an animal with a very large brain, an animal with…with great powers of being able to dive to…to great depths in the ocean and survive, and so on. Um…the whale is seen as a symbol of…of a…a…a life of freedom and…er…it evokes all kinds of…of non-culinary thoughts. So that the whale is…is now seen as something that has to be preserved an…and kept in respect in the ocean. And whether you go out on a whale-watching trip and see the whale for yourself or whether you just know that it's in the ocean, tha…that is what is important and…and the people who go out and hunt the whale for commercial purposes are very much seen to be…er…not the kind of people that you'd want to associate with any more.

So, it…the whale is no longer a…a renewable resource, but a…um…a…a figure to be seen as…as symbolising so much more for many people.

★★★

PRESENTER: Ray is obviously passionately involved with whales. What is it about the whale that stirs him?

RAY: They really are very exciting animals. Um…the large whales are *very* large. Er…to see a blue whale, which is the largest animal that…that has ever lived in the ocean…er…on…on this earth, and to see it turning and moving, twisting, so completely at home in the water, i…it's a very exciting sight. To see a…a large animal like a humpback whale leaping right out of the ocean is a very spectacular event to…to actually see this happen. So they…they are dramatic animals in that sense. And some of them are very big, yes, a blue whale is like a, you know, a couple of buses end to end, i…it's of that size, a hundred feet long, 150 tons perhaps of living, mobile animal.

And they do have very large brains. And so there is the sense that, you know, maybe they have a…a form of intelligence that…that . . . it's difficult enough to…to measure human intelligence, measuring the intelligence in…in another species altogether is…is really quite difficult. But the fact of the…the very large brain suggests that there is…um…you know, a degree of…of affinity with man which has the large brain use o…on land. These have been described as 'our cousins in the ocean'. There…we feel a…an affinity of some kind.

When you've…um…have the chance to…to…to get close to a…a dolphin – I've been in a…a rubber dinghy with a wild but a sociable dolphin swimming around – when it comes and…and peers at you out of the water, it's like looking into the eye of s…your pet dog, you think, 'There must be something in there, if only I could…could make contact with it.' It's the same with the dolphin, it's the same with the whale, that…that there is some kind of…of instinctive bond that you feel. They…they are impressive animals in terms of size and ability, and…and there is this sense that there's…there's more than…than we can grasp at the moment. There's something more that…that we may find out in the future. They…they really are very exciting animals.

C 👥 If you haven't used the extra follow-up discussion questions at the end of **10.1**, this might be a good time to introduce them.

▶ 10.3 The Third Chimpanzee

READING

Background   This passage is from *The Rise and Fall of the Third Chimpanzee* by Jared Diamond, a well-known American ecologist and physiologist. He is also the author of *Guns, Germs and Steel (A Short History of Everybody for the last 13,000 Years)*, a marvellous account of human development and history from the first farmers to the present day. Both fascinating, thought-provoking – and funny too!

If possible, ask everyone to read this passage before the lesson. The questions are similar to Part 5 of the Use of English Paper.

Although there are no discussion questions in the Student's Book, encourage everyone to share their reactions to the issues raised by the writer. Here are some questions to start things off:

- What did you think of the passage?
- What was the most interesting point the writer made?
- Would you like to read more from this book? Why (not)?

ANSWERS

1 humans and pygmy chimps (if chimpanzees are 'the first chimpanzee')
2 humans depend completely on tools to make a living
3 none
4 lions
5 elephants (and others)
6 (see below)

10.3 Model summary

Anatomically humans and chimpanzees are very similar: the only differences are that chimpanzees have more hair and they don't walk upright – and they don't wear clothes. If the zoologist from outer space didn't notice (or couldn't understand) human speech he would think them to be very similar species. He would discover after doing genetic tests that humans and chimpanzees have over 98 per cent of their genes in common, which makes them more similar than closely related bird species.

Leo Jones *New Progress to Proficiency*

This document may be photocopied.
© Cambridge University Press, 2002

ANSWERS

¶ 1   minutest
¶ 2   gulf   darker   attributes   rudimentary   eclipse
¶ 3   intimated   initially
¶ 4   affinities   grunting
¶ 5 & 6 baggage
¶ 7   precursors
¶ 8   propensities

10.4 Conditionals – 1   GRAMMAR REVIEW

SUGGESTED ANSWERS

1 I **feel** upset **when** I **think** about the destruction of the rainforests.
 – *Every time I think about them, I feel sad*
 I**'d feel** upset **when** I **thought** about people destroying the rainforests.
 – *I used to feel sad every time I used to think about them*
 I**'d feel** upset **if** I **thought** about the rainforests being destroyed.
 – *Sometimes I thought about them and I used to feel sad then*
 or *If I let myself think about it I would feel upset, so I don't let myself think about it*
 I **feel** upset **if** I **think** about the destruction of tropical rainforests.
 – *Sometimes I think about them and it makes me sad*
 I **felt** upset **when** I **thought** about jungles being destroyed.
 – *I felt sad every time I thought about them.* This is pretty much the same as *I'd feel upset when . . .* except that this suggests I didn't feel upset for quite so long. *When* suggests a more frequent occurrence than *if* in the above examples.

2 If you **don't leave** now, you**'ll** be late.
   & **Unless** you leave now, you**'ll** be late.
   – *You really ought to leave in case you're late*
   If you **left** now, you **wouldn't** be late.
   – *You probably don't intend to go now, so that means you will be late*
   If you **leave** now, you **won't** be late.
   – *You'll probably be going now, so that means you won't be late*
   If you **didn't leave** now, you**'d** be late.
   – *I'm fairly sure you're going, but supposing you stayed, you would be late*

3 If you**'re** interested **I'll** tell you about my dream.
   – *Let me know if you're interested, and if you are, I'll tell you my dream*
   If you **were** interested **I'd** tell you about my dream.
   – *I know you aren't interested, so I won't tell you*

4 **When** I **have** time, I**'ll feed** the cat.
   – *I'll open the tin later, when I'm not busy*
   If I **had** time, I**'d feed** the ducks.
   – *I'm very busy, so I can't/won't feed the ducks*
   If I**'d had** time, I**'d have fed** the dog.
   – *I was very busy, so I didn't feed it*
   If I **have** time, I**'ll feed** the goldfish.
   – *I may be too busy, but if I have a spare moment I'll feed them*
   If I **had** time, I**'d have fed** the birds.
   – *I'm very busy, so that explains why I didn't feed the birds*
   When I **had** time, I**'d feed** the rabbits.
   – *I used to feed the rabbits when I wasn't too busy*

B

SUGGESTED ANSWERS

1 If you go too close to that dog it may/might/will bite you.
2 If I'd realised that you needed help, I could have given you a hand.
3 If the amount of carbon dioxide in the atmosphere is not reduced, the ozone layer will be permanently damaged.
4 If the forests hadn't been cut down, they might still cover most of Europe.
5 If people were less ignorant about the effects of pollution on the environment, there might be less of it.
6 If animals could speak in their own defence, we wouldn't have/need to speak up for them.
7 If everyone drove more slowly, there would be less pollution.
8 If there wasn't/weren't any acid rain these lakes would still have fish in them.
   If it weren't for acid rain, these lakes . . .

C

POSSIBLE CONTINUATIONS

1 If he hadn't been so generous, **he might still have some money left.**
2 If you aren't careful, **you'll fall off the ladder and break your neck.**
3 If she doesn't phone me by Friday, **I'll have to go round and see her.**
4 If everyone cared more about the environment, **they would do more to protect it.**
5 If any species becomes extinct, **it can never be replaced.**
6 If human beings became extinct, **there would be plenty of other species to take our place.**
7 Unless the governments of the world cooperate, **there is no chance of the global environment being adequately protected.**

D   1 👥👥 This open-ended discussion leads to paragraph-writing.

   2 🖊 Actually writing the summary could be set as homework.

There's more in **13.4 Conditionals – 2**.

Background Gerald Durrell (1925–95) ran his own zoo on the island of Jersey, and was a well-known broadcaster and zoologist. His books are mostly about his amusing encounters with animals and are full of anecdotes, notably: *The Overloaded Ark, The Bafut Beagles, The Drunken Forest, A Zoo in My Luggage. The Stationary Ark,* from which this extract is taken, is one of his more serious books.

His best-known book is *My Family and Other Animals,* the opening paragraphs of which are included in **13.3 Family life**.

A

> **SUGGESTED ANSWERS**
>
> **1** appalling **2** feel very strongly **3** rabid (= mad, raving) **4** far **5** just as
> **6** just as **7** ancient **8** obliterate

B Begin by looking again at the first extract. Ask the class to spot some more examples of emotive language. Here are some examples:

I must agree with you . . . a few are excellent . . . zoos can and should be of value . . . I feel very strongly that . . . a great many rabid opponents . . . the rolling vistas, the ancient trees . . .

> **SUGGESTED ANSWERS**
>
> It is odd how comforted people feel . . . purely to make money. No thought of science or conservation sullied their primary conception. . . . unpleasant fungus, . . . disgraceful . . . appalling. . . . I would like to stress that . . . totally impossible . . . rare beasts
>
> I am not against . . . I am against . . . of immense conservation value . . . animal abattoirs in a sylvan setting
>
> I feel therefore . . . not simply clamour . . . acumen and far-sightedness
>
> . . . all of us . . . already too hard pressed by our unbeatable competition . . . even the few good ones . . .

C **1** Here students should make their own choices of phrases they want to remember – preferably ones that they don't already use in their own writing.

2
> **SUGGESTED ANSWERS**
>
> **1** disgraceful
> **2** There is no doubt that
> **3** Quite frankly   appalling
> **4** am against   – in spite of this
> **5** Clearly   absurd
> **6** It seems to me that   but you must agree that   absurd

D Before writing the paragraphs, students might like to exchange ideas on the topics listed. Alternatively, the written paragraphs can be shown to the other members of the group to start off a discussion.

Although this section doesn't take up much space, it may take longer than you anticipate.

A   ANSWERS

1 I wish that dog **would** stop barking.
– *It's barking and I don't like hearing it, but there's nothing I can do about it*
I wish that dog **didn't** bark.
– *Whenever the dog barks I find it annoying*
I wish that dog **had stopped** barking.
– *It went on barking a long time (maybe all night), which was very annoying*
I want that dog **to stop** barking.
– *It's barking and I don't like hearing it, but there's nothing I can do about it*
or *You must order the dog to stop barking (said threateningly to its owner, perhaps)*

2 It's time **for you to do** the washing-up.
– *You asked me to remind you of the time, that time has now come*
It's time **you did** the washing-up.
– *You offered to wash up and you should have started by now*
or *You never wash up but you ought to do it*

3 If only it were Friday!
– *I wish it were Friday*
Only if it was Friday . . .
– *This could only happen if today was Friday*
or *That could only happen on a Friday, not another day*
If it were only Friday . . .
– *If today was Friday, not a later day, then . . . (. . . maybe the situation might be different)*
If it's only Friday . . .
– *As today is Friday, not a later day (we still have plenty of time left)*

4 Would you rather I didn't help you?
& Would you prefer it if I didn't help you?
& Would you prefer me not to help you?
– *Do you want me to refrain from helping you?*
Would you rather not help me?
– *Do you want to do something else, rather than help me?*

5 I **was going to** phone her tonight.
& I **intended to** phone her tonight.
& I **was to have** phoned her tonight.
– *I was planning to ring her this evening (but now the plans have changed – maybe it's no longer necessary or possible)*
I **am to** phone her tonight.
– *It's been arranged for me to ring her this evening*

6 I wish I **knew** the answer.
– *I don't know the answer unfortunately*
I wish **to know** the answer.
– *Please tell me the answer*

B SUGGESTED ANSWERS

1 wouldn't keep interrupting/disturbing
2 was done to stop/prevent
3 it if you arrived/you to arrive
4 had been more aware of
5 I was brave enough to / knew how to
6 were/was something we could do
7 were going to come
8 you played your saxophone/hifi
9 time we went / time for us to go
10 was fed / had its food

10.7 Biological diversity

A Some of these questions are quite tricky – as they will be in the exam!

> **ANSWERS**
>
> 1 d   2 a (research into DNA hybridisation)   3 a   4 b   5 c   6 b   7 d   8 a

B

> **ANSWERS**
>
> ¶ 1 anathema   cook up   ¶ 2 argue   ¶ 4 thesis   ¶ 5 reaper-man   permed   ¶ 7 yield

Afterwards, discuss the students' reactions to the article.

10.8 *put* and *set*   VERBS AND IDIOMS

A

> **ANSWERS**
>
> *put*   pressure on someone   two and two together   someone at their ease   a question
>   to someone   a stop to something   someone in the picture   pen to paper
> *set*   a trap for someone   your teeth on edge   a good example   fire to something
>   your watch   the scene

B

> **ANSWERS**
>
> 1 said something thoughtless which embarrassed him
> 2 cost me   put an end to
> 3 depend on the success of one scheme or action
> 4 make him lose concentration and upset him
> 5 ascribed   discourage
> 6 asserted your authority
> 7 delayed
> 8 founded   intended/aimed
> 9 humiliating   put yourself in my place
>   gives people an unfavourable impression of us both
> 10 wouldn't be surprised if / consider him capable of (making . . .)
>   trying to deceive me

C

> **ANSWERS**
>
> 1 put   up to
> 2 set up
> 3 putting   across/over
> 4 put   out   put   up
> 5 put up with
> 6 put in
> 7 putting aside/putting away/setting aside
> 8 sets out
> 9 put in
> 10 sets in

As a follow-up: arrange the class into pairs and ask the students to write their own 'fill the gaps' exercise for another pair, using expressions from this section.

This section deals with degrees of formality in vocabulary and also in grammatical structure. A 'neutral' style (one that is neither too colloquial, nor too formal) is likely to be appropriate in most types of composition that students will have to do in the exam – unless they choose to write a personal letter, for example.

 1   ANSWERS

Different forms are more interesting to admire and study than lots of things that look the same.   **– neutral**

It's a lot more interesting to admire and study different forms than lots of things that look the same.   **– informal**

Different forms are more interesting to admire and study than a large number of similar looking species.   **– formal**

I do like little kittens and puppies – they're ever so sweet, aren't they?
                                                                                 – informal/colloquial

I consider young kittens and puppies to be the most endearing creatures.   **– formal**

Small kittens and puppies are delightful, I think.   **– neutral**

2 There are many examples of neutral style in the first half of **10.7**. Here are some of them:

The idea . . . gives most people a warm feeling inside.
. . . But what, exactly, is diversity?
. . . And which kind is most worth preserving?
. . . all species should not be equal.
. . . they suggest that preserving the rarest is not always the best approach.
. . . They reckon that if choices must be made . . .
. . . This makes sense from both a practical and an aesthetic point of view.
. . . saving one is nearly as good as saving both.
. . . Six species of crane are at some risk of extinction.
. . . Breeding in captivity might save them.

 Many variations are possible.

SUGGESTED ANSWERS

2 I hope your father has fully recovered (from his illness).
3 She was furious when she was told that she'd lost her job.
4 Organic fruit and vegetables are cultivated without the use of artificial fertiliser.
5 We were terrified when a large dog came bounding up to us.
6 Please be careful with the knife (you're using).
7 Testing cosmetics and shampoo on animals is not only pointless, it's also cruel.
8 You should have turned off the light when you left the room.
9 I think it's likely to rain fairly soon.
10 Instead of throwing your litter in the street, you ought to put it in a litter bin.

C Many variations are possible.

SUGGESTED ANSWERS

2 According to the experts, global warming is speeding up.
3 Even a small rise in temperature may have a big effect on the ice in polar regions.
4 Throwing cans and bottles away is an unnecessary waste of energy and materials. It's much better to recycle them.
5 Lunch is served from 12 o'clock.
6 Please be careful when getting off the train.
7 You're not allowed to use personal stereos or musical instruments here.
8 Although no vegetarians eat meat, vegans don't eat either fish or dairy products.

Extra activity   Step **2** of this activity (**Rewriting in a neutral style**) could be set as homework. Alternatively, the informal writing could be set as homework to be done before the next lesson, exchanged during the next lesson, and completed after the next lesson as further homework.

1 👥 🖊 Write a paragraph giving your views about being economical with energy (turning off lights and heating, driving slowly, etc.) in the style you'd use in an informal letter to a friend.

2 👥 🖊 Pass your paragraph to another pair, who should rewrite it in a more neutral style.

10.10 Use of English Part 1   EXAM PRACTICE

Background   This passage is from a book by Sir David Attenborough which accompanied the TV series *Life on Earth*. David Attenborough is well-known as a TV presenter and enthusiastic naturalist. His other books, also accompanying TV series, include *The Living Planet*, *The First Eden: the Mediterranean World and Man*, *The Trials of Life* and *Life in the Freezer* about Antarctica.

A   In the exam it's always advisable to read the passage quickly through for gist before filling in the gaps.

B   **1 & 2** 👥   In Part 1 of the Use of English Paper, candidates don't get several words to choose between, as in a multiple-choice test. This exercise reminds students that they should run through the various possibilities in their minds, rather than assume that the first word that comes to mind must be the best one. Here, more than one word is OK in some gaps. In the exam, usually, only one is possible, but sometimes there may be more than one correct answer. In the exam candidates should only write ONE word. (The answers used in the orginal text are in **bold print**.)

> **SUGGESTED ANSWERS**
>   **2** come across **discover** find
>   **3** **shining**
>   **4** **collect** discover gather
>   **5** **disguised**
>   **6** **enormous** huge immense
>   **7** **creatures** insects types
>   **8** experts people **specialists**
>   **9** **concerned** themselves
>   **10** exactly **just** precisely quite
>   **11** biggest **richest** strangest
>   **12** **exist** remain survive
>   **13** **forms**
>   **14** **careful** fortunate
>   **15** attacked **bitten** stung

10.11 Save the Earth   SPEAKING AND COMPOSITION

A   👥👥 This is intended to be an entirely open-ended discussion. Remind students that this is a topic that may well come up in the Interview in the exam.

👥 After a while, in order to encourage an exchange of views, the groups could be broken up into pairs consisting of students from different groups. Then each student has to summarise what his or her group has discussed so far before continuing the discussion.

Here are some more quotes to write up on the board, to fuel the discussion, if necessary:

'The future will either be green, or not at all.' – Jonathon Porritt

'Man is the only animal that blushes: or needs to.' – Mark Twain

'Small is beautiful.' – E. F. Schumacher

'Nowadays we don't think much of a man's love for an animal; we laugh at people who are attached to cats. But if we stop loving animals, aren't we bound to stop loving humans too?'

– Alexander Solzhenitsyn

'No gain without pain.'

'The wounds we have inflicted on the Earth can be healed . . . But if it is to be done, it must be done now. Otherwise, it may never be done at all.' – Jonathon Porritt

B Make it absolutely clear that students must make notes before writing – the difficult part about this task is likely to be restricting the essay to 350 words. (Sorry if the quotes seem crass, but they do reflect what some people may feel even if they don't say so publicly!)

10.11 Model version

"The future of the planet looks bleak, but there's nothing I can do about it."

Scientists and experts are continually warning us that our planet is doomed. Again and again, we hear the same depressing phrases: global warming, pollution, over-fishing, tropical rainforests . . . All because of what human beings have done and are still doing. Not enough people are worried about the future. Can anything be done? What can I do?

Global warming is often cited as the most serious threat. Temperatures are rising and climate patterns are changing as the amount of carbon dioxide in the atmosphere rises. Greenhouse gases, which are emitted by burning fossil fuels in cars and power stations, are responsible for this. These emissions must be stopped if we want to stop global warming, and it's up to the politicians to enforce this. What can I do? Only vote for politicians who are going to be green. Every vote counts when a government has a narrow majority.

Pollution is contaminating our rivers, lakes, seas and air. As more and more people are aware of this, there is going to be more pressure on polluters. Air pollution from traffic must be controlled if our cities are going to be places fit to live in. But if polluters themselves loathe pollution, it will stop. What can I do? Make more people aware. And technology is developing new ways of powering cars which we cannot imagine today. Before too long there may be new environmentally-friendly cars, eliminating the need for petrol and pollution.

Fish stocks in every ocean are getting smaller all the time, due to over-fishing. Many fish never reach adulthood because of intensive fishing. We depend on fish as an important part of our diet. We need to control fishing, to conserve the stocks and allow them to regenerate. What can I do? Eat less fish and only eat fish that is caught by non-intensive methods.

Once destroyed, a tropical rainforest cannot be replaced. But it can be managed by controlled forestry. What can I do? Only buy tropical hardwood from managed forests.

If it was only me, as an individual, doing all the things I've suggested, it would have no effect. What I must do is persuade everyone else to share my views. What can I do? Support pressure groups like Friends of the Earth, who can influence the actions of governments and corporations. This may help our planet to survive a little longer for the benefit of our children and our children's children.

Leo Jones *New Progress to Proficiency*

Another world

11.1 **Enjoying reading**   LISTENING AND TOPIC VOCABULARY

 🖊 Although this is quite long, each part will probably only need one playing. Note that Christine appears twice: first at the beginning of the programme and again at the end.

ANSWERS

1 C   2 K + C   3 J + W   4 K   5 C   6 K   7 W   8 K   9 J   10 W + C + K

TRANSCRIPTS   *6 minutes 45 seconds*

INTERVIEWER: We talked to four people about reading. First here's Christine. What kind of books do you read?

CHRISTINE: I love detective fiction, I have to say. And I think that to me detective fiction has been a respite, it's been a treat, from serious grown-up reading. I learned to love books as a very little girl with my Dad who took me to the library twice a week, and I learned a great respect for plot...um...and for story-telling. And just loved the cliff-hanger story and still love it. Because I can get quite lost in one of those and I...I'm a very fast reader, and my desire to work out who did it and what happened next is so great that it overpowers everything else and I will disappear into a book for hours and not speak to a soul. But I get that from my father who is exactly the same, my Mum has never been a great reader and my Dad and I drive her mad, because we will sit for hours contentedly reading when we're together and she thinks this is awfully boring and...and unsocial. But my Dad is never not reading and that's where I got it from.
★★★

INTERVIEWER: Jonathan, what kind of books do you enjoy reading?

JONATHAN: Well, I always enjoy reading cook books. I'm quite a keen cook...um...so I get new ideas for recipes and things. But I just enjoy reading them as...as almost as fiction.

INTERVIEWER: Mhm. And...er...when...when do you read them?

JONATHAN: I will read them...mm...they're not books I tend to read at bedtime, they're more daytime books. If I have a...a few minutes to kill, I'll pull one on...off the shelf and have a browse.

INTERVIEWER: Mhm. And...er...what's your favourite book?

JONATHAN: Well, my favourite cook book would probably be Jane Grigson's *Vegetable Book*. She's a fantastic food writer anyway and I'm not a vegetarian, I love meat, um...but her *Vegetable Book* is fascinating because she covers each vegetable, each major vegetable in turn, gives you a bit of historical background and then all sorts of recipes involving the vegetable, and other ingredients as well. And it has a...a sense of history about it that I find very ap...appealing.

INTERVIEWER: Mhm. And why do you enjoy reading?

JONATHAN: Well, I enjoy reading cook books, I think, largely because even if you're not cooking the recipes you're reading it conjures up a sense of other places, other flavours, other times in your life when you might have eaten something similar. And the promise of happy times in the future if you do cook this food for somebody else.
★★★

INTERVIEWER: Karen, how about you? What do you enjoy about reading?

KAREN: The immediate thing about a book is that is...just it takes you into a different world, you can immediately find yourself introduced to a whole set of behaviour or w...or ideas that, you know, you wouldn't easily come across in your own life. You can just shut the door and that's it. I mean, I think it's much more, I mean, it's much more pleasurable than television, although I mean, I'm interested in television and film as well, but you know obviously you can take it at your own pace, and you can read again and you can savour certain passages. And...um...I think it's just the idea...getting into one person's head, and sort of seeing how they see things. And just having...also, you know as I said before about readability, being caught up in a good story. I mean, you're lost for a few hours, aren't you? You're in a different world for a few hours. And that...and also just the tactile pleasure of holding a book, of a book as an object. I mean, I like books as objects, I can never never throw them away ever, I could never give any...even a scrappy old paperback I could never give it to a jumble sale.
★★★

INTERVIEWER: What kind of books do you enjoy reading, William?

WILLIAM: Er...I enjoy the classics. And...er...novels that are set in a different period of history. Um...I particularly like reading about periods of history I don't know anything about.

INTERVIEWER: And when do you read?

WILLIAM: Um...well, I'm a compulsive reader, um...so whenever I get the opportunity really, whether it's...er...on a journey, or when I'm at home with nothing to do, er...if I'm on holiday. Er...but any opportunity I get really I'll be into a book.

INTERVIEWER: And...um...what's your favourite book?

WILLIAM: Um...well, a book I've enjoyed recently was *Perfume* by Patrick Süsskind. Um...again a book set in a different period of history. Er...but this book in particular is fantastic because it is all about somebody...er...who notices the smells of things...um...much more than we would and...er...can actually tell what has happened in a...different areas of town by the smells that he can pick up there. Even things that have happened a long time beforehand. So it's a…it's a book that's written but has, you know, a great sort of sensual…er…feel to it.

INTERVIEWER: Mhm. And…um…what is it about reading that you enjoy?

WILLIAM: Um…I think it's just that, being able to transport yourself somewhere else…er…for whatever period you're reading for. Um…I think it's a great medium for creating…er…something that you don't know anything about and I'd actually rather read a book than watch a movie. I find it much easier to…er…escape somewhere else…um…when I don't have somebody's pictures showing me what it looks like. I can imagine it, a certain amount of it, myself and just enjoy the reading.

INTERVIEWER: Mhm, thank you.

★★★

INTERVIEWER: Finally, Christine again, why do you enjoy reading?

CHRISTINE: It's another world, it's going into a world…um…that somebody makes convincing, where there are characters in that world about whom you have a concern and you want to know what happens to them, and…um…it matters to know what is going to unfold and what happens next. And it's about expanding your picture of the world. It's taking you into bits of people's experience that you haven't got for yourself. Um…but the best book is one where you find the environment and the situation and the conflict if there is one, because most literature involves some kind of conflict. Er…the resolution of that conflict, or whatever, it…y…you just desperately want to know what it is. And it's that…um . . . it's that commitment to the creation the author has made that keeps you reading absolutely desperately to the last page. Um…and it's about…er…magic as well, it's about being taken into a world that just transports you and you forget the here and now, you know, I…I could quite forget to feed the pussies if they didn't jump on my head if I were really engrossed in a book. And I regret the fact that I seem to have so little time to read these days. Um…one of my resolutions every year is to make more time to do it, and one of these days I will, you know, because I love reading.

B Encourage 'non-readers' to talk about what they **DO** read (if not fiction, then maybe magazines, newspapers, non-fiction, brochures, catalogues . . .).

C

> **ANSWERS**
> 1 best-sellers   thrillers   whodunits
> 2 contents   blurb   dustjacket
> 3 dedication   foreword   preface
> 4 anthology   book   collection
> 5 complex   intricate   involved
> 6 get   struggle   wade
> 7 chapters   sections   units
> 8 figuratively   metaphorically   symbolically
> 9 message   purpose   side
> 10 readable   thought-provoking   well-written

D The Latin is given for your information only.

> **ANSWERS**
> e.g. = **for example** (Latin: *exempli gratia*)   etc. = **and other things** (Latin: *et cetera*)
> i.e. = **that is** (Latin: *id est*)   cf. = **compare** (Latin: *conferre*)   ff. = **and the following pages**
> pp. = **pages**   ibid. = **from the book already mentioned** (Latin: *ibidem*)
> viz. = **namely** (Latin: *videlicet*)   N.B. = **note well** (Latin: *nota bene*)   sic = **spelt in this way (probably misspelt) in the original work from which we are quoting** (Latin: thus)
> © = **copyright**   ¶ = **paragraph number**
>
> Most of the abbreviations can also be written without full stops:
>   eg   etc   ie   cf   ff   pp   ibid   viz   NB

11.2 'My last novel is the best work I can do'   LISTENING

Background

William Boyd (b. 1952) is a writer whose early work deals humorously with the English abroad, but his later books are more serious and each one covers a quite different theme. Boyd's books are consistently well-written and thought-provoking.

His best-known books include: *A Good Man in Africa*, *An Ice Cream War*, *The New Confessions*, *Brazzaville Beach*, *The Blue Afternoon* and *Armadillo*.

The opening of *Brazzaville Beach* is in **11.3**.

A Anticipating some of William Boyd's answers will make it easier to follow what he says later.

B Pause the interview at the places marked ★★★.

ANSWERS

1 film and theatre
2 two to six in the afternoon
3 people he knows / his own life
4a masculinity and femininity / gender
4b personality
5 being autonomous   feeling free   being self-sufficient
6 think themselves lucky / realise that others are worse off / stop moaning / not be so pathetic
7 university libraries / noisy, distracting places
8 first draft
9a second guess / anticipate
9b true
10 *Armadillo* (his most recent novel)

TRANSCRIPT   *12 minutes 50 seconds*

NARRATOR: You'll hear an interview with William Boyd, the author of *A Good Man in Africa*, *Armadillo*, *The Blue Afternoon*, *An Ice Cream War* and *Brazzaville Beach*. Fill each box with a word or short phrase.

WILLIAM: My name is William Boyd, and I'm a novelist. Er…I also write short stories and scripts for films.

INTERVIEWER: And how did you start?

WILLIAM: I started…um…really when I went to University. Um…I did a lot of journalism, a lot of student journalism, I was a TV – er…not the TV critic, the film critic and the theatre critic of the university newspaper. Nice job! And…um…but I wrote a lot of stories and I actually wrote a…a novel while I was at university, which I never published or I never tried to publish, it was a…an autobiographical novel all about me and I had to get it out of my system. But…um…it was…er…really my university days that saw the beginning of my writing career.

I think also maybe deep down I realised I could never work for anybody! I was…I was…er…destined to be a freelance, and the wonderful thing about writing, I think, being a novelist, it is…it is the ultimate 'one man band', and…er…you are completely free and I think that i…if I had to sum up, you know, what does writing mean to me in one word, it would be 'freedom'.

INTERVIEWER: That's nice, that's lovely. And I mean, on a typical day when you're actually writing, how do you…are you quite disciplined with yourself?

WILLIAM: Quite disciplined. I mean, er…when I'm writing a novel I try to write every day…um…but sometimes you can't because you've got a life to live, and…er…er…the central heating needs fixed, or you've got to go and do some shopping or something. But…um…I try to do, you know, is…try to write every day as many days of the week as is possible, and…er…I don't have any rigid discipline, like I sit down at my desk at eight o'clock and rise from it at half past eleven for a cup of coffee. I…I can write for about three to four hours…um…and sometimes that's in the morning. And more recently I find that something's happened to my biorhythms or something, I find I'm writing more in the afternoon now after lunch from sort of…two to six is my normal stint. Um…but of course as the novel goes on and I get more and more caught up in it I begin to work longer days and seven days a week until by the end it's kind of a frantic sixteen-hour day going on. ★★★

INTERVIEWER: Now how do you come up on your characters?

WILLIAM: Well, sometimes they just s…suggest themselves to you. Um…sometimes they're maybe drawn from bits of life – I'm never…I'm not an autobiographical writer so I don't use my own life and the people I know as material for my fiction. Um…and sometimes you just have to sit down and invent them. Um…you know, I've…I've written from the point of view of a woman, and I…I knew that…er…I knew that was the first thing and then I had to think, 'Well, what kind of woman would she be?' And so I just…er…invented her, I invented her personality, and her…her physical appearance. And I think I am very much that type of writer, I do use my imagination. I don't go to life for inspiration. I'm quite happy to sit and…and dream in a way, dream up things, and then there's another whole question of making it…them seem lifelike. But…er…a lot of it is…is a conscious act of…of choice and it's very much a question of…of me deciding and of…and of just setting my imagination to work.

INTERVIEWER: In *Brazzaville Beach* I…I loved the way that you were able to write as Hope Clearwater, and she was so real, she was just like it…um…she was, well, she was like a woman. I mean, was that difficult to write?

WILLIAM: Well, it was a difficult…er…process to…to get to the right method. And I think I have found the right method and I think it works both ways, I think if you are a woman wanting…wanting to write from the point of view of a man you should adopt the same method I did, which was to forget all questions of masculinity and femininity, to forget gender completely, and to concentrate entirely on personality.

And I think it's a kind of…we in a w…we're a bit knee jerk in the way we think, 'Oh, women are sensitive and warm and giving, and men…er…cannot commit and are cold and are frightened of their emotions'. Well, you know, that's a generalisation, um…you can't write a novel based on generalisations. So the more precise you are, the more idiosyncratic the character is, the more real he or she will appear in the…in the novel.

★★★

INTERVIEWER: What do you really enjoy about what you do?

WILLIAM: Well, I think the main thing I enjoy about it, or…is my complete and absolute self-sufficiency. Um…and I'm also deeply conscious of how lucky I am to be able…to be, as Chekhov said, 'a free artist'. Um…I don't live in a country that's oppressed…um…I am uncensored. I can…I can earn a living…er…at what I want to do more than anything else in the world. I can decide not to work one day or work flat out for three months. And I think it's that absolute liberation, that absolute autonomy, that…er…is the thing I cherish most and which I would think I would feel most…er…um…unhappy about if it was removed. Um…and…um…as a result…um…I don't take it for granted, and then there's the compensation of…of being an artist practising your art form, um…which has its bad days and its exhilarating days, but I think it's really within the context of…of this…this absolute freedom and autonomy…um…that makes it…er…you know, so fulfilling.

INTERVIEWER: Is there anything you don't like about being a novelist?

WILLIAM: Well, I've got lots of grumbles and complaints but really…um…I think they're pathetic. [No, I'm sure they're not!] I…I…I remember once being asked a question, when I was giving a reading and somebody said 'Er…do you suffer for your art?' And I immediately said, 'But of course I do'. And then I thought, 'Hang on a minute, what…what exactly do I suffer?' [Having to talk to such a bloody idiot!] 'What suffering are we talking about here?' So I really think it's a…a luxury…er…to complain. And…er…maybe if I was suffering from a terrible writer's block or if I was constantly being trashed by the critics and couldn't sell a copy, then I would be a more tormented soul. But…um…the little, you know, um…'slings and arrows of outrageous fortune' that you encounter in the writing life are…are…are as nothing beside the more serious injustices and grievances that…er…the world hands out. So I think those of us who…um…you know, moan and complain about, 'Oh, it's so hard and so difficult!' um…really don't know they're living.

★★★

INTERVIEWER: Can you write anywhere? Can you write here or do you prefer writing in a…um…particular location?

WILLIAM: No, I can write just about anywhere. And I think this is something because I started writing in universities and university libraries, people wandering around or whispering, and…so I've never needed solitude and I still write in libraries, I still go to…um…a library to…er…to write sometimes. I also work in my house in my study but if the phone rings I'll answer it, if there…somebody knocks at the door I'll break off and go and answer the door. Um…and I've written on planes and in cafés and, you know, hotel rooms, all sorts of things. So I don't need the…those kind of, you know, special conditions which I think are actually a, well, an excuse for not working!

INTERVIEWER: Do you write…um…freehand or put it all on your…on a laptop or . . .?

WILLIAM: Well, I write…er…I write my novels…the first draft I write…I write in longhand, in pencil – it's very low tech! Um…because I think there's something…er…missing if there isn't a manuscript stage. I mean this is just for my case, I think that there's something about the head, the hand, the page link which is fundamental to writing prose, and I suspect, well, certainly for me, and I suspect it's to do with things like sentence length, and inner rhythm and cadence to a sentence. And also the act of crossing out and the act of inserting other words. Um…on the screen of a computer that's gone, it's always looks pretty much perfect, but you can see on a manuscript just from the scribblings and the second thoughts and the third thoughts the whole process of your fiction evolving and…er…it's a very curious indication about something that's going well, or something that's going badly. Um…if you've written five lines for example in longhand and you haven't put a full stop there's something at the back of your mind saying this sentence is getting far too long. You never get that feeling if you're typing it onto a screen on a computer because there's…everything is there but not there and endlessly malleable, but you've made those marks on the page and there's something about that act which I still feel is fundamental to my fiction writing. And so even though I've been using a computer now for seven years, and I write journalism on it and…and screenplays and so on, whenever I start a novel or a short story or a work of fiction I…er…always do the first draft in…in longhand and then I type it on to the screen, and edit it on the screen.

INTERVIEWER: And when you're writing, do you write in your head to an individual or are you writing…um…to the world?

WILLIAM: No, I think you…er…probably write for yourself, I think that you write the books you like to…would like to read. And I think it's always a mistake to try and second-guess your ideal reader…um…because…er…you will possibly not be true to yourself, your sincerity, your integrity. I think you have to really do what you want to do and not what you think you ought to do, and that way even if the book is, let's say, terrible and an awful failure, at least you will…will have been true to yourself, and you've got no one else to blame.

★★★

INTERVIEWER: Have you got…er…one of your novels that's your favourite?

WILLIAM: Um…I have sort of an answer to this which is a bit of a cop-out or it seems a bit of a . . . But I actually think . . .

INTERVIEWER: You don't mean you've been asked this before!

WILLIAM: I have been asked this before, but I always give the same answer, which is…sounds a bit of a . . . but I think that if you…if I had to choose one book to represent me, as it were, for posterity, it would always be my last book because I think that . . . Haha, I know! It's a . . . But it's true because in a writerly sense everything that's in your last book is as good as…as I can get at the moment. I mean, people have . . . I've…I've written seven novels now, and some people like my first novel better than any others, some people like my fourth novel better. But in my…from my point of view I know that my last novel *Armadillo* is the…is the best work I can do at the moment, though it's going to be supplanted by the novel I'm going to write next of course, which is going to be in…in writerly terms, better, more sophisticated, more mature. I'm more experienced, I've...I've learnt more, and that may not be evident in the success of the novel or the apparent perceived success of the novel, but it will be evident to me as the writer of it.

INTERVIEWER: Does it surprise you still that you have that ability?

WILLIAM: Sometimes it's amaz...you are amazed at what you have thought up, because it's spontaneous in the act of writing, something unplanned. You, you know, I do plan everything in advance, I sit down to write Chapter Five and I start writing it and I get an idea – out of the blue – and everything...everything changes. Um...so...er...it's almost functioning independently sometimes of me, and that's when I'm...er...astonished and I think, 'What on earth made me think of that?'

INTERVIEWER: Oh, it's exciting.

WILLIAM: Yes, it is, it is, and you hope it won't go away, that's the other thing, you hope this faculty will remain with you and...er...will in a way...er...continue to enrich what you write.

C   At the end, ask each group to recommend a favourite book or author to the rest of the class.

11.3   Setting the scene . . .   READING AND SPEAKING

Background

We heard an interview with **William Boyd** in **11.2**.

The protagonist of *Brazzaville Beach* is a woman who, against the background of civil war in an African country, is studying chimpanzees and makes the alarming discovery that they engage in warlike activities with each other, just as humans do.

Barbara Vine is the pseudonym of the crime writer Ruth Rendell (b. 1930). Her books written under this name are more imaginative and strange than her more routine Inspector Wexford mysteries. She is a very accessible, stylish writer whose work dwells on life's losers and the darker side of human nature.

All of her Barbara Vine novels are highly recommendable: *A Dark Adapted Eye, A Fatal Inversion, The House of Stairs, Gallowglass, King Solomon's Carpet, Asta's Book, No Night is Too Long* and *The Brimstone Wedding*.

A Fatal Inversion concerns obsessive family relationships and a murder, the perpetrator of which is due to be executed as the book opens. During the rest of the book, the situation leading up to the murder slowly unfolds in flashbacks.

David Lodge (b. 1935) is a humorous writer whose work has a serious edge. Many of his works are concerned in some way with university life, and the worlds of game-playing, sexual intrigue and Catholicism.

His best-known books are: *Changing Places, Small World, Nice Work, Paradise News, Therapy* and *Thinks . . .*

The main characters of *Nice Work* are Vic Wilcox, the managing director of a struggling engineering firm, and Robyn Penrose, a feminist university lecturer. The book explores their different worlds and the developing relationship between two very different people.

Here and in **11.9** we have the opening paragraphs of some well-known novels, which I hope will whet students' appetites, encouraging them to want to read more.

A For this, **B** and **C**, the questions should be discussed in pairs. If you form an even number of pairs now they can combine into groups of four when you reach **D**.

> **SUGGESTED ANSWERS**
>
> 1 She (or he) lives in a beach house somewhere in Africa, where she/he just happens to have landed up and is unlikely to stay for ever. She/he seems to be single. [The reader discovers later that the narrator is a woman – some readers may recognise that the beach is in a Portuguese-speaking country.]
>
> 2 None (apart from '*some workmen*' and '*everyone else who lives round here*') – it gives a mood of isolation or self-containment
>
> 3 The narrator lives in a house on a beach: this is described in some detail in the last paragraph together with its garden – it is 'a few years' after 1964
>
> 4 Six: four of which are in the phrase '*Brazzaville Beach*', the title of the book – it seems that the beach is likely to be the main setting of the story

5 In ¶ 1 we find out where the narrator lives and we may be intrigued to know how she ended up there – the imagery of the *spar of driftwood* to which the narrator compares herself is striking

In ¶ 2 we find out the origins of the name of the beach, but without understanding what *Quadros* means in Portuguese or knowing about the conference in 1964, we are none the wiser. The style is very matter-of-fact

In ¶ 3 the reader is introduced to the political background of the story. The questions asked stand out stylistically

¶ 4 gives a detailed description of the house and its garden – the use of *I* and *my* emphasises that the house belongs to the narrator, she considers it to be her home. The style makes the place sound very attractive

B

SUGGESTED ANSWERS

1 Very little: she is going to die at exactly 8 o'clock, her home is in the country, she is probably the narrator's aunt (her father's sister). We don't know why she is going to die at 8 o'clock: it is a mystery

[The reader later discovers that she is going to be executed.]

2 Four times – not all that many, but enough to set a mood of gloom

3 She reads poetry (Browning); she doesn't get on well with her father

4 The narrator awakes in her parents' house in a leafy suburb on a Thursday in August 30 years ago

C

SUGGESTED ANSWERS

1 He often wakes up early and can't go back to sleep, because of his worries at work; he works in industry in a senior position; he is married and has a son called Gary

2 She is Victor's wife: she is overweight, she takes sleeping pills, she reads in bed before going to sleep

3 Victor awakes in his bedroom very early on Monday January 13th 1986

4 Twelve: it makes us realise that he has a lot of problems – they attack him like alien spaceships in a video game. The technical terms (*fettling shop, core blowers*, etc.) are puzzling to the reader, but they mean a lot to Victor

5 ¶ 1 begins like a diary entry, followed by terse scene-setting sentences, and then we share Victor's thoughts and the questions in his mind

In ¶ 2 his worries are listed and made to seem like attackers in a video game

In ¶ 3 we are introduced to his wife – a series of actions are described, like a blow-by-blow account of a fight

D 👥👥 Perhaps tell the class some of the information given in the **Background** notes above at this stage.

11.4 Describing a book   SPEAKING AND COMPOSITION

A 👥 Maybe ask everyone to concentrate on the first half of the discussion questions at this point, and return to discuss the others later, after they've written the composition.

B ✒ If there is too much to condense into 350 words, you might ask the class to focus on certain aspects of the book, rather than all six suggested.

> **11.4 Model version**
>
> *Leviathan* by Paul Auster
>
> *Leviathan* is a fascinating blend of detective story and literary novel by Paul Auster, an American writer whose other novels combine fantasy and realism, with an element of autobiography. The narrator of this story has a lot in common with Auster himself, but he is someone else.
>
> The story starts with an explosion on a remote roadside in Wisconsin, USA. A man is

blown up by the side of a road and nobody knows who he is except Peter, the narrator of the novel. The rest of the story is about Peter's memories of his own encounters with former friend Benjamin Sachs and his journey across America meeting other people who knew Sachs. He is trying to piece together what happened to his former friend and what led to his death. What terrible things happened to him? Was his death an accident, suicide or murder?

As we find out more about Sachs, we also find out about Peter himself. Peter tells us about his encounters with Sachs over the fifteen years of their intermittent friendship. Years pass and many things happen as they lose touch with each other for a couple of years, and then meet again. We meet Fanny, Lillian and Maria and find out about their different relationships with Sachs — and with Peter himself. Seen through the eyes of each of these women, Sachs seems to be different people. How can the same man be so different?

The whole story is like a puzzle. Gradually, as we learn more about the characters, the pieces fit together and the whole picture starts to become visible. But the writer keeps us guessing until the very end. And the style of writing is clear, clever and thoughtful.

One of the themes of the novel is that nobody is what they seem. We present different faces to different people, and as we grow older and move to different places we can become different people. We don't stay the same person.

Leviathan is a thought-provoking and rewarding book. I can't wait to read it again.

Leo Jones *New Progress to Proficiency*

Prescribed reading

Question 5 in the Writing Paper gives candidates a chance to write about the prescribed book or 'set book' they have read. This is optional, but highly recommended.

New Progress to Proficiency does not contain questions on particular books, as these change each year. Choosing one of these books not only gives students an extra topic to choose from in the Writing Paper, but also gives them a good chance to improve their reading skills and enrich their vocabulary. It's a really good idea to recommend one of the books to your students and discuss it regularly in class. One of the others might also be recommended as reading for pleasure. A wide range of tastes is catered for in the selection of texts, as the list for 2002 shows:

Anne Tyler: *The Accidental Tourist*
John Wyndham: *The Day of the Triffids*
Graham Greene: *Our Man in Havana*

(Actually, all of those books are entertaining and well worth reading!)

The latest Examination Regulations contain each year's list of prescribed books.

Written work should be set on the particular book chosen: the kind of questions that might be asked would relate to the characters, plot, style and relevance of the particular book.

Here are three sample questions from the UCLES CPE Revised Specifications, just to give an idea of what students might expect:

Based on your reading of one of these books, write on **one** of the following. Write **(a)**, **(b)** or **(c)** as well as the number **5** in the box.

(a) Anne Tyler: *The Accidental Tourist*
'There was no room in his life for anyone as unpredictable as Muriel.' Write an essay for your tutor discussing that statement, comparing the personalities and lifestyles of Macon Leary and Muriel Pritchett and illustrating the comparison with events from the novel.

Write your **essay**.

(b) John Wyndham: *The Day of the Triffids*
Your local newspaper has invited readers to send in articles entitled 'It kept me awake…' on books they have read. Write an article about *The Day of the Triffids*, focusing on what makes the book frightening and how the suspense in the book is maintained.

Write your **article**.

(c) Graham Greene: *Our Man in Havana*
A library is about to have an exhibition on fathers and daughters in literature and has asked its readers for some ideas. Write a letter to the library staff recommending *Our Man in Havana* as a possible book to appear in the exhibition. You should briefly describe the characters of Wormold and Milly and discuss their relationship and its importance to the novel.

Write your **letter**. Do not write any postal addresses.   © UCLES, 2000

The following topics might come up, but the questions would of course refer to specific characters and ideas in the particular book:

- A quotation from the book, which candidates are asked to comment on and relate to some of the characters or the story
- The importance of certain characters in the book
- Looking at the situations certain characters find themselves in and considering what they could have done. Or considering what would you have done in the same situation
- Reasons for the book's popularity
- Insights into life in the period the book is set, or the place the book is set
- Present-day relevance of the book's themes and ideas
- Film or TV versions of the book, and how they compare to the original

For more examples of typical questions, see the most recent *Cambridge Proficiency Examination Practice.*

11.5 **Conjunctions and connectors – 1**   GRAMMAR REVIEW

A **1** Discourage the students from highlighting words they already use frequently.

2

> **SUGGESTED ANSWERS**
>
> **2** Many blockbusters, such as James Mitchener's *Alaska*, are over 1,000 pages long.
> **3** He enjoys reading biographies, particularly ones about politicians.
> **4** Science fiction is an acquired taste – at least that's what sci-fi fans say.
> **5** She prefers reading non-fiction books, which means that she enjoys biographies, history books, as well as other similar books.
> **6** The reason why the book was a best-seller was that it contained a lot of explicit sex and violence.
> **7** He doesn't read much apart from thrillers.
> **8** Reading is not only an inexpensive hobby but it is also enjoyable.
>   Not only is reading an inexpensive hobby, it is also enjoyable.

B

> **SUGGESTED ANSWERS**
>
> **1** apart from / with the exception of
> **2** what is more
> **3** in particular / above all
> **4** even though / although   in other words
> **5** for example   consequently
> **6** nevertheless / however
> **7** at any rate / at least
> **8** above all / in particular / particularly / especially

Extra activity Even though students should be encouraged to use a variety of conjunctions and connectors in their compositions in the exam, *and* or *but* are often perfectly adequate to convey most meanings, especially in straightforward narratives and reports – as this **Extra activity** shows.

 Look again at the three extracts in **11.3**:
- How many times is *but* used?
- How many times is *and* used to connect clauses?

- How many of the phrases listed in **11.5 A1** are used in the three extracts?

There is more on this topic in **15.4 Conjunctions and connectors – 2**.

11.6 Collocations: idioms

VOCABULARY DEVELOPMENT

ANSWERS

1 pros and cons	7 thick and thin
2 facts and figures	8 wear and tear
3 ups and downs	9 over and above
4 swings and roundabouts	10 few and far between
5 law and order	11 bread and butter
6 touch and go	12 safe and sound

Ask the class to think of further similar phrases. Here are some more examples:

airs and graces   an open and shut case   cut and dried   far and wide   free and easy
here and there   neat and tidy   part and parcel   rank and file   rough and ready
round and round   out and about   spick and span   to and fro   up and about

SUGGESTED ANSWERS

a/an basket of fruit   bucket of water   bunch of flowers   carafe of wine/water
cup of tea   flight of stairs   flock of sheep   gust of wind   herd of cattle
item of luggage   jug of milk   loaf of bread   pack of cards   pair of tweezers
piece of equipment/cake   pot of honey   puff of smoke   range of hills
sack of potatoes   school of whales   slice of cake/bread   spoonful of sugar
spot of bother   team of helpers   tin or can of beans   tube of toothpaste

Other humorous variations are possible!

SUGGESTED ANSWERS

1 a range of hills	6 a team of helpers
2 a bunch of flowers	7 a spot of bother
3 items of luggage	8 a flock of sheep/swarm of bees, etc.
4 a pack of cards	9 a flight of stairs
5 gust of wind	10 a pair of tweezers

ANSWERS

She's as blind as a bat
The sea was as calm as a millpond
She's as free as the air
He's as cool as a cucumber
She's as hard as nails
He's as quiet as a mouse
She's as fit as a fiddle
He looked as white as a sheet
That story is as old as the hills
She looked as pretty as a picture
The children were as good as gold
She's as light as a feather
We were as warm as toast

11.7 **A good beginning**

(A) 👥 This is an open-ended discussion. It might be a good idea to pick out some of the useful vocabulary in the passage, which is the first part of a longer article. To do this, go through the passage with a highlighter, selecting words your students will find useful.

(B) 👥→👥 No suggested answers here: but you should choose your own favourite opening lines so that you can enter into the discussion.

(C) **1 & 2** There are no suggested answers for these tasks. The extracts are genuine students' work.

(D) **1 & 2** 👥 ✒ This is what we have been leading up to, and it's important that enough time is devoted to it.

11.8 **It . . . constructions**

(A)

ANSWERS

1 Did Jane Austen write *Emma*?
   – *slight emphasis on the last item mentioned: the book. However if a stress is put on different words in the sentence, the emphasis and implications change:*

Did Jane Austen write *Emma*?	–	*. . . I insist that you tell me*
Did **Jane** Austen write *Emma*?	–	*. . . or was it <u>Anne</u> Austen?*
Did Jane **Austen** write *Emma*?	–	*. . . or was it another author called Jane?*
Did Jane Austen **write** *Emma*?	–	*. . . or did she edit it?*
Did Jane Austen write ***Emma***?	–	*. . . or another book?*

Was it Jane Austen who wrote *Emma*?
– *more emphasis on the author's name*
Was Jane Austen the author of *Emma*?
– *emphasis on the author*
Was the author who wrote *Emma* Jane Austen?
– *emphasis on* the author. *(This structure sounds clumsy here with the two names juxtaposed)*
Was *Emma* written by Jane Austen?
– *emphasis on the author's name*
Was it *Emma* that Jane Austen wrote?
– *. . . or was it another book? Emphasis on the title, suggesting that this is the only book she was famous for (cf Was it* Wuthering Heights *that Emily Brontë wrote?)*
Was Jane Austen the author who wrote *Emma*?
– *emphasis on* the author. *(It seems unnecessary to use the term author here, and maybe woman might be more usual)*

2 What I enjoy reading is thrillers.
   – *emphasis on* thrillers – *this structure helps to create suspense as we wait for the main point to be mentioned*
   Thrillers are what I enjoy reading.
   & It's thrillers that I enjoy reading.
   – *emphasis on* thrillers
   I enjoy reading thrillers.
   – *no special emphasis, as written. In speech we might put stress on* enjoy *or on* thrillers

3 It was me who borrowed your book.
   – *emphasis on* me *as the person responsible*
   I borrowed your book.
   – *no special emphasis*

SUGGESTED ANSWERS

1 surprising/remarkable   get to the summit
2 wrote
3 a good job   warned/told
4 is unfriendly/unlikable   is very shy
5 long/too long   realised/discovered   we had made
6 is it   never arrive anywhere
7 'll be/will be   who answers/picks up
8 to be   who was   is/'s me who reads

C **SUGGESTED ANSWERS**

1 It was only yesterday that she finished reading the book.
2 Is it the humour of her stories that you enjoy?
3 Was it *Emma* or *Persuasion* that you read recently?
4 It was because I was feeling worn out that I went to bed early.
5 It was a strange noise that woke me up in the early hours.
6 It was half past four in the morning when I heard the noise.
7 It was when I looked out of the window that I realised what had happened.
8 It was then that I found I couldn't get back to sleep.
9 It was about eight o'clock when I finally did get to sleep.
10 It wasn't until lunchtime that I woke up.

11.9 Three American novels

READING

Background

Ernest Hemingway (1899–1961), despite his image of being a hard-drinking, macho man of action, had a genius for evoking a time and a place in his writing, by means of a delightfully simple style. His prose is particularly accessible for foreign learners.

His best-known books include: *Fiesta (The Sun Also Rises), For Whom the Bell Tolls, The Old Man and the Sea, Men without Women* and *To Have and Have Not.*

A Farewell to Arms is a love story set against the background of the First World War.

John Steinbeck (1902–68) wrote about the lives of simple, ordinary people in America. His best-known books are: *Of Mice and Men, Cannery Row, Tortilla Flat* and *East of Eden* (the film of which starred James Dean).

The Grapes of Wrath is the story of dispossessed farmers driven off their land in Oklahoma, to search for a better life in California, which was 'the land of milk and honey'.

Paul Theroux (b. 1941) is a travel writer as well as novelist. His travels have taken him all over the world and are described in such books as: *The Great Railway Bazaar: By Train through Asia, The Old Patagonian Express, The Kingdom by the Sea, Riding the Iron Rooster, The Happy Isles of Oceania* and *The Pillars of Hercules.*

His novels are full of imaginative detail and exotic locations, each one quite different from the other. Particularly recommendable are: *Picture Palace, The Family Arsenal, O-Zone, My Secret History* (the first paragraphs of which are in **13.3 Family life**), *Milroy the Magician* and *Hotel Honolulu.*

The Mosquito Coast is the story of a family who abandon civilisation in the USA, and go to live in the jungle of Central America, hoping to build Utopia for themselves. But life becomes a nightmare. The novel is a compelling creation of an obsessive central character ('Father') and is told through the voice of his young son.

 If this is set for homework, students have time to do this at their leisure. The purpose of this section and the next is to encourage students to appreciate the style of the writing in the three extracts.

  SUGGESTED ANSWERS

1 Extract 1 is from *A Farewell to Arms* by Ernest Hemingway (1929)
Extract 2 is from *The Grapes of Wrath* by John Steinbeck (1939)
Extract 3 is from *The Mosquito Coast* by Paul Theroux (1981)

2 Extract 2: *May   day after day* the changing weather
the growth of green weeds and their subsequent dying back
3 Extract 1: *Troops went by the house and down the road   the leaves fell*
troops marching along the road   the soldiers marching   the use of prepositions and
particles: *across, along,* etc.
4 Extract 3: *savages   awfulness   dope-taking, door-locking,*
ulcerated danger-zone of rabid scavengers . . . a piling-up of words that suggest decay
and violence
5 See the quotations in Answers 2–4 above
6 Extract 1 (Hemingway)
7 Extract 2 (Steinbeck) – or 1?
8 Extract 3 (Theroux)
9 Extract 2 – and 1?
10 *for discussion*

11.10 The future of reading?   SPEAKING AND COMPOSITION

A (The Rocket eBook is a real product.)

B Remind everyone to make notes before they start writing.

11.10 Model version

I couldn't wait to try out my new eBook! It looked wonderful when I tried it out in the shop, but would I still love it when I used it at home?

When I got home I plugged it in and left it to charge its battery while I went out to my evening class. When I got back it was ready to use.

I began reading in the kitchen with the eBook resting on the table as I had a drink and a snack. The screen was easily visible, but not as clear and sharp as a page in a normal book. To change the page on an eBook you just press a button, or you can scroll the text if you prefer. You don't have to hold the pages open, like you do with a book, and you can change the font and font size to make it easier to read comfortably.

I took my eBook to bed with me. This was when I discovered its best feature: you can read in bed in the dark! You don't need a light because the screen is bright. And if you fall asleep while reading (as I did!) the eBook turns itself off after a few minutes, keeping your place in the book till the next time you turn it on.

The next day, I had a long train journey to make. I read my eBook with my Walkman playing, easily ignoring the other passengers' conversations and mobile phone calls. The time flew by and I was sorry when the journey was over.

During the rest of the week and at the weekend, I read in public and in private. I read on the bus, in the park, in cafés, at home. But not in the bath and not at the beach — the eBook is splashproof but I didn't want to risk dropping it into water or getting it dirty or stolen.

My verdict? Well, a paperback book is lighter, and a printed page is certainly easier to read than the eBook screen. The darker the surroundings, the easier it is to read. But you can store dozens of different books and magazines on one eBook. And you can also download newspapers, which makes reading on the train or on the bus easier than folding and unfolding a newspaper — and cleaner, because you don't get inky fingers.

But technology is developing all the time with incredible rapidity. How long will it be before my lovely new eBook is superseded by something lighter, cheaper, more versatile and easier to read?

Leo Jones *New Progress to Proficiency*

The cutting edge

12.1 Science and technology

TOPIC VOCABULARY

 To settle any arguments, the photos show:

the surface of a compact disc, a microchip and Velcro.

The *cutting edge* refers to the very latest technology.

 ANSWERS

1 application	**2** meteorology	**3** zoology	**4** anthropology
5 computers	**6** knob	**7** generation	**8** controlled
9 inspiration	**10** impractical	**11** equipment	**12** patent
13 think up	**14** socket (US outlet)	**15** trial and error	

Finish by discussing the wrong answers and considering why some of them are wrong in context.

12.2 The Freedom Ship

LISTENING AND SPEAKING

🔊 Allow everyone time to read the questions through first, before playing the recording. (For more information about the Freedom Ship, go to their website: www.freedomship.com)

ANSWERS

1 20,000   **2** $138,000   **3** $7 million   **4** by ferry   **5** 75%   **6** 1,316 metres
7 220 metres   **8** 2 years   **9** 40-seater jets   **10** mostly in warm climates
11 school and university   **12** none   **13** employee leasing services
14 it will be incinerated (burnt to produce energy)   **15** diesel fuel
16 no worries: you'll hardly feel the waves

TRANSCRIPT   *5 minutes 20 seconds*

NARRATOR: Listen to part of a broadcast about the Freedom Ship.
PRESENTER: Have you ever wanted to travel the world and still stay at home? It's soon going to be a possibility if Norman Nixon's plans work out. He's building a floating city and he's calling it the Freedom Ship. To tell us more about it, here's Sandy Harrison. So Sandy, tell us about the Freedom Ship.
SANDY: Yeah, well, the Freedom Ship is going to be nearly a mile long and it'll be home to 40,000 people. There will be 20,000 homes on board. The cheapest is going to be $138,000 for a 3 metre by 10 metre room with a fridge and microwave – that's bigger than the largest suite on a cruise liner! And the most expensive will be $7 million for a 450 square metre ocean-view residence. Most of the units will have a sea view, and the very cheapest ones will overlook a park or open courtyard. There'll be 10,000 staff, who run the ship and provide all the facilities.
PRESENTER: Right.
SANDY: Yeah, well, the idea is that it will slowly travel the world, pausing a few miles out from chosen destinations such as ports or exotic tropical islands that can only be reached by sea. It will be on the move for twenty-five per cent of the time and otherwise anchored off different ports. It won't go into the port because it's too large. There will be ferries to take people to and fro.
PRESENTER: And where is it going to be built?
SANDY: The ship will actually be built at Puerto Castilla in Honduras. It'll be five times larger than the largest cruise liner afloat. 1,316 metres long, 220 metres wide, 100 metres tall. But it's not a cruise liner, it's a city.
PRESENTER: Right, and…er…what will be on board?
SANDY: Well, there'll be a school and a university on board, a runway for planes, a fully equipped hospital, and hotels for people who want to spend a holiday on the Freedom Ship. The shopping mall, one of the world's largest, will also be one of the most beautiful. And per…in other words, it will be the first self-contained city that not only floats, but moves. The plan is for it to circumnavigate the globe every two years, going into port for the benefit of its residents and for tourists, who will come on board and shop at duty-free shops.
PRESENTER: What else?
SANDY: Well, let's think now. Um…a free public tramway will carry people around the ship. There will be small aircraft and hydrofoils to ferry people to and from shore. Also hangars, marinas, and repair and

machine shops for private aircraft and boats. The runway won't be long enough to take a jumbo jet, or even a normal airliner, but it will be able to take 40-seat commuter jets and the runway can always be moved to face into the wind.

PRESENTER: Ha, of course!

SANDY: As the ship will spend most of its time in warm climates, people will want to enjoy the open air. It'll have 80 hectares of open space outside and this'll include tennis courts, parks and promenades with waterfalls, ponds, and extensive landscaping. Inside, most levels will feature large saltwater aquariums.

PRESENTER: Right.

SANDY: Entertainment facilities, including movies, theatres, clubs, casinos – also restaurants designed to appeal to a wide range of palates.

PRESENTER: So…um…what kind of people are going to live there?

SANDY: Well, Norman Nixon hopes that it'll become a 'global environment' with a…a large mixture of different nationalities and ages. It's not meant to be seen as a retirement cruise ship, but one where people could run their businesses and educate their children. And there will be no local taxes to pay.

PRESENTER: Ahh!

SANDY: Yeah, Freedom Ship may sound like a sort of resort city only for the rich. Yet there will be ample employment opportunities. Businesses can use the ship's 'employee leasing services' where workers will be trained, given uniforms, and provided with room and board on the lower decks.

PRESENTER: And all the latest technology I suppose?

SANDY: Oh, yeah, everything will be as environmentally-friendly as possible. Everything that can be recycled will be. And waste, sewage and non-recyclable materials will be incinerated and produce energy. Nixon plans for a pollution-free, energy-efficient and safe ship that will exceed current standards for both ships and land-bound cities. Standard cruise ships are, obviously, notorious polluters, but state-of-the-art technology will be used to make Freedom Ship as safe and environmentally-friendly and non-polluting as possible. The engines will use clean diesel fuel, not dirty marine fuel.

PRESENTER: Well, Sandy, it'd be no good for me. I get seasick when I go on a ship.

SANDY: Well, no worries there, apparently. Because of its size the Freedom Ship won't be vulnerable to hurricanes and storms. You'll hardly feel the movement of the ocean.

B **1–3** 👥👥 The discussion could last quite a long time if students get really interested in giving a presentation. If they do, some written follow-up describing their scheme is recommended.

12.3 Design flaws

READING

Background

Bill Bryson was born in Des Moines, Iowa, in 1951. He settled in England in 1977. His books are often laugh-out-loud funny and describe his travels and experiences of everyday life. His best-known books are: *The Lost Continent* and *Notes from a Big Country* (about the USA), *Notes from a Small Island* (about Britain), *Neither Here Nor There* (about Europe) and *Down Under* (about Australia). He also writes about the English language and its history in *Mother Tongue* and *Made in America*.

Design flaws is one of the humorous articles in *Notes from a Big Country*. Another article from this is *Why no one walks in the USA*, which you can read in **17.4 A**.

A **1** If possible, ask everyone to do this (and maybe also **A2** and **B**) for homework, to save time in class. Highlight the parts that you found amusing, so that you can compare your reaction to your students' reactions. (Humour is a matter of taste, and Bryson's humour is not to everyone's taste.)

2
ANSWERS
¶ 3 limitless ¶ 4 dress ¶ 5 font ¶ 6 imbecilic ¶ 7 blunder (on)
¶ 8 indentation ¶ 9 spontaneously ¶ 10 manifold ¶ 10 envision
¶ 11 moaning

B
ANSWERS
1 d 2 a 3 c 4 b 5 c 6 b

C 👥👥 The discussion returns to the humour and style of the article.

1

ANSWERS

combine something **with**	engage **in**	part **with**
compare something **with/to**	invest **in**	reason **with**
contrast something **with**	lean **on**	rely **on**
depend **on**	mistake it/them **for**	separate something **from**

2

SUGGESTED ANSWERS

agree **with** someone **about** something	insist **on**	smell **of/like**
apologise **to** someone **for** something	interfere **with/in**	struggle **with/against/for**
	intrude **on**	succeed **in**
approve **of**	negotiate **with** someone **about/for** something	suffer **from**
bargain **with** someone **for** something	object **to**	talk **to/with** someone **about** something
care **for/about**	quarrel **with** someone **over/about** something	vote **for/against/on**
decide **on/against**	resign **from/over**	watch **for/over**
experiment **on/with**	retire **from**	worry **about**
hope **for**		

3

ANSWERS

admire him **for**	deliver it **to**	thank her **for**
blame her **for**	punish him **for**	threaten them **with**
congratulate him **on**	rescue them **from**	use it **for**
consult her **on/about**	respect her **for**	warn him **against/about**
convince them **of**	take it **from/to**	

B

ANSWERS

1 through	**2** in	**3** through	**4** for	**5** with	**6** of	**7** through	**8** of
9 from/at	**10** through	**11** by	**12** with	**13** on	**14** of/on	**15** in	
16 in/with	**17** By	**18** in/on	**19** with	**20** of	**21** With	**22** for	
23 at	**24** for						

See also **14.4 Word order: phrasal verbs, 15.3 Prepositions–2** and **17.5 Adjectives + prepositions**.

1

ANSWERS

1 c	**2** i	**3** d	**4** a	**5** e	**6** b	**7** g	**8** h	**9** e	**10** f

2 Comments are *in italics.*

SENTENCES REPHRASED IN THE ACTIVE

1 Candidates may not use dictionaries in the examination.
   – *Emphasis on* candidates *as the people who are involved*

2 His father criticised him but his mother praised him.
   – *Emphasis on* father *and* mother

3 People have/Everybody has misunderstood him and made him feel inadequate all his life.
   – *As the people involved are not important, this sounds strange in the active voice*

4 The college authorities have decided to restrict parking by students in the grounds.
   – *Emphasis on the people who made the decision, rather than the decision itself*

5 Dangerous drivers (??) have injured several people in accidents at this junction.
— *We don't know who was responsible for the accidents (maybe the people themselves were partly responsible) so this sounds strange*
6 We heated the solution to boiling point and then allowed it to cool to 20°.
— *Emphasis on* we, *which is unusual in a report of a scientific experiment*
7 Although we arrived early, someone/the people in the office kept us waiting for an hour.
— *Emphasis on the people who caused the waiting*
8 We arrived late because bad weather/heavy air traffic delayed our flight.
— *Emphasis on the cause of the delay*
9 Someone/Sandy/My assistant (?) is photocopying the documents at the moment.
— *Emphasis on the person who is doing it*
10 Someone has/You have taken some money from my room.
— *Emphasis on the person, not the theft*

B **ANSWERS**

1 She's fed up with being looked down on.
2 The children were looked after by their grandparents.
3 This matter is being dealt with by my assistant.
4 All breakages must be paid for.
5 Tony can't be relied on to finish the work on time.
6 The repairs will be seen to right away.
7 Her apartment had been broken into during the night.
8 Scientists are often looked on as experts.
9 It was pointed out to me that I was wearing odd socks.
10 He might be referred to as 'technophobic'.
11 Until permission is granted they can't expand the airport.
12 Some people might be intimidated by electronics, but not me.
13 How can all these old magazines be disposed of?
14 Those old magazines will have to be got rid of.
15 All the survivors of the accident have been accounted for.

12.6 *give* and *take*   VERBS AND IDIOMS

A **ANSWERS**

give   advice to someone   an answer   an explanation   encouragement
evidence   permission   someone a kiss   someone a lift   someone a ring
someone a shock   someone some help

take   a liking to someone or something   a photograph   pride in something
an interest in something   issue with someone   part in something
pity on someone   your time over something

B **SUGGESTED ANSWERS**

1 assume   put up with hardships as well as easy times   start
2 be resentful   accepted it without resentment
put his side of the argument as well as I did
3 surprised   accepted
4 liked   (only used in the passive)
5 deceived   revealed what was supposed to be secret
6 raised an objection   be so familiar with him that she didn't appreciate him
7 show your feelings by attacking   raise the matter
8 invite out   help you stop thinking about your problems
9 imitate/mimic   removes   has no patience left
10 absorb

ANSWERS

1 took   away
2 taking down
3 given over to
4 take out
5 taken on   taking   out   take   off
6 have given   up   take up
7 taking over
8 take back

12.7   Suffixes

VOCABULARY DEVELOPMENT

If in doubt about the definitions of any nouns, you should consult a dictionary. If there seem to be more words than you have time to deal with, ask everyone to pick out, say, eight pairs of words to deal with.

Here are a few more examples to start things off.

An *administrator* is employed to run an organisation, but a *dictator* runs a country undemocratically.
They're both in control of other people.

A *chauvinist* believes that men are superior to women, or that his nation is superior to other nations.
A *feminist* believes that women should have the same rights as men.
They both have strong beliefs.

An *employer* is someone who employs people.
An *employee* is someone who is employed by an employer or a company.
They both work, but in different capacities.

Abstract nouns and verbs   (Where no abstract noun or verb exists and a phrase or an unrelated word has to be used, these are *in italics*.)

administration · dictatorship
chauvinism · feminism
employ/employment
mine · *being under age*
persecute/persecution · prosecute/prosecution
research · search

attack · hijack
council · counsel/*advice*
fortune-telling/*tell fortunes* · storytelling/*tell stories*
pawn · *dealing in shares*
occupy the position before · *follow*
own/hold shares · *own a house*

serve drinks · moneylending/lend money
demonstrate · spectate
owning land · *like to be alone*
pay/payment
psychology · psychiatry
solve problems/deal with trouble · make trouble

Extra activity

And here are few extra pairs which might be discussed as a warm-up or follow-up to **A**:

auctioneer · mountaineer   brewer · reviewer   burglar · gangster   commuter · computer   forefinger · fishfinger   impersonator · operator   juror · insurer   messenger · passenger   part-timer · old-timer   perpetrator · commentator   viewfinder · reminder   well-wisher · publisher

B ANSWERS

deafen emphasise familiarise generalise glamorise loosen moisten
nationalise sharpen straighten strengthen subsidise summarise sweeten
sympathise synthesise thicken tighten victimise visualise widen

C **1 & 2** 👥 These follow-up activities give students time to decide which words to memorise, and a chance to use them in sentences of their own devising.

12.8 ## Thinking about the reader READING AND WRITING SKILLS

A **1** Before embarking on the questions, encourage students to highlight vocabulary which they want to remember in the passage.

2 👥 SUGGESTED ANSWERS

1 'Humans do not always err. But they do when the things they use are badly conceived and designed.' (line 7)
'To me it sounds like equipment failure coupled with serious design error.' (line 20)
'While we all blame ourselves, the real culprit – faulty design – goes undetected.' (line 25)
2 Eighteen – it makes the text very personal
3 we   three times   ourselves   twice
4 None
5 Only once: Consider the phrase . . . (line 13)
6 Fifteen – it raises questions that the reader is encouraged to think about
7 The first five questions are answered, three of them with quotes:
'Pilot error . . . human error . . . Human error.'
The next questions are all unanswered, until Human error? in line 20.
The last three questions are answered with While we all blame ourselves, the real culprit – faulty design – goes undetected
8 Very well, by involving the reader in the questions to think about and by encouraging the reader to share the writer's personal experiences, as if in a diary or personal letter
9 Perhaps: A reader who might share his concern for accidents at nuclear power plants and the causes of airline crashes. A reader who is sympathetic to his ideas, and is not an expert or a technologist. An educated person
10 a He doesn't presuppose any technical knowledge and gives information that can be followed by any layperson. He is trying to interest and persuade the reader to share his views and not to give information.
   b Perhaps: Using the first person frequently and having so many questions, makes a direct appeal to the reader, whom he assumes to be in sympathy
   Or, perhaps? The overloading of first person pronouns and questions makes an assault on the reader, beating us into agreement

B **1 & 2** 👥 ✏️ The paragraph could be planned in pairs in class, but written up as homework.

12.8 Model paragraph

Traffic has always ruled my life and restricted my enjoyment. When I was little I wanted to go and play in the park on the other side of the main road, but my mother wouldn't allow me to cross the road. Why? Because of the traffic. When I was older I wanted to go out with my friends on our bikes, but my father told me I mustn't ride on the main road. Why? Because of the traffic. Now I want to learn to drive and buy a second-hand car. But there's no point. Why? Because it's quicker to walk than drive and there's nowhere to park anyway.

Leo Jones *New Progress to Proficiency*

If possible, get everyone to do some research before the lesson, perhaps by assigning the Activities in **A2** to each student in a previous lesson, so that **A** and **B** can be done in one go without a break.

(A)

1 👥👥👥 These discussion questions, together with the photos, lead in to the **Communication Activity**. They could be done as a whole-class discussion.

2 👥👥👥 Student A looks at **Communication Activity 6** on page 200, Student B at **19** on page 204 and C at **28** on page 206. Each activity contains a list of questions to consider and to discuss with their partners.

(B)

1–3 👥👥👥👥 ✎ Unless some research is done earlier, as suggested above, these steps might be best done after a break, so that students have time to think about the issues raised in **A1** and **2**.

12.9 Model version

Modern electronic devices like videos and televisions embody increasingly sophisticated technology. They're capable of performing multiple functions and there are numerous adjustments that can be made. But when you play a video do you use all the buttons on your remote control? No, you only use these: Play, Stop, Rewind, Fast Forward and Pause. Are they the most prominent or accessible controls? Probably not. Why can't those controls be bigger than the rest? And why can't all the other controls be underneath a plastic flap, which you can open when you *do* need to use them? And why do they all have black buttons which you have to examine closely to see which is which? Why can't the most frequently-used buttons be different colours, which light up when you press them, like mobile phones?

Even everyday non-technological equipment is badly designed. For example, going in or out of buildings can be quite hazardous. Some doors open inwards, some outwards — with a handle both sides. This means that doors have to have "Push" or "Pull" on them — and everyone has to read the sign before they can go in or out. How many times have you pulled when you should have pushed? Having a handle on the push side is totally unnecessary and confusing. There just needs to be a handle to pull on one side and no handle on the other side. Then every user would know what to do and there would be no confusion.

Revolving doors are much more annoying. In supermarkets and airports they have to be large enough to accommodate trolleys as well as people. This is fine unless too many people and trolleys try to go through at the same time, and everyone gets stuck. Inside the door is a very small sign saying "Do not push". If you do push, which is what you intuitively do to make it go faster, the whole thing stops, trapping everyone inside. There are even doors at Heathrow Airport with built-in revolving shop windows showing products you can buy in the Duty Free shops, making even less room for people and their trolleys! Whose bright idea was that?

The problem is that designers are people who like things to look nice. If something looks elegant and attractive, they like it. But people need things to work properly and easily. Elegance is no substitute for user-friendliness.

Leo Jones *New Progress to Proficiency*

13

Just good friends?

 A Treat this warm-up discussion as the kind of conversation about photographs that students will encounter in the exam Speaking Paper.

This is the complete picture – the one in the Student's Book shows a part of this:

B The picture in **Activity 7** on page 201 is part of Edward Hopper's *Room in New York*, 1932. The one in **Activity 20** on page 204 is part of Edward Hopper's *Four Lane Road*, 1956. As the relationship between the people is ambiguous, this should provoke some differences of opinion. At the end, ask the pairs to report on their impressions of the relationships.

C

ANSWERS

1 R + S   **2** W   **3** W + S   **4** R + W   **5** W   **6** R + S   **7** S   **8** R

TRANSCRIPTS   *8 minutes 10 seconds*

NARRATOR: Listen to Ruth, William and Sarah talking about friendship.

INTERVIEWER: Ruth, who is your best friend?
RUTH: My best friend is a girl called Kerry.
INTERVIEWER: When did you meet?
RUTH: Kerry moved to my home town when she was fifteen and I was fifteen and…er…her parents bought the hotel at the top of my road and so she used to walk to school…er…down my road every day and…er…one day I just caught up with her and…er…we started walking to school together.
INTERVIEWER: Why do you get on well?
RUTH: Um…we've definitely got the same sense of humour. We share the same sense of humour about a lot of things, I think that's really, you know, what it is that helps us to get on so well.
INTERVIEWER: How much time do you spend together and wh…what do you do?
RUTH: Well, I must be honest, er…we used to spend a lot more time together…er…before we got married and…er…had kids and stuff like that. Um…you know, we used to go to a lot of rugby matches together, er…rugby international matches. We used to go to Scotland and Ireland and…and stuff, and…um…just have a really good laugh. Er…but then, you know, marriage sets in and…um…children and things and so we don't actually see each other that often, but when we do, we just always have a really good time.
INTERVIEWER: What do you disagree or fall out about?
RUTH: Well, Kerry very much likes to stay in the past. And she loves to talk about the past, which I like doing as well. But she…she doesn't like changes very much and…um…you know, she likes to kind of…er…do things that we used to do when we were fifteen. So she'd still be happy to go…er…to Scotland to watch a rugby match, whereas that really has absolutely zero appeal to me now. Um…so I think maybe our kind of perspectives on life have changed and, you know, she'll say to me, 'Oh, you've become so boring, this, that and the other!' And I'll say, 'Well, you just live in the past.' So I

think that…that's the only . . . We don't really disagree really badly over that, but that's certainly a
difference between us now.

INTERVIEWER: Why is friendship important to you?

RUTH: Well, I think you go through life…um…and you have all these experiences, um…some good, some
bad, and it's good to have people around you who have known you…er…for a long, long time, who
can act as…um…a real support and…er…help you through good times…er…help you through
bad times and share the good times with you. Um…and it's important to have people who
understand you and who you can unload a lot of your feelings onto and…er…and ask opinions on,
ask for help…er…about. Um…and…er…just have that kind of support network, and I think it's a
very much a two-way system.

INTERVIEWER: How do you make new friends?

RUTH: Well, in the work I do I'm always meeting new people all the time and…um…I would say there's a
difference between friends and acquaintances. Because I think it takes a long time to actually
become close friends with somebody. Um…whereas you might make acquaintances, who you might
kind of go out with and go to the cinema with or whatever, but you won't have that same
established history. Um…so I think as you get older, it's more difficult to make friends than it is
when you're younger.

★★★

INTERVIEWER: William, who's your best friend?

WILLIAM: Er…my best mate is Geoff Buxton.

INTERVIEWER: When did you meet?

WILLIAM: Oh, we've known each other since we were kids. Er…our parents were friends together, we lived in
the same street and we've known each other since we were about four.

INTERVIEWER: And why do you get on so well?

WILLIAM: Um…because of that really, I think. You know, we've…er…we've spent a lot of our lives together.
We grew up in the same street and…er…grew up as kids, we went to the same school. Um…we
went to the same secondary school, we even went to the same university. Um…we do quite similar
things. We're, you know, different people but we have similar interests and stuff, so I think it's
probably that.

INTERVIEWER: And how much time do you spend together and what do you do?

WILLIAM: Um…well, we both…er…live in the same area of town, um…so we…er…see each other, not every
day but, you know, quite a few times during the week. Um…we play football together, um…we go
out…er…with a similar group of friends. So…er…we socialise a lot together. So…um…you know,
we go out to see the football and…er…watch films and go out drinking, stuff like that.

INTERVIEWER: And what do you disagree or fall out about?

WILLIAM: Um…ahh, that's difficult really. I mean we agree on most things. Er…I'm not too sure about his
taste in music. Um…I'm not too sure about his taste in women sometimes. Um…I don't think
we've really had too many girlfriends that the…either of us, you know has liked. Um…but we, you
know, we're working on that.

INTERVIEWER: And why is friendship important to you?

WILLIAM: Um…I don't know, I think it's important to have someone who can…who's sort of fairly constant in
your life, you know, who's there…er…no matter who you might have had an argument with, you
know, someone who's…you can always run to and talk about things and…er…someone…er…who
can tell you you're behaving like a bit of an idiot really, and you won't be offended by it.

INTERVIEWER: And how do you make new friends?

WILLIAM: Um…well, I suppose I meet people at work…um…or people that…er…Geoff might meet or . . . I
quite enjoy meeting people that are complete strangers really on a night out or whatever.

★★★

INTERVIEWER: Sarah, who's your best friend?

SARAH: My best friend is a mad girl called Tonya.

INTERVIEWER: When did you meet?

SARAH: I met Tonya, I'd been in the UK for about two years and…er…we became sort of acquaintances
and from there we worked on the friendship and now we're best of mates.

INTERVIEWER: Why do you get on well?

SARAH: Er…we've both got a warped sense of humour. And also we need people. I live on the other side of
the world from my family, so I sort of need a new support system. And she has no mother or father
any more, they passed away, so we understand about the same things. So for that we sort of have a
common bond and from that we've grown.

INTERVIEWER: How much time do you spend together and what do you do?

SARAH: We can't actually spend that much time together because of our work schedules. She now is in
movie production so the…she's on set for hours, and of course I'm up and down the country or
overseas, doing work. So…er…we spend a lot of time on e-mail and telephone. Um…it's a very
expensive friendship! And…but whenever we get together we try to go away for weekends or even if
it's just a girlie giggle over dinner, it's…we…we make an effort to do it when we're back in…both
in the same place at the same time.

INTERVIEWER: What do you disagree or fall out about?

SARAH: What we actually fall out about is men. She's got the worst taste in men I have ever seen!
And…er…she keeps falling for the same mistakes, so I end up going, 'Oh, my God, here we go
again!' But you've got to be a friend and always be there when they do fall.

INTERVIEWER: Why is friendship important to you?

SARAH: Er…friendship's important because life can get so hectic and busy and…and…and you've got to
put a lot of sort of energy into relationships, whether it be a personal relationship, you know, with a
partner, or whether it be with friends, and if you have someone that knows you really well, you can
just come home from a hard day and say, 'Ohh!' and you can rant and rave and you know that you
don't have to explain why you're feeling that way. They can sort of go, 'Oh, here she goes again,
yeah, yeah, yeah, yeah, yeah.' And…um…it makes you feel better that you're not bitching to the

wrong people or you're…you've got confidence. As I said I live on the other side of the world, so friendship's very important, that I have a gr…a group of people, or even just one or two people around me to be there in the ups and downs.

INTERVIEWER: How do you make new friends?

SARAH: Making new friends is really hard as an adult. I think it's a lot easier as a child. But as an adult when you come to another country, people are already stuck in their little ways, they've got their partner, they've got their group of friends who know them, and they've got no need to make a new friend. They might like you as an acquaintance. But making friends with someone you really trust, and you want to open your soul and . . . That's tough! And it took me many years to get a very close group around me that I trusted, that I adored, that I had a lot in common with, that I felt safe with, and I wanted to make the effort with. Um…but as adults it's…it gets harder.

D You might like to add this extra question to the discussion – but not if any members of the class are each other's 'enemies':

- Do you have/Have you had any 'enemies'? Describe them and explain why you dislike/disliked them.

E 1–3 Some qualities that are missing from the first list are:

adaptability   communication   frankness   honesty   tolerance   trust

F 1 This part doesn't need to be done immediately after **E**. If it's more convenient, it can be done in another lesson.

Students will probably need to hear the recording once right through to get used to the voices before they attempt the questions.

> **ANSWERS**
> 1 despondent *or* timid?
> 2 jaded
> 3 anxious
> 4 businesslike *or* impatient?
> 5 sarcastic *or* annoyed?

TRANSCRIPT   *2 minutes 10 seconds*

PRESENTER: Now listen to the following speakers and select a suitable adjective to describe their mood or tone. *(The Presenter gives the number before each speaker)*

SPEAKERS: Well, good evening. Thank you both for getting here on time and for waiting so patiently. Everyone else seems to be rather late, or maybe they haven't been able to make it. Anyway, we'll make a start I think, and if any of the others do come we can always fill them in on what's happened so far, can't we? *(The exact words used vary slightly from speaker to speaker)*

2 You'll probably have to play the recording again for this step.

3 Facial expressions may give the game away here, so each speaker should turn away from the listener, or use a sheet of paper as a screen while they're speaking. Remind everyone that in real life we can usually see a person's mood, but on the phone we have to rely on vocal signals.

13.2 ## As the saying goes . . .   GRAMMAR REVIEW

A These sentences contain structures that have been reviewed in previous **Grammar Review** sections. Questions based on proverbs like these are **NOT** likely to come up in the exam.

> **SUGGESTED ANSWERS**
> 1 (unlike a *fair weather friend*)
> 2 When there **is a quarrel**, both parties **are responsible**.
> 3 What really **counts is what you** do, not **what you** say.
> 4 The world is **full of many different kinds of** people.
> 5 Be **tolerant** and **allow others to do** what they want to do.
> 6 You couldn't **have foreseen what would** happen.
> 7 Family **relationships are stronger than** other relationships.
> 8 A son tends **to behave in a similar way to his** father.

9 A remark **that is made jokingly may contain hidden truth**.
10 Absent friends **are quickly forgotten**.
11 When people **are parted from each other, they grow to appreciate each other more**.
12 After someone **has helped you, it's only fair to do something for them in return**.
13 If you **want something badly enough, you'll find a way of achieving it**.
14 Everyone **falls in love**, but they **recover from it** eventually.

B It might be interesting, particularly in a monolingual class, to compare these English proverbs with proverbs in the students' own language.

Perhaps warn everyone against trying to impress native speakers with their knowledge of idioms and proverbs. Overusing them can sound silly:

Oh goodness me, it's raining cats and dogs again.
– Yes, it never rains but it pours.
Still, every cloud is supposed to have a silver lining, isn't it?

13.3 Family life   READING AND SPEAKING

Background

Gerald Durrell – see page 123.

Ian McEwan (b. 1948) is well-known for his short stories and novels which explore the slightly sinister and bizarre world of people who are leading seemingly normal lives. Particularly recommended are *The Child in Time, The Comfort of Strangers, The Innocent, Black Dogs, Enduring Love* and *Amsterdam*.

The Cement Garden is a disturbing story about a brother and his sisters who, after the death of their father, keep the death of their mother secret from the neighbours, and go on living as a family.

Paul Theroux – see page 139.

A The questions are intended to encourage everyone to look closely at the style of the extracts and discuss the content. They aren't exam-style questions.

> **SUGGESTED ANSWERS**
> 1 The first is from *My Family and Other Animals*, the second from *The Cement Garden* and the third from *My Secret History*.
> 2 *Question for discussion* (The second seems to be the most intriguing – but the first is more amusing.)
> 3 They are all told in the first person 'I . . . '
> They are about events that happened when the narrator was young (10, 13, 15)
> The narrator seems to be an independent sort of child
> 4 The first extract is the only humorous one
> The second extract is full of foreboding and menace, with its references to killing, death and ghostly faces
> The third extract is more philosophical and the narrator is analysing his own character
> 5 In the first extract, the narrator was ten years old: he has a good sense of humour
> In the second extract, the narrator was thirteen years old and though still a child in his ways, wished he could be more grown-up and fit in with adult male society
> In the third extract, the narrator is a loner and an outsider, who up to the age of fifteen kept his second life concealed. He was a dreamer and, at fifteen, lonely
> 6 The family '*took over*' the book as he wrote it – their personalities were too strong for him to control, even when sitting alone writing
> They behaved strangely
> 7 He probably had nothing else to do and was bored
> He wanted to appear older so that he could relate to the driver and his mate
> 8 Poor people are not regarded as full members of society – they are outsiders

9 In the first extract he regards his mother and brothers (Leslie is a brother) and sister as amusing characters and as his equals, even though he was considerably younger than they were at the time

In the second extract, the narrator didn't like his father (perhaps feared him), describing him as '*irascible*' and '*obsessive*'. We don't know if his mother was living. We don't know about his relationship with his sisters

In the third extract, no members of his family are mentioned

B 👥 → 👥 As with **13.1 E1**, ask the class to suggest which are the most important features from the list – and which are the least important.

C Even though there are no vocabulary questions in this section, the extracts should be treated as a potential source of new words.

13.4 **Conditionals – 2**   **ADVANCED GRAMMAR**

A **1** 👥   **SUGGESTED ANSWERS**

1 If it **weren't** for the children they would have split up by now.
  – *fairly formal*
If it **wasn't** for the children they would have split up by now.
  – *fairly informal*
Were it not for the children they would have split up by now.
  – *very formal*
If they **didn't have** children they would have split up by now.
  – *informal*

2 If you **should** see Terry could you give him my regards?
  = You're not very likely to see him . . .*(rather formal style)*
When you see Terry could you give him my regards?
  = You probably will see him . . .
If you **happen to** see Terry could you give him my regards?
  = You're not very likely to see him . . . *(informal style)*
If you **see** Terry could you give him my regards?
  = You may see him . . .
Should you see Terry could you give him my regards?
  = You're not very likely to see him . . . *(very formal style)*

3 If you **wouldn't mind** waiting I'll let them know you're here.
  = Please wait for a moment . . . *(very polite)*
If you **don't mind** waiting I'll let them know you're here.
  = I know you have no objection to waiting (maybe because you just told me that you've got plenty of time) . . .
If you **wait** I'll let them know you're here.
  = You have to wait (and not be impatient) . . . *(not polite)*

4 **Had** it not been for your help, I couldn't have done it.
  – *very formal*
Without your help I couldn't have done it.
If it **hadn't** been for your help I couldn't have done it.
& If you **hadn't** been so helpful I couldn't have done it.
  – *fairly informal*
I'm glad you helped me, **otherwise** I couldn't have done it.
  – *very informal*

2 They would ALL be easier to understand with commas separating the clauses, except for the sentences using *but for* . . . and *without* . . . .

B

SUGGESTED ANSWERS

1 If you'd like to take a seat, I'll bring you some coffee.
2 Had they been more compatible, their relationship might have stood a better chance of surviving.
3 Should I miss my connection, I'll try to call you to let you know.
4 But for their parents' objections, they might have got married.
5 If you should have time, I'd like you to come and see us.
6 Had there been less traffic, we wouldn't have been (so) late.
7 If she were to tell him she is leaving, it would upset him.
8 Were it not for their wonderful relationship, they might not have decided to get married.
9 If it weren't for her patience and loyalty, she would have left him by now.
10 Without working hard at a relationship it's not likely to last.

C   **1 & 2** 👥 🖊 If students don't wish to write about their personal relationships, these sentences could be fictional – or if they're studying a prescribed book, they could be about the characters in the book.

13.5   . . . till death us do part?   READING

". . . to have and to hold from this day forward, for better for worse, for richer for poorer, in sickness and in health, to love and to cherish, till death us do part." (from the Church of England marriage ceremony)

Background

Tom Sharpe (b. 1928) is well-known for his comic novels, several of which are about the technical college lecturer, Henry Wilt. Sharpe himself used to teach at 'the Tech' in Cambridge. Among his other books are *Riotous Assembly, Porterhouse Blue* and *Blott on the Landscape.*

   In *Wilt*, Henry Wilt is suspected of murdering his wife after she has mysteriously gone missing and he has been seen dumping a life-sized inflatable doll in a building site hole . . .

Nigel Williams (b. 1948), also a comic novelist, has written other novels set in the South London suburb of Wimbledon: *They Came from SW19* and *East of Wimbledon.*

   The Wimbledon Poisoner humorously describes a series of murders which are committed in Henry Farr's suburban road – but not by him. Mrs Farr is not one of the victims.

Another amusing novel about wife-killing is **Michael Dibdin**'s *Dirty Tricks*, in which an EFL teacher marries a rich widow and tries to get his hands on her money.

A   **2**

SUGGESTED ANSWERS

1 Mrs Wilt
2 Clem, the dog
3 a small house (semi-detached)
4 Because he was a pedigree dog
5 Because he was not wealthy
6 He daydreamed
7 Losing his wife   becoming rich   becoming powerful and influential
8 He tended to lose them
9 He teaches (we can infer this from his wish to be Minister of Education – the Tech is the local Technical College)
10 A contrived accident – or murder
11 It seems to depersonalise her (making her seem less like a character in her own right, perhaps)
12 It emphasises his strange-sounding name (reminding us of *wilting flowers*, perhaps)

B   **1 & 2** 👥 These are questions for discussion. (In the end neither wife is killed, by the way.)

Associations and underlying meanings are usually hard to explain, but they give some words richer meanings.

A

SUGGESTED ANSWERS

yoga exercises	– middle-class? women rather than men? keeping fit? dieting?
Rovers and Mercedes	– better-off people? middle-class?
a semi	– less well-off people, suburbs, not as small as a terrace house or a flat but smaller than a detached house
an itinerary	– route provided by guide or travel agent, business travel, planned route
a pilgrimage	– religion, visiting religious sites
parried	– boxing, martial arts, fencing
the Tech	– further education? lower level than a university? students on sandwich courses? less motivated students?
fulfil his latent promise	– children or students who have so far underachieved, letters of reference for less able students

B The words with more pejorative associations are <u>underlined</u> here.

ANSWERS

<u>cautious</u> · prudent   cooperative · <u>obedient</u>   difficult · challenging
<u>dreamer</u> · idealist   <u>frank</u> · sincere   <u>gullible</u> · trusting
<u>humble</u> · modest   laid back · <u>lazy</u>   light-hearted · <u>frivolous</u>
<u>moody</u> · depressed   <u>naive</u> · innocent   optimistic · <u>impractical</u>
oversight · <u>mistake</u>   realistic · <u>pessimistic</u>   solemn · serious
<u>stubborn</u> · resolute   <u>studious</u> · hard-working   tease · <u>mock</u>

C **1 & 2** Students should do this quite quickly, noting the first words that come to mind.

Extra activity

It's often hard to differentiate between associations and collocations – as this pseudo-Freudian word association game may show:

> Take it in turns to say the first word or phrase that comes into your mind, like this:
>
> 'Word' 'association' 'football' 'referee' 'whistle' 'flute' 'violin' 'musician' 'conductor' 'train' 'educate' and so on . . .
>
> If you perceive no connection, ask your partner to explain why she or he said that word:
>
> 'Why "train"?' 'Because you have to show your tickets to the conductor on a train.' 'Ah.'

Background

Margaret Drabble (b. 1939) is one of Britain's best-known writers. Her books, though touched with humour, seriously address the consequences of social change upon families and couples. Her best-known books include: *A Summer Bird-Cage, The Waterfall, The Needle's Eye, The Middle Ground, The Radiant Way, A Natural Curiosity, The Gates of Ivory* and *The Witch of Exmoor.*

The Millstone is about a young woman who has an illegitimate child, a poignant story which is both funny and sad.

A

1 She seems to be very aware of her shortcomings, and doesn't take herself seriously
 She admires her own confidence and wishes she were braver
2 *... if I remember rightly ... I do remember rightly ...*
3 humorous self-mocking/self-deprecating literate, educated and possibly slightly pretentious (the use of words like *au fait, ascertain, our destined hotel*, etc.)
4 She presumably signed her own name in the hotel register: a puritanical receptionist may have refused to accommodate an unmarried couple, or at least asked embarrassing questions
  The fact that she is 'still not married' is a fact of some significance. The mixture of confidence and cowardice is going to play an important part in the story
  The story is probably going to contain a series of misfortunes, described with wry humour. *Having a millstone round your neck* means having a problem that won't go away. (Rosamund has an illegitimate child)

B 1   SUGGESTED ANSWERS

Using the first person means that the narrator can legitimately be expected to know everything about her own emotions. It makes the story more personal and is rather like a confession or diary. A third-person narrator wouldn't normally be expected to know so much.

Compare this version – the details at the end of the first paragraph would almost certainly be omitted in a third-person narrative:

Rosamund's career had always been marked by a strange mixture of confidence and cowardice: almost, one might say, made by it. Take, for instance, the first time she tried spending a night with a man in a hotel. She was nineteen at the time, an age appropriate for such adventures, and needless to say she was not married. She is still not married, a fact of some significance, but more of that later. The name of the boy was Hamish ...

Hamish and Rosamund had just come down from Cambridge at the end of the Christmas term: they had conceived their plan well in advance, and had each informed their parents that term ended a day later than it actually did ...

2 SUGGESTED ANSWERS

In **13.5**, it seems to be more amusing to view Wilt and Henry Farr through a third-person narrator's eyes, than to hear them speak for themselves. Compare these rewritten versions:

Whenever I took the dog for a walk, or, to be more accurate, when the dog took me, or to be exact, when my wife told us both to go and take ourselves out of the house so that she could do her yoga exercises, I always took the same route. In fact the dog followed the route and I followed the dog. We went down past the Post Office ...

I did not, precisely, decide to murder my wife. It was simply that I could think of no other way of prolonging her absence from me indefinitely.
  I had quite often, in the past, when she was being more than usually irritating, had fantasies about her death. She hurtled over cliffs in flaming cars or was brutally murdered on her way to the dry cleaners. But I was never actually responsible for the event.

In the extracts in **13.3**, the use of the third person would make them sound less convincing, perhaps.

C **1 & 2**   This may be set as homework, but allow time for comparing paragraphs together in class afterwards.

13.8 Writing a proposal

 A   Maybe brainstorm some ideas with the whole class if the pairs find it hard to think of many.

 B   Discuss the kind of section headings that might be appropriate, before the students write their proposal for homework.

13.8 Model version

Lion Yard Student Centre

The need for a Student Centre
Research has shown that many students find it hard to make friends, particularly from different courses and faculties. A new Student Centre would encourage students from all faculties to meet in one central place, and make new friends.

Location
Lion Yard is a historic building, built 200 years ago as a warehouse. The building is derelict and is being offered to the community by its present owners for conversion into a Student Centre. The conversion would have to preserve the historic character of the building, as well as its façade. To achieve this, the interior walls would need to be demolished and new partitions erected to accommodate the facilities proposed below. There are three floors in the building, each of which would house different facilities.

Ground floor
The ground floor is an ideal location for a gym/fitness room and sports hall. The sports hall should be large enough for a basketball court or indoor soccer pitch. The gym/fitness room will need up-to-date equipment, but some of this could be obtained later. There will also be changing rooms and shower facilities. A staircase would lead from the main front door to the first floor.

First floor
This would be the main focus area of the centre, with a café, cafeteria and common room. Here students could meet over coffee, a meal or just sit together in the common room, which would be equipped only with sofas to encourage students to sit together. This would be a strictly non-smoking area. Smokers would be obliged to use the outside yard area in all weathers.

Second floor
For the moment this can remain empty. In the future this floor could accommodate study facilities or other social facilities, such as a bar or Internet café.

Cost
The cost of conversion and providing the facilities would be high, but I recommend that sponsors are found for each facility in the building. Thus each room would be named after its sponsor: the 'Cambridge University Press Café', the 'UCLES Cafeteria', etc. Former students of the University would also be invited to make contributions, and encouraged to donate equipment and furniture.

   Staff costs would be relatively low, as all the staff would be students working part-time or even voluntarily.

Leo Jones *New Progress to Proficiency*

All in a day's work

14

A **1** Pause the recording after each speaker to allow everyone time to make their notes.

> **SUGGESTED ANSWERS**
>
> Shazia enjoys working with people, being part of a team
> Shazia doesn't enjoy the long hours, staying in the hospital overnight
>
> James enjoys the variety, thinking on his feet, organising things, being left to his own devices, travelling, helping people to have a good life
> James doesn't enjoy computers going wrong
>
> Tessa enjoys the unpredictability, meeting interesting people, seeing her work in print
> Tessa doesn't enjoy things going wrong: film, equipment, sometimes people

2 👥 Also ask the class to talk about their reactions to what they've heard, and then discuss the pros and cons of:

- Being a single parent, having to earn a living and raise a young child
- Working as a woman in a man's world – or as a man in a woman's world
- Doing an unchallenging or routine job

TRANSCRIPTS *9 minutes 15 seconds*

NARRATOR: You'll hear a doctor, a butler/house-manager, and photographer describing their jobs. Make notes on what they enjoy and don't enjoy about their jobs.

SHAZIA: My name is Dr Shazia Afridi…um…I live in London and I am a doctor. Um…I work as a neurologist…um…I work in…in a hospital in the centre of London…er…called Queens Square, which is part of the University College, London. Er…it's what's called a tertiary referral centre, which means that…um…it's…it deals with the very specialised cases of neurology and people come from all over the country.

INTERVIEWER: And what do you particularly like about your job?

SHAZIA: Um…I like…I like a number of things about my job, I like…I like working with people primarily, which is partly why I went into medicine. Er…I also like the fact that…um…I see new people every day…um…and I meet a wide…a variety of people and I like working in a team, which is something which is very important in medicine.

INTERVIEWER: Now is there anything you don't like about your job?

SHAZIA: Um…yes, I don't like the long hours. Er…unfortunately, being a doctor means you do have to work very long hours and you have to do what are called 'on called' which means you stay in the hospital overnight…um…and this affects your…your social life quite considerably and also means I'm away from my husband a lot of the time.

INTERVIEWER: If someone wanted to go into medicine, what advice would you give them?

SHAZIA: Um…I'll…well, I'd want them to know exactly what they're going in for. Um…so I think…er…working…work experience is a…is a very…er…beneficial thing to do. Er…they…they should probably attach themselves to a doctor and just follow them around for at least a week or…just to see exactly what the doctor does.

★★★

JAMES: I'm James Charles and I'm a butler and house-manager.

INTERVIEWER: And what happens on a typical day?

JAMES: Um…well, I…I open the post, I deal with…um…any post that's come in, anything that needs urgent attention gets done. I go on to the Net and check the e-mail and obviously check for faxes and things like that, that's the first…the first job really. Then there'll be a list of things to do, I mean, it maybe…um…anything, it may be that one of the cars needs to go in for service, it may be that…um…something has gone wrong with the telephones and I need to deal with that. I may have to go out, there may be something that I need to buy, so I, you know, I may take the car or one of the cars and go and…and do some shopping, and there may be research to do into a project that's going on at the moment, which…which can take some time…um . . .

INTERVIEWER: And can you tell me some of the things you enjoy about your work?

JAMES: Um…I like the variety, I like the fact that no day is the same as a different day. I like the…um…I like the reward that comes from thinking on my feet…um…organising things almost before the people that I work for know that they need things to be organised. I like the fact that I'm left quite a lot to work on my own devices. My boss works away or travels a lot, so I'm often there just on my own looking after the house or, you know, whatever goes on in the building…um…and I like the fact that occasionally I get to travel as well, not as often as I'd like probably, but…er . . .

INTERVIEWER: But you've been quite…to quite a few places with him, haven't you?

JAMES: Yeah, yeah, we have a…an associate company in California, where I…I go now and again. I've been involved in some business on his behalf in Australia…um . . .

INTERVIEWER: And has he got properties elsewhere?

JAMES: Yes, yeah, he has a holiday home in Jamaica and another holiday home in Italy in Umbria.

INTERVIEWER: And can you tell me some of the things you don't enjoy so much?

JAMES: Um…I don't like it particularly when computers go wrong. I'm not a great lover of…of technology and of course one has to use technology but it sometimes goes wrong in…er…in ways that are quite simple but beyond my brain.

INTERVIEWER: And does he expect you to be able to fix it as you're the butler/manager?

JAMES: Yeah, he has a habit of buying new technology and then not reading the book but expecting me to know how it works. Even though I haven't read the book either, of course.

INTERVIEWER: And if someone came to you and said, 'I've decided what I'd like to do is be a butler/house-manager', what advice would you give them?

JAMES: Be prepared to work very hard, be prepared to work long hours…um…and don't go into it unless you actually do care about helping people to…well, helping people to have a good life really. To…um…to make the path of their life as smooth as possible because that in itself is the major reward I think of this kind of job.

INTERVIEWER: What makes a good butler then?

JAMES: Lists, lists, lists. Very…you know you have to be very efficient. You can't afford to forget things so we all find a different way of doing it. I personally, you know, obviously I use computers and things but I make lists of things to do today and tick them off so that nothing as they say falls through the cracks. You have to be…you have to be cool, calm and collected too, you know. I mean, whether…whether people are annoying you or whether somebody's being over-demanding or whatever, you know, at the end of the day you are in a service position, if you like, and it's your job to…er…to do whatever, you know, somebody wants, you know, and if you don't like that then you're probably in the wrong business.

★★★

TESSA: I'm Tessa Holman, I'm a photographer…studio-based photographer.

INTERVIEWER: And can you tell me some of the things about your work that you really enjoy?

TESSA: I think probably the most enjoyable aspect is the…um…freedom of…of what I do, and also the lack of predictability. Um…I very much enjoy working with different people, meeting different types of people…um…having…er…a…a…different week every week, it's almost something different every day, never being able to predict what I might be photographing…um…from one week to the next really, and I've done some very interesting things and I've met an awful lot of interesting people.

INTERVIEWER: And are there any things about being a photographer that you don't like, or that you don't enjoy?

TESSA: The only thing that I…I s…find sometimes frustrating is that there's so many…um…things that can go wrong, from film to equipment to y…all the other variables that…um…er…human variables as well. Um…sometimes you feel that things are a little bit beyond your control when something happens that hasn't happened to you before…um…but other than that, no, I don't think there is. I think it's…um…a great job, a great job and I think I'm very privileged to do it. You know, it's…it's great to meet people, particularly if you…you admire them, you like them anyway, and then to…um…photograph them, I…I f…find incredibly exciting.

INTERVIEWER: And do you always photograph them not smiling, or not…er…you know, trying to look serious?

TESSA: It's very hard sometimes. The…the one person that I…I managed to photograph not smiling and looking very unlike herself was Julie Walters, who's a great…um…er…sort of comic actress, and…er…try as I might I couldn't raise a smile, she was not having a good day! One of the thing about…things about what I do is that…er…very often actors, actresses particularly sort of the…the very successful ones have to publicise a film, for example, that they've done and they'll be sent…um…seven photographers during the course of a day, to take their picture for various different magazines and newspapers. Um…and it's incredibly tiring for them, poor dears, but…um…you know, it…it's quite…it's quite difficult to…when you're only sort of number four or number five in the day when they really would like to go home, put their feet up and see their kids…um…to try and get them to be…um…original for you, is quite an uphill task…um…and that's why I think if you do manage to…to get something that's…that's really quite…er…other…as original as possible under the circumstances it's quite an achievement. And um…I think with Julie Walters, she was exhausted at the time that I met her, so that was…um . . .

INTERVIEWER: But you were still happy with the photos?

TESSA: Oh, very much, and she was incredibly pleasant and very, very nice, and…er…you know, expressed an interest in seeing the pictures, felt…er…felt herself that she was the best thing that she'd done that day.

INTERVIEWER: That's great.

TESSA: So that was…so that was nice that…er…to…to hear.

INTERVIEWER: Have you ever been surprised or disappointed by the results from a photo shoot?

TESSA: Um…I've been disappointed a couple of times…um…and yeah, also surprised. I think when you've gambled on…on a…on a…you're not quite sure if something's going to work, but you gamble on it, and it does come out and it does look very good, that's a…that's a really satisfying…um…you know, f…feeling. But also, because you have to hand your photographs over to a magazine or to a…to a newspaper…um…they can do, ultimately really what they want with it, you know, they can make a layout look good or bad. Um…it's always very surprising when you get a…a magazine back that's got your photograph in it, and they've done a lovely job, or maybe given you a full page when you didn't expect that, and…and you sort of think, 'Yeah, I'm really proud of that, that looks great'.

B ANSWERS

1 D   2 C   3 D   4 A   5 C   6 B   7 B   8 A   9 C   10 B   11 D
12 D   13 B   14 D   15 C   16 B   17 A   18 C

A **1**

SUGGESTED ANSWERS

waves break   traffic lights change, but they can also break (stop working)
a boy's voice breaks (becomes deeper), but it can also change   a storm breaks
the weather can break (change for the worse), but it can also just change
your mood can change   day breaks

2

SUGGESTED ANSWERS

You can **break** . . .   a promise   a world record   an appointment (?)   crockery
someone's heart   a habit   the ice   the law
news to someone   the silence   your arm   your leg

You can **change** . . .   a promise (?)   a world record (?)   an appointment
a tablecloth   crockery   direction   gear   money
the bed or the sheets   a habit (?)   the law   the subject
trains   your clothes   your mind   your shoes

B

ANSWERS

You can **follow** . . .   an argument   a line of argument   a route or directions
a story   a trade or profession   advice or instructions
someone's example or their lead   an idea   a football team
a football match   the fashion or a trend

You can **lose** . . .   an argument   control over something   face   heart
a football match   interest in something   the thread of a story
track of something   weight   your job   your nerve
your temper   your voice if you have a cold
your way or bearings

C

ANSWERS

1 ask   lend   lifting
2 open   supply
3 cancel   placed   changed
4 pay   raise   collect
5 offered   resist   accept   lose
6 leads   running   strike
7 throw   drawing   bear
8 raised   reached   hold

14.3 **A good ending** WRITING SKILLS

A

Thanks to: André Meier, E.H. Limpens, Helmut Binder and Arianna Tommasini for allowing
us to use extracts from their work.

COMMENTS

1 Not very appealing – it seems the applicant stands to get more from the arrangement
than the employer. It's unwise to write this, even if it may be true
2 Seems fine, but maybe lacks a final punch
3 This is OK, though maybe rather dull
4 This is nice, though possibly rather pushy. (Moreover, typing a job application on
pink paper is not such a good idea!)

B COMMENTS

9.3 ". . . And that is why I'm giving up."
– *short and punchy, sums up the whole of the article*

9.7 ". . . Once you start to think strategically, you begin to take control of your studies rather than letting them swamp you."
– *sums up the whole article, but rather wordy perhaps*

10.7 ". . . With clearer goals established, economic theory can then tell environmentalists where to go."
– *a measured conclusion to the article, looking forward to further developments and progress*

12.3 ". . . In either case, it really isn't fair."
– *nice personal touch, encourages the reader to share the writer's feelings*

12.4B ". . . The scientists say the penguin is a better bet than human transport because it holds its body still as it swims."
– *some extra information is given which looks forward to further developments. A pleasantly colloquial final sentence*

12.8 ". . . It is time for a change."
– *short and simple, looking forward to better things in the future*

14.5 ". . . In fact that's not the case at all. Unfortunately, the only thing that seems to matter to some people is being better off than the next person."
– *rather disappointing as Prof Argyll's views on lottery winners only relate vaguely to the theme of happiness, and it's also a rather depressing ending*

The least effective seems to me to be **14.5**, but there are several contenders for 'most effective'.

C ✐ Please make sure enough time is allowed for this part – it's the most crucial part of this section. Students should not only discuss improvements but write them.

If the members of the class don't have their recent compositions with them, postpone this activity until the next lesson and impress upon them that they *must* bring them along next time.

14.4 Word order: phrasal verbs GRAMMAR REVIEW

A The lists contain mostly verbs that students should already be familiar with. However, they should highlight and look up any unfamiliar ones.

More information

Some phrasal verbs can be transitive or intransitive, depending on their meaning:

I told him to **clear out**, but he refused to leave.
I told him to **clear out** his room because it was so untidy.

clear out	= go away / make tidy	**drop off**	= deliver / fall asleep
look up	= use reference book / raise your eyes	**miss out**	= not include / be unlucky
pay off	= make payment / succeed	**pick up**	= lift / improve
turn up	= make louder / arrive unexpectedly	**work out**	= calculate / keep fit

ANSWERS

1 a shop around
  b spoke up
  c had worn off
2 a pay it back / pay you back
  b won over
  c had left him behind
3 a saw them out
  b show her around
  c invite her/Pam out

4 a missing out on
  b checking up on you
5 a came up against
  b leading up to

 B

ANSWERS

 1 tear it up   pay up
 2 dream up   explain it away
 3 hand in   talk him out of it   stay on
 4 stick up for me / sort things out
 5 caught out!
 6 trade it in
 7 wait up for me
 8 climbed down
 9 cracking down on
10 grew out of it

14.5 **Learning to be happy**   READING

A This discussion is a lead-in to the rest of the (long, but easy-to-read) article.

B If convenient, and possible, ask everyone to read the article before the next lesson.

ANSWERS

1 are passionate about
2 see eye to eye
3 some people
4 demanding jobs
5 reflecting on how they spend their time
6 not everyone can be happy
7 are less worried about being successful
8 become very unhappy

C

ANSWERS

¶ 1	exercised	= kept busy
¶ 1	end	= goal
¶ 2	concludes	= judges
¶ 3	innocuous	= innocent
¶ 5	euphoria	= exhilaration
¶ 10	adrenalin-driven	= motivated by excitement
¶ 12	couch potatoes	= people who watch too much TV
¶ 17	mingling	= socialising
¶ 18	devout	= believing
¶ 23	inverting	= reversing
¶ 26	flipside	= less good side

D This is a follow-up discussion.

14.6 **Beat the clock**

ANSWERS

1 C   2 E   3 B   4 A   5 D

1 The 'most important' points are a matter of opinion. But generally, in this kind of article, the main point is likely to be in the last (or possibly the first) sentence of each paragraph.

2 👥 At the end, ask everyone what kind of training they have thought of for people attending interviews. Would any of these ideas be useful training for the Speaking Paper of the exam?

14.7 **Looking for a job?**   **LISTENING AND COMPOSITION**

🔊 Before listening to the recording, it's a good idea for students to look at the questions and pencil in any answers that they can guess. The task is tricky because some of the information is implied by the speakers, but not actually expressed. And when they express agreement, this means they both express the same view.

ANSWERS

1 Kerry	2 Neither	3 Neither	4 Neither	5 Anne	6 Anne
7 Kerry	8 Neither	9 Kerry	10 Neither	11 Both	12 Neither
13 Neither	14 Kerry	15 Anne	16 Neither	17 Neither	18 Kerry
19 Neither	20 Kerry				

TRANSCRIPT *4 minutes 50 seconds*

NARRATOR: Listen to part of a seminar for job-seekers.

CHAIRPERSON: . . . and…er…we've…er…we've discussed several ideas now and…and you've all had a chance to do some role-play of interviews, so I…I think it's time now for our two experts to give some final tips. Er…Kerry, let's take the application form first, because that's the first hurdle, isn't it?

KERRY: Yes, yes, that is the first hurdle. Um…now…er…my suggestion may sound silly but…er…it's not. Um…what you should do is…is actually photocopy the application form and practise filling in the copy so that you don't make any mistakes…er…when you do the final version.
Um…and…er…always use the space provided, don't…you know, don't go on, don't exceed the space that you're…you're given, now this is important as well. Um…you may not know this but 95% of applicants are rejected on the basis…on the basis of the application form alone, it's very important. You see…um…people are so overworked, the selectors don't have time to…to read everything. Er…there…there may be 100 applicants for…for the job that…that you go after. Um…so they…they often skim the form, and they look for the important things…er…and the simple things: spelling, presentation and also vagueness, a lack of precision.

ANNE: Mm, yes. I agree with Kerry…um…but I would also stress that it is important to use words that actually show your interest in high achievement. Um…now, I'll explain what I mean: er…words like 'success', 'promotion'…er…'ambition', 'responsibility'. Er…it…it also helps if you've got something interesting or unusual to put on your form…um…this actually makes you stand out from the rest and it gives the interviewer something to talk to you about apart from anything else. Um…for instance, an adventurous holiday, er…a holiday job that you've done…um…an unusual interest you've got, as long as it's not too weird, you know, that sort of thing.

CHAIRPERSON: Mm, yes, I see, thanks. Now, about the interview itself…er…we've emphasised already the importance for the interviewee to ask plenty of questions, not just to sit there and be the passive partner. Um…Kerry, what do you have to say about that?

KERRY: Yes, that's…that's…that's very true. Always be positive, don't…um . . . Be confident, don't undersell yourself and always do lots of homework about the company that interviews you, find out about it, about…everything you can about it: it…its activities…er…its…if it has any policies…er…that…um…differ from other companies of that sort…er…and its subsidiaries…er…e…even its competitors.

ANNE: Mm, and the other thing to…to really be prepared for are some surprises at the interview. I've known all sorts of things happen, I've known applicants being asked to solve *The Times* crossword or sort through today's in-tray putting letters in order of priority. Er…the other thing that's quite common nowadays are group interviews with a few other applicants. Um…y…you might find that you're expected to spend a day with the personnel manager…er…having lunch with him, possibly even assisting him.

CHAIRPERSON: Another surprise technique that sometimes happens is…um…to provoke the candidate, the interviewer insults him or…or gets up starts shouting or something like that. And well wh…what should one do if that situation arises?

KERRY: Well, I mean, it…it's…it's pretty obvious: just don't lose your cool. You know, just…er…be…er…if you think about it, if…if you just keep it in your mind that that might happen, you'll prob…probably be all right but…er…with most surprise techniques it's…it's…it's impossible to be prepared for them, you just…um…have to learn to expect the unexpected.

ANNE: Yes, that's right, yes. And of course, don't panic. The…the best way to prepare yourself is just to practise being interviewed. A…and as…as Kerry said it's vital to present yourself positively as somebody who's socially sensitive, sparkling, has a sense of humour, adaptable and intelligent – if all those things are possible!

KERRY: But…haha…but if…er…if…er…in spite of all the…the advice we give you, you…you keep losing out…um…it's always good to try the technique of creative job searching.

CHAIRPERSON: Creative job searching? That's a new one on me!

KERRY: No well, it's…it's quite simple and you've probably done this sort of thing already. Decide on the kind of field that you want to work in and res…research it…er…do…do plenty of research and…and get in touch with the companies in that field and…er…oh, do…do everything you can: talk to people who work in…in these companies…um…an…anything to show your interest. If you can, um…get them to allow you to spend a day there to see what goes on and…um…who knows, in the end . . .

ANNE: They'll give you a job to keep you quiet?! Haha.

KERRY: Haha. No, but…er…if there's an opening, you'd be surprised, you'll be the person they think of to fill it.

CHAIRPERSON: Kerry and Anne, that's a great help, thanks a lot…er…I think it's about time for coffee now, don't you?

ANNE: Mm, good idea.

KERRY: Mm.

B 👥👥 Maybe also ask the groups to discuss which advice would hold good for the Speaking Paper in the exam – not all of the advice does.

C 🖊 Perhaps bring some English-language newspapers into class, and do the 'job-searching' in groups, looking at real advertisements. Then the planning can also be done by students working together.

However, you might prefer to photocopy this ad, which is similar to the kind of text candidates might encounter in Part 1 of the Writing Paper:

WORK IN
BERMUDA!

ACME Atlantic are a well-known and respected trading company. We handle imports directly from manufacturers in 35 different countries, often to our own specifications, and currently export to 46 different countries worldwide.

We are looking for enthusiastic people to work in our office in Bermuda on temporary 3-, 6- and 9-month contracts. Applicants must be able to speak and write at least one foreign language fluently and can be nationals of any country.

Experience in import/export will be an advantage, but as special training will be available this is not essential. The main requirements are a willingness to work as a member of a team, to cope with pressure, to use the telephone in a foreign language and in English and to be prepared occasionally to work long hours when necessary.

There are several posts available and long-term prospects are good, though initially all successful applicants will be contracted for a maximum of 9 months.

The salary we will offer is excellent. We will pay for your return air fare and provide adequate accommodation at a nominal rent.

Please apply in your own handwriting, enclosing your résumé, to Charles Fox, European Sales Office, ACME Atlantic Ltd, 45 Pentonville Road, London EC2 4AC.

from *New International Business English* by Leo Jones and Richard Alexander

---

Leo Jones *New Progress to Proficiency*

Extra activity

Role play the interview following the job application you made in **C**. Take it in turns to be the interviewer and the interviewee.

14.7 Model version

Dear Mr Fox,

I wish to apply for one of the temporary positions in your Bermuda office, as advertised in today's Daily Planet.

I am __ years of age and a citizen of __. I am at present in my second year studying __ at the University of __, which is a four-year course. When I finish my studies I am hoping to begin a career in the __ business, where I will be able to use my languages.

I speak English fluently, as well as Spanish and my own language. My written English is good. I am at present studying for the University of Cambridge Proficiency examination, which I will be sitting in June this year. My plans after this are to find work in another country before the new University semester begins in October.

I have worked during previous vacations in the local office of Acme Inc, where I was a member of a team dealing with enquiries from clients and suppliers from many different countries, using e-mail and the telephone. My line manager, Ms Muster, complimented me on my performance and would be happy to supply you with a reference regarding my character and suitability for a position with your company.

I am a hard worker, and I enjoy meeting people and dealing with people from different cultures. I enjoy work that is challenging and not routine, where each day presents new experiences and problems to deal with. I particularly enjoy working as a member of a team. The position you advertise seems exactly what I would be good at. I feel sure that my knowledge of __ as well as English would be a particularly useful contribution to the success of your team.

I am a calm, intelligent person and respond well to stress and pressure. I enjoy using the telephone and have plenty of experience in speaking to native speakers of English on the phone, as well as to other people who do not speak my language.

I am available from June 15 until October 15.

I enclose my CV which gives full details of my education, experience and background.

Looking forward to hearing from you,

Yours sincerely,

Leo Jones *New Progress to Proficiency*

14.8 # Use of English Parts 1 and 2

EXAM PRACTICE

Spelling is important here! A word spelt even slightly wrong loses a mark in the exam.

 These are the words in the original article, but several variations may be possible.

SUGGESTED ANSWERS

1 forced   2 approached   3 product   4 name   5 research   6 sale
7 exports   8 profits   9 hand   10 hope   11 developed   12 output
13 process   14 launched   15 benefit

ANSWERS

16 scientists   17 invention   18 technological   19 aromatic   20 production
21 consumption   22 dependence   23 uncertain   24 diversify   25 seller
26 continental   27 decaffeinated   28 striking   29 relationship   30 product

Is it art or entertainment?

15.1 The tingle factor

READING

If possible, ask everyone to read the article before the lesson. The questions only touch on some of the ideas in the article, which is what happens in Part 4 of the Reading Paper.

> **ANSWERS**
> 1 C   2 D   3 B   4 C   5 B   6 A

B   👥👥 Music is a hard subject to discuss, but the article gives plenty of background information and ideas to fuel the discussion and provoke agreement or disagreement. At the end, ask each group to report on their discussion.

15.2 'You're being paid to be a child!'

LISTENING

Background

Simon Russell Beale (b. 1961 in Penang) is one of Britain's most famous actors. Since the interview was recorded, he has played Hamlet at the Royal National Theatre to great acclaim. His best-known TV performance was as Kenneth Widmerpool in Anthony Powell's *A Dance To The Music Of Time* on Channel 4.

> **ANSWERS**
> 1 D   2 C   3 D   4 D   5 D   6 C   7 A   8 C

TRANSCRIPT   *10 minutes*

NARRATOR: You'll hear an interview with the actor Simon Russell Beale, who has performed at the Royal National Theatre and with the Royal Shakespeare Company.

SIMON: I'm Simon Russell Beale and I'm an actor.

INTERVIEWER: And you've just returned from a world tour of Shakespeare's *Othello*, er...where did you go?

SIMON: We went to Austria, Poland, the United States of America, er...Japan, Korea, China, Australia, New Zealand. It was an amazing experience.

INTERVIEWER: And what's it like playing Shakespeare to a non-British audience?

SIMON: Um...yes, that's quite a difficult question to answer because I don't...I mean, I...I felt, after I'd played eight weeks in front of non-English speaking audiences, that...that my own performance, and indeed the whole show, was beginning to try too hard. It was...um...it's quite difficult to explain, but we were present...over-presenting it. Um . . .

INTERVIEWER: Were you aware then that the audiences were listening in a...to a language that wasn't their first language?

SIMON: Yes, although amazingly, and shamingly, the knowledge of Shakespeare in all those audiences was phenomenal and...um...er...they'd studied it, they knew exactly what Shakespeare was about, they knew exactly what *Othello* was about. So in that sense...er...the response was actually in some ways...er...quicker and faster than you find sometimes in...in...playing it in London. Um...but there was a diff...there were different reactions in different countries, um...and different things that made people laugh and different things that made people cry.

INTERVIEWER: And how do you think performing Shakespeare is different from performing more modern...er...plays?

SIMON: Well, it's a hugely disciplined thing to have to do because of course it's written in verse, and one must never forget that Shakespeare's a great poet, as well as a great playwright. Um . . . it's to do with the...it's to do with the rhythm really. You have to, in a verse play, um...l...lull the audience in a way into this rhythmic heartbeat...er...that goes right the way through the play. And it...it's very interesting, it's...it's a...it should become a sort of subconscious thing in both the audience's ear and brain and indeed in the actor's...um...er...ear and brain as well. Um...but if it goes wrong you know it does. There's a sort of lurch, or there's a sudden break in the rhythm which you know is actually not what Shakespeare meant. He...he means a h...there's a th...a th...a gentle thud right the way through the play, it's just a heartbeat as I say right through the whole play. Um...and if you observe that, then oddly a lot of the emotional work that you have to do...er...as an actor is done for you by the playwright because he is so good.

INTERVIEWER: And how do you feel when Shakespeare's transported from Elizabethan times to modern day?

SIMON: Well, sometimes it works and sometimes it doesn't. I mean, one can't be prescriptive about these things. I...I think...um...certain people hate the idea of modern dress Shakespeare, and there are times even in our production of *Othello* when you think, 'Oh, hang on a minute, they...why do they use a gun when they...they're always talking about swords and things like that?' which is . . . I, in fact, in the end shoot somebody dead rather than stab them. Um...and I...I think in *Othello* actually, as...as it happens, it works extremely well because it's been very carefully done. I think that's the rule, if you're going to...if you're going to put it into a different era just...just be careful in the direction. Just make sure you don't make too many glaringly obvious...er...mistakes or anachronisms, er...that...that's going to jolt the audience out of concentrating on the play itself. But as a general principle I think there's no harm at all in...in setting it where you want to set it. You can set it on the moon if...if that's . . .

INTERVIEWER: Oh, I agree with that, I think audiences'll...will accept a convention...um . . .

SIMON: As long as it's clearly presented and as long as, yes, as long as, as I say, you're not jolted out of concentrating on the really important thing which is the words.

INTERVIEWER: Has anything surprised you about...um...during your time as an actor?

SIMON: Um...gosh! That's a tricky question. Um...I have to say there are things like I think actors and...um...people in the theatres that I've worked in, which is mostly Royal Shakespeare Company and the National Theatre, are...um...much kinder and much less insincere that the...than the popular image...er...portrays them as. And they're a...actors are essentially a very generous bunch of people. They're also a very bright bunch of people. Um...I've had to...had the luck to act with some, you know, extraordinarily bright and generous people. Um...so I suppose that, in a sense, is not a surprise but it's something that it would...I would like to be able to say is not the common perception.

INTERVIEWER: And how is performing on stage different from working in television or film?

SIMON: Um...somebody described it to me, a film director that I was working with...a television director said...er, 'Acting in film is like being a sprinter, and acting on stage is like being a...um...you know, a 400-metre runner'. There's a...there's a different type of energy needed in both. Um...there's long hours of waiting on film sets and then you suddenly have to do something extraordinary or emotional or funny or whatever...um...after hanging around for a whole day. Um...which I have to say I find difficult. Um...although I find the process of film-making intriguing and...and fascinating. Um...the...acting on stage is...is...requires a completely different energy...um...and it requires a different type of physicality. Um...again it's difficult to explain but there are certain actors who work very well on stage and don't work very well on film, and vice versa. And I think that's partly to do with their...the source of their energy which sounds very pretentious but I think stage actors...stage actors need a source of energy right down in their belly somehow, um...to produce the type of...of largeness of performance that can reach the back of an auditorium. Whereas film of course is a different...is...is much more internalised, and...er...and also you have...you have no responsibility in film on the pace of what you're doing. It's the...it's almost the first lesson I learnt when I first...er...started doing some serious filming which was only a couple of years ago, and...er...I suddenly realised I'd done a scene and the director came up and just said, you know, 'Just take your time. It's up to me as a...and my editor to make it pacey if that's what we want, but it's up to you to be as truthful as you can possibly be'.

INTERVIEWER: And...er...what do you really, really enjoy about being an actor?

SIMON: Oh, gosh! Um...well, I've been very lucky in that I've had to do...I've been asked to do great works of literature, which I have to say makes an enormous amount of difference, and that even includes the...the television that I did. Um...and exploring...exploring a...um...a character like Iago, you know, who's...borders on the psychopath. Er...it's just a fascinating journey. The other thing is, and this sounds very corny but it's true, is the camaraderie of the people that I have met through the thirteen years that I've been working, and some of whom have remained friends for many, many years.

INTERVIEWER: And always will.

SIMON: And hopefully always will.

INTERVIEWER: And the fun, I always think it must be terrifically good...good fun.

SIMON: Oh gosh, yes! Yes, yes, also there is...there is a bit of a...a...a thing in...in every actor, isn't there, that . . . I talked about it as res...responsibility earlier, in a sort of odd way we never really have total responsibility and...and again that can be frustrating and sometimes you think, 'Oh I wish I could...I wish...I'd like to direct or I'd like to produce.' And lots of actors do that or write, where you have much more responsibility. But part of the fun of acting is the fact that it's still playing, isn't it? It's still being a child.

INTERVIEWER: But you're being paid to be a child.

SIMON: Yes, exactly, which is quite nice!

INTERVIEWER: And what do you not enjoy?

SIMON: Quite specifically learning lines, which is...it's . . . People ask, 'How do you learn lines?' It's just that that's a hard slog. That's just simply sitting down and like every job has a boring aspect, well that's the boring aspect of . . .

INTERVIEWER: Because Iago is the...one of the biggest Shakespeare characters?

SIMON: Yes, I think, well, I keep...I keep on being told it is the largest, that it's larger than Hamlet. I d...that might be...might very well be true in terms of number of words, um . . .

INTERVIEWER: And how on earth do you unwind after um...say, you've done two shows of *Othello*?

SIMON: You don't need to un...unwind after two shows of *Othello*, I'd fall over I think after two shows of *Othello*! Um...but I, you know, have a pint of beer in the...in the bar, you know, and there's usually people in, which is nice, friends...um...I'd always like to have a drink with them. Um...but I'm usually in bed within two hours of finishing a show. So I . . .

INTERVIEWER: That's because you . . .

SIMON: I...I don't find it particularly difficult to switch off.

INTERVIEWER: And lastly if...um...someone came to you and said they wanted to be an actor, is there anything...any advice you'd give them?

SIMON: Only to do it. I mean, I...I...I've been asked that a lot obviously and...and...and, you know, I used to think, 'Oh gosh, I ought to really...er...ad...advise them wisely and say, "Be wary, and it's a difficult business, and . . ." ' but eventually I...I...I've come round to the idea that if you...if you've got any idea that that's what you would like to do you've got to try it, and...um...for the ...er...obvious and old reason that if you don't try it you'll regret that and it would be awful if you've...you know, you're sixty and you say, 'I wish I...I'd tried it.' So my only advice is: if the...if you want to do it, do it.

15.3 Prepositions – 2 GRAMMAR REVIEW

A

ANSWERS
1 beside/next to   with
2 at   in   over   below
3 in   in   over
4 by   on/in   on
5 opposite   from   from   to   on
6 on   in   in
7 in   in front of   in   in   during/about
8 Besides   at
9 after   in   before
10 on   for   in/during
11 in   under   in   behind/in/on top of/under/next to
12 into   in   in   by/beside/next to/under   with   on

B

These are the prepositions used in the original text; some variations are possible.

ANSWERS
1 with   2 to   3 of   4 in   5 of   6 about   7 on   8 of   9 at   10 of
11 of   12 on   13 of   14 in   15 of   16 in   17 to

C

 Draw everyone's attention to the real size of the painting (it's one metre tall) before they discuss their reactions.

15.4 Conjunctions and connectors – 2 ADVANCED GRAMMAR

A

ANSWERS
1 Despite my relative lack of knowledge of art, I know what I like.
2 Besides painting in oils, he (also) paints watercolours.
3 Without going to the box office today, you won't get seats for the show.
4 Due to the illness of both the tenor and soprano, the performance was cancelled.
5 Except for jazz, I like all kinds of music.
6 As well as missing his wife, he was missing his children (too).
7 Like you, I didn't enjoy the film.
8 But for the pianist's wonderful performance, I wouldn't have enjoyed the concert.

B

SUGGESTED ANSWERS
1 Some people say that modern art is overrated, but **all the same I find the work of Pablo Picasso really fascinating**.
2 **It is sometimes said that** artists lead a good life: their hobby is their profession, but **they may have trouble making ends meet if they can't sell their work**.
3 **On the whole** Hollywood movies are ephemeral, **but every so often** you see one that you can't forget.
4 **To some extent** watching television is rather a waste of time, **but now and then you do see worthwhile, interesting programmes**.

5 **As a rule** politicians are honourable, dedicated people, **but there are exceptions to every rule and there are some who are corrupt or dishonest.**

6 **Many people believe that** reading is a wonderful source of pleasure; **however, some books are very badly written, and may not be worth reading at all.**

7 **To a certain extent,** people work because they have to, not because they want to, **but all the same many people do get a lot of satisfaction and pleasure from their work and their contact with people at work.**

8 **Generally speaking,** I enjoy all kinds of music **except for jazz.**

C 1 Allow everyone enough time to notice what's happening in the picture and to make notes.

2 **Activity 1** on page 199 contains W.H. Auden's *Musée des Beaux Arts*, a poem about the painting and its implications.

3 ✎ This task should be done as homework. (This is not an exam-style task.)

15.4 Model version

It is the end of a normal working day. In the foreground a farmer is still ploughing his field, half asleep, following his horse down a slope. Behind him a shepherd, with his dog and flock of sheep, is gazing up into the sky. However, we cannot see what he is looking at. Behind them both, stretching to the horizon, is the sea: an inlet or a bay surrounded by cliffs, with a magical city in the distance on the left, an island in the centre and castles and rocky mountain peaks on the right. A ship with its sails flapping in the strong wind is sailing close to the coast on its way to the open sea, sailing towards the west. The sun is just about to set. We notice, lit up by the last rays of the sun, the bare legs of a young man who is about to drown. Without knowing the title of the picture we would not realise this is Icarus, who has fallen out of the sky and splashed into the sea. No one has noticed except perhaps for one person: a man sitting alone on a grassy bank in the bottom right-hand corner. But there is nothing he can do apart from watch, powerless.

Leo Jones *New Progress to Proficiency*

15.5 Use of English Part 5: *Guernica*   EXAM PRACTICE

A 1 The actual painting is nearly 8 metres wide. It can be seen in the Prado Museum in Madrid.

2 This is a difficult passage. Consider it as a yardstick of your students' ability to get to grips with abstract ideas, and cope with an uncompromisingly erudite style and a plethora of unfamiliar vocabulary. If they can manage this, they can probably cope with anything that the examiners might throw at them!

The piece is taken from a history of twentieth century art, published to accompany a series of TV programmes. Robert Hughes is art critic of *Time* magazine.

SUGGESTED ANSWERS

1 Could make the general public talk about pictures or paintings
2 From the mass media
3 Because television is now most people's principal source of images
4 To emphasise that although political art exists, it is not effective
5 To emphasise the difference between the two meanings of value: price and worth
6 Wallpaper for the walls of the powerful: it is now completely without influence
7 He regrets it

B 👥👥👥👥 In this follow-up discussion, the students are encouraged to talk about the role of art, and the role of the critic.

C 👥👥 The exam tips at the foot of page 161 are for discussion. Pool ideas if there are any further tips that members of the class come up with.

15.6 Two reviews   READING

A The two dreadful films have been chosen because it's often more fun to compare experiences of bad films than good ones – and it's more fun to write a review of them.

> **ANSWERS**
> 1 c   2 a   3 c   4 c   5 c   6 d   7 c   8 a

B **1** 👥👥 At the end, ask the pairs to report on the worst films they've seen.

2 👥👥 Here the students exchange information about movie clichés, as explained in the introduction. One student looks at **Activity 5** on page 200, the other at **18** on page 203. They should exchange information in their own words, not just read aloud to each other.

15.7 Writing Part 2   EXAM PRACTICE

A 👥👥 Pool ideas after the pairs have discussed the advice. The most crucial thing in the exam is to ANSWER THE QUESTION!

B **1** 👥👥 Exchange ideas when the pairs have finished.

2 👥👥 The film needn't be a bad one if some pairs prefer to write about one they recommend.

C 🖋 There's no model version here because the two reviews in **15.6** are both exam-length. If you want to find reviews of recent movies, look at the Empire website: www.empireonline.co.uk. See also **15.8** for a more favourable review from the same source.

15.8 Reading Part 1   EXAM PRACTICE

Discuss the annotated answers with the class before they answer questions 7 to 12.

> **ANSWERS**
> 7 B   8 A   9 D   10 B   11 C   12 A

15.9 Use of English Part 4   EXAM PRACTICE

Discuss the annotated answers with the class before they answer questions 4 to 8.

> **ANSWERS**
> 4 is expected to be poorly
> 5 is no question of me/my paying for
> 6 's previous film before *The Beach* was
> 7 was a fool to turn down the offer
> 8 never occurred to me to take up

15.10 *good* and *bad*

In this section, and also in **16.12**, there are plenty of idioms, but no phrasal verbs.

SUGGESTED ANSWERS

1 can be used/in a satisfactory condition
2 That is a difficult/impossible question to answer – or one that I'm not willing to answer
3 reluctantly/unwillingly
4 in addition/extra
5 a favour
6 permanently
7 restless, sleepless night
8 considered to be impolite/rude
9 deteriorated even more
10 to my advantage
11 completely useless   dishonourable person
12 is valid

ANSWERS

1 make good money
2 in good time   makes a good impression
3 as good as her word
4 as good as new
5 a bad leg/ankle/knee
6 in a bad way
7 've a good mind
8 put in a good word
9 gave it up as a bad job
10 while the going's good
11 in good faith
12 a good job

And here are some more idioms which your students might find useful or interesting:

a good deal of
a good talking to
in his own good time
make good the loss
make good = succeed
the good old days
a goody-goody
all in good time = there's no rush
do more harm than good

bad language
give a dog a bad name
a bad debt
bad blood

Look after yourself!

16

A

ANSWERS

1 B   2 B   3 B   4 B   5 D

B

 Remind the students to note down any useful vocabulary that comes up in their discussion. Ask them what you'd call someone who always thinks they're ill (*a hypochondriac*).

C

ANSWERS

1 flabby   plump   stout
2 a consultant   a specialist   his GP
3 skinny   slim   thin
4 stress   tension   worry
5 fainted   lost consciousness   passed out
6 twinges   ache   pain
7 vaccines   preventive medicine   healthy living
8 a sedative   a pain-killer   a tranquilliser
9 capsules   tablets   pills
10 pull through   get better   get well
11 rash   swelling   inflammation *(some people, particularly hypochondriacs, might go to the doctor about any of these problems)*
12 catching   contagious   infectious
13 an examination   a check-up   a medical
14 pulled a muscle   sprained her ankle   fractured her wrist
15 alternative   complementary   fringe

D

Alternatives with incorrect spellings like 1 and 2 would **NOT** appear in the exam, so maybe they're a bit unfair in this kind of exercise.

ANSWERS

1 psychosomatic
2 anaesthetic
3 unbalanced
4 transmitted
5 gynaecologist
6 threw up
7 allergy
8 eradicated
9 stomach
10 agoraphobia

E

 On the recording there is a collection of 'doctor, doctor' jokes for you to share with the class, just for fun really. In some of them the 'doctor' is a psychiatrist, one assumes.

TRANSCRIPT   *1 minute*

PATIENT: Doctor, doctor, I keep thinking there's two of me.
DOCTOR: One at a time please.

PATIENT: Doctor, doctor, I've lost my memory.
DOCTOR: When did this happen?
PATIENT: When did what happen?

PATIENT: Doctor, doctor, my little boy's swallowed a bullet. What shall I do?
DOCTOR: Well, for a start, don't point him at me.

PATIENT: Doctor, doctor, I keep thinking I'm a pack of cards.
DOCTOR: Sit down. I'll deal with you later.

PATIENT: Doctor, doctor, I keep thinking I'm a dog.
DOCTOR: Lie down on the couch and I'll examine you.
PATIENT: I can't. I'm not allowed on the furniture.

PATIENT: Doctor, doctor, people keep ignoring me.
DOCTOR: Next please!

PATIENT: Doctor, doctor, I keep thinking I'm a spoon.
DOCTOR: Well, sit there and don't stir.

PATIENT: Doctor, doctor, I feel like a pair of curtains.
DOCTOR: Pull yourself together, man!

PATIENT: Doctor, doctor, my hair's coming out. Can you give me something to keep it in?
DOCTOR: Certainly. How about a paper bag?

PATIENT: Doctor, doctor, my wooden leg's giving me a lot of pain.
DOCTOR: Why is that?
PATIENT: My wife keeps hitting me over the head with it.

16.2 Speaking

EXAM PRACTICE

Ask everyone to remind themselves what happens in the Speaking Paper before they embark on this mock exam.

A 👥 It's OK to spend a bit longer than 3 minutes on this.

B 👥 It's OK to spend a bit longer than 4 minutes on this.

C 👥 Each 'long turn' should take the stipulated 2 minutes.

At the end, ask each pair to report on what happened by asking these questions:
- Which part was the hardest?
- Did both of you manage to take an equal part in the discussion?
- If you could do it again, what would you do differently?

Then . . .

Ask everyone to repeat all three parts of the mock exam and try and do it better – maybe with a different partner this time.

(See **17.9** on page 196 for the Assessment criteria used by the Assessor and Interlocutor in the exam.)

16.3 Relative clauses

GRAMMAR REVIEW

A 👥 **ANSWERS**

1 The doctor I spoke to yesterday told me not to worry.
  – I've talked to other doctors about my problem, but the one I consulted yesterday tried to reassure me *(informal or neutral style)*

  The doctor, **whom** I spoke to yesterday, told me not to worry.
  – I normally consult only one doctor and when I talked to him/her yesterday, I was reassured *(formal style)*

  The doctor, **who** I spoke to yesterday, told me not to worry.
  – I normally consult only one doctor and when I talked to him/her yesterday, I was reassured *(informal or neutral style)*

  The doctor **to whom** I spoke yesterday told me not to worry.
  – I've talked to other doctors about my problem, but the one I consulted yesterday tried to reassure me *(formal style)*

  2 He told us about the treatment, **which** made him feel better.
     – Just telling us about the treatment improved his health, not necessarily the
       treatment itself
     He told us about the treatment **that** made him feel better.
     – It was the treatment itself that improved his health

  3 They operated on the first patient **who** was seriously ill.
     – Several other less sick patients were not operated on: the very ill one got
       preferential treatment
     They operated on the first patient, **who** was seriously ill.
     – Patient number one was very ill and he/she was operated on

B   COMMAS have been added where necessary.

ANSWERS

The Californians have come up with a device for people **who**[1] have their own small
swimming pool**, which**[2] should transform their lives as much as those indoor exercise
bikes **which**[3] were so popular in the 1970s did. Swimming**, which**[4] is recognised to be one
of the best ways of keeping fit**,** is impractical in pools **that/which**[5] are too small
for serious swimming. But the *Hydroflex* is a new device **which/that**[6] can keep swimmers
in the same spot and still allow them to do all the strokes. It consists of a plastic bar
which/that[7] is attached to the side of the pool by two lines and to the swimmer by a waist
belt. The swimmer**, whose**[8] legs are protected from the lines by the bar**,** remains
stationary while swimming. It sounds like an activity **that/which**[9] is only suitable for
people **whose**[10] desire to keep in shape helps them to ignore the taunts of neighbours
who[11] happen to spot them in the pool.

C   COMMAS have been added where necessary.

SUGGESTED ANSWERS

  1 He's the only person I know **who runs/swims/walks** ten kilometres a day before
     breakfast.
  2 I swam twenty lengths**, which took** me a long time.
  3 He has two sisters both **of whom are** doctors. The younger of the two**, whose name is**
     Jane, qualified last year. He also has two brothers**,** neither **of whom** knows anything
     about medicine.
  4 One of the children must have swallowed the pills **which had been/were** left in the
     bathroom.
  5 All **of the things that/which** people say about hospitals is true.
  6 She loves talking about her operation**, which made** us all feel ill.
  7 The matron is the **person who** is in overall charge of the nursing staff.
  8 Taking a degree in medicine**, which takes much** longer than most other university
     courses**,** is the only method **by which/by means of which** one can become a doctor.

16.4 Listening Part 1   EXAM PRACTICE

 To simulate exam conditions, allow everyone 15 seconds to look at questions 1 and 2.
Then play Extract 1, then rewind and play it again. Pause for another 15 seconds. Then follow
the same procedure with Extracts 2, 3 and 4.

At the end, discuss with the class what they found difficult about this exercise. And finish by
putting the class into pairs to talk about their reactions to what they heard in the four extracts
and the topics raised:

  1 unsympathetic doctors
  2 homeopathy and other complementary medicine
  3 'the body's vigorous powers of self-healing'
  4 dreams

TRANSCRIPTS   *5 minutes 40 seconds*

1

DOCTOR: Ah, Jim, good morning.

PATIENT: Morning, doctor.

DOCTOR: Have a seat. Right, now what seems to be the trouble?

PATIENT: Agh. Well, mm…I've got this awful pain in my chest. [Mhm.] I think I may have cracked a rib or something. It really hurts a lot, especially when I move. [Right.] I hoped it'd get better over the weekend, but on Monday it was even worse, and today if anything it's still worse again.

DOCTOR: Right, OK, well, let's have a look. [Thanks.] Does it hurt when I do this?

PATIENT: Aaah! Yes, it does.

DOCTOR: And this?

PATIENT: Oooh! Oh!

DOCTOR: Hmm. OK, well, when did you do this?

PATIENT: Oh, that's the funny thing. I'm not really sure when it happened. It just started hurting on Thursday when I woke up. [Mhm.] I…I thought I must have been lying awkwardly in bed, you know, like a crick in the neck. Th…then I thought back over the previous day and the only thing I can think of is that…what happened when I was in the supermarket. I was bending over the freezer and someone got me with the corner of their trolley. [Right.] It didn't really hurt at the time.

DOCTOR: OK, well, that must be it, I imagine. Well, there's not a lot I can do. Um…there's no point in…in…in going to have an X-ray. Er…I think you'll just have to let it get better by itself.

PATIENT: How long will that take?

DOCTOR: A couple of months.

PATIENT: A couple of months!!

DOCTOR: Yes, you just have to take it easy and rest. Take…you can take pain-killers if it gets too bad.

PATIENT: Mm. Oh, well, thanks a lot.

DOCTOR: That's all right. Er…come back and see me in a…in a month. OK?

★★★

2

REPORTER: Well, homeopathy was invented by a German chemist called Samuel Hahnemann. At that time it was already known that quinine, which is made from the bark of a tree that grows in South America, could be used to treat malaria. Hahnemann gave very strong doses of quinine to himself, his family and friends, who were all perfectly healthy people, and he found that they all developed exactly the same symptoms – it was as if they actually had malaria, which they didn't really, of course.

Then he carried out more experiments, using his friends and his pupils as guinea pigs, getting them to take doses of hundreds of other substances. [*actually only 100*] Including lots of different herbs and even metals like gold and copper, to find out what the effect of each one was – to…to find what symptoms developed. In this process of 'proving' the substances, he discovered that, for example, taking regular doses of arsenic caused vomiting and diarrhoea. So, in other words, he produced 'artificial' diseases.

Well, I suppose the crucial connection he made was between the cure and the illness, and this is one of the fundamental principles of homeopathy: treating like with like. He discovered that if patients suffering from the same symptoms, from natural diseases, were given minute doses of the same substance that caused the equivalent artificial disease, they actually got better. And he used the 'single blind' technique whereby none of the patients knew if they were taking an inert powder or the medicine itself – only he knew.

★★★

3

DOCTOR: Well, I'm a doctor and I've spent my life dealing with people who seek cures, and just want to get better. Er…they may find a…a…a smart office with framed diplomas on the wall reassuring, and enjoy being listened to sympathetically. But what counts for them is results. And the most impressive way to present results is in the form of testimonials from satisfied customers.

But anyone who's done any sort of…er…service job knows just how easy it is to acquire flattering testimonials. I mean, I have drawers full of grateful letters from patients who survived my treatment, thanks more to their luck than my judgement. And the fact is that anyone who treats patients can earn the same kinds of tributes, thanks to the body's vigorous powers of self-healing. And…um…I'm not suggesting that most of my patients are hypochondriacs!

★★★

4

MAN: I had a really strange dream last night.

WOMAN: Oh, don't tell me about it, please!

MAN: I wasn't going to. It just made me think about this piece I read the other day by J.B. Priestley. [Uh?] He says that he really likes dreaming, going to bed and lying still and then, oh, what did he say? Mm, 'By some strange magic, wandering into another kind of existence.' He said it was as if there were at least two extra continents added to the world . . .

WOMAN: What?

MAN: Uh… and, oh…er…'lightning excursions running to them at any moment between midnight and breakfast'. Then he wrote about 'huge mysterious anxieties, with…er…luggage that can't be packed and trains that refuse to be caught' and 'there are thick woods outside the bathroom door' [Bathroom!] and 'the dining-room is somehow part of a theatre'. And then, oh, what did he say? Oh, yeah, 'then there are moments of desolation and terror in the dream world, that are worse than anything we've known under the sun'.

WOMAN: Like?

MAN: Well, I'm not sure, but…but…ah, then on the other side of that the, you know, sometimes this other life can be very attractive and every now and then 'a serene glow or a sudden ecstasy, like glimpses of another form of existence altogether, that we can't match with open eyes'. Mm? I…I agree with him, dreams are wonderful. What do you think?

16.5 Use of English Part 2   EXAM PRACTICE

Spelling must be correct for a mark in the exam!

> **ANSWERS**
> 1 themselves 2 conference 3 loneliness 4 difficulty/difficulties 5 persistent
> 6 embarrassment 7 failure 8 outside 9 inadequate 10 conditioning
> 11 pre-disposition 12 psychologists 13 self-conscious 14 thought 15 partly

16.6 Listening Part 2: Was Freud a fraud?   EXAM PRACTICE

To simulate exam conditions, allow everyone 45 seconds to look at the questions, then play the recording, pause for 10 seconds and play it again. (After this there is a whole minute's silence before Part 3 is heard.)

A

> **SUGGESTED ANSWERS**
> 1 got worse 2 a good story / fiction 3 novelist/writer 4 slip of the tongue
> 5 disregarded / poorly reviewed 6 pleasure 7 not original / not invented by him
> 8 discouraged/restricted 9 fooled

B Suitable words to describe Professor Abrahams:

vehement sarcastic scathing brusque urbane malicious energetic erudite quick-witted

A *psychologist* studies human behaviour, a *psychiatrist* treats people who have mental or emotional problems.

TRANSCRIPT *4 minutes 40 seconds*

PRESENTER: In most people's estimation the Viennese psycho-analyst Sigmund Freud ranks with Copernicus, Galileo, Darwin and Einstein as one of the greatest scientists of all time, in fact a true genius. Well, how true is this? Professor Carl Abrahams says we've all been fooled too long. Is that right, Professor Abrahams?

ABRAHAMS: Yes, the truth is that Freud is one of the most successful charlatans who ever lived. He pulled the wool over his contemporaries' eyes and his followers continue to pull the wool over people's eyes today. Now, just for a start: there's no evidence whatsoever that psycho-analysis has ever cured anyone of anything. Ha…it's become clear that Freudian psycho-analysis is pure hokum according to over 500 empirical studies of patients. Now, those who supposedly benefited from psychiatrists' treatment fared no better than those who were left to their own devices, indeed there's good evidence that it made some patients worse. Now, most professional psychiatrists know this very well, but the world is full of amateur psychiatrists like teachers, social workers, probation officers, and even parents, who attempt to apply misunderstood and speculative Freudian ideas.

PRESENTER: Speculative?

ABRAHAMS: Yes, yes. Freud's so-called apparatus for explaining human behaviour is pure speculation. Also there…there's no concrete evidence that his methods even worked for him. For example, the so-called 'wolf-man', this man who had dreams of wolves sitting in a tree outside of his house: now, he had exactly the same symptoms and the same problems for the rest of his life after supposedly being cured by Freud successfully. Freud concocted a beautifully literary story but he omitted certain factual details and he actually added his own imaginative content. Now, this has been proved by detective work in other patients he treated. Very often he clearly made an erroneous diagnosis and his treatment was unsuccessful but he chose to ignore these cases. In other words, Freud appears to have been a brilliant novelist but a lousy doctor.

PRESENTER: Now, Carl Jung's main criticism of Freud's work was that he placed excessive emphasis on sexuality and on childhood experiences as being the origins of neurotic disorders, wasn't it?

ABRAHAMS: Absolutely, his equation of pleasure with sexuality was unjustified. Now, it's caught the public's imagination and kept it for the whole of this century. Take the Freudian Slip that people refer to when they make a slip of the tongue…er…for instance: 'the breast thing to do' instead of 'the best thing to do', you see. Now this is popularly supposed to be due to a man's desire to return to his mother's body, like Oedipus, but it's…ha…it's all absolute rubbish of course.

PRESENTER: But how did Freud manage to fool people in the way you say he did?

ABRAHAMS: Ah, well, it's very interesting. Firstly he consciously set out to create a myth of himself as the misunderstood and persecuted hero, whose books were disregarded and poorly reviewed. Well, nothing could be further from the truth. Now, just look at the medical journals of the time and you will find long and enthusiastic reviews of every one of his publications. Some were even commenting back then on his genius. Indeed, the greatest myth of all is that Freud was a genius, that…that his was a truly original mind at work. He is popularly supposed to have invented the unconscious. Well…ha…again this is utter nonsense. People had been writing about the unconscious mind for 2,000 years before Freud, indeed it was being widely discussed by educated people long before Freud claimed it for his own.

For example, his so-called Freudian symbolism was common knowledge in Greek and Roman times and his supposedly new method of free association had been publicised by Sir Francis Galton years before Freud claims to have invented it. Now, other theories he claimed as original had been proposed by…er…Pierre Janet, for instance, and so on and so on.

PRESENTER: Well, all right, so Freud may have been a fraud, but how has his influence been harmful?

ABRAHAMS: Well…er…three instances. Number one: by encouraging speculation instead of experimental studies. Er…number two: by encouraging…er…nebulous philosophising and so on. And number three: by discouraging rigorous clinical trials. Now, although Freud is not taken seriously by any self-respecting professional any more, the psycho-analysts of the world are making a very good living from the gullibility of…er…the public, who still believe that Freud can not only explain their problems but even that he…that he knows how to cure them. In short, it'll be a long time before the myths, the utter myths, that Freud himself so…so artfully created can finally be expunged.

PRESENTER: Professor Abrahams, thank you.

ABRAHAMS: You're welcome.

16.7 Synonyms and homonyms VOCABULARY DEVELOPMENT

A **1 & 2** 🔊 Students may need reassuring that *bored, unemotional* and *sad* voices sound very similar. Without seeing the speakers' faces, it's difficult to tell which is which. Some answers may have to be worked out by a process of elimination.

Suitable synonyms and phrases which could also describe the tone of the speaker are given in *italics*.

ANSWERS

1	furious	– *livid, vehement*
2	cross	– *annoyed, indignant, upset*
3	kind	– *sympathetic, amiable, affectionate*
4	bored	– *jaded, weary, fed up*
5	unemotional	– *phlegmatic, matter-of-fact*
6	friendly	– *cheerful, reassuring, welcoming, pleased, glad, positive*
7	sad	– *depressed, despondent, upset*
8	amused	– *delighted, enchanted, taking it as a big joke, finding the situation hilarious*

TRANSCRIPT *2 minutes 30 seconds*

PRESENTER: Listen to each speaker and select a suitable adjective to describe their mood or tone.
(The Presenter gives a number to introduce each speaker)

SPEAKERS: Ah there you are. I was wondering where you'd got to. Luckily I had some work to get on with so I wasn't bored. Anyway, even if the film has started by the time we get there, I don't think it'll matter – do you?

(The exact words used vary slightly from speaker to speaker)

B Note that the contexts and collocations of the words in the lists may not be the same and this should be discussed with the class. There are few exact equivalents when it comes to synonyms. Ask the class to suggest phrases incorporating the adjectives and participles with suitable collocations.

ANSWERS

amazed = *astonished*   annoyed = *indignant*   clever = *talented*   confused = *bewildered*
cured = *better*   depressed = *despondent*   determined = *persistent*   different = *diverse*
disappointed = *disillusioned*   dull = *dreary*   encouraged = *heartened*
exciting = *thrilling*   frightened = *scared*   glad = *delighted*   respected = *admired*
revolting = *disgusting*   shocked = *horrified*   upset = *distressed*   worried = *anxious*
worrying = *disturbing*

 SUGGESTED ANSWERS

1 Surfing can be **risky**, but hang-gliding is **a far more hazardous pastime**.
2 There are many **effective** ways of keeping fit **and jogging is a particularly effective way of keeping in shape**.
3 I was **delighted** to meet my old friends again. It was **wonderful to have the chance to talk** about old times.
4 I'm sorry that you were **under the weather** yesterday. You look **as fit as a fiddle** today.
5 It was **very generous** of you to offer to help, but the work wasn't **particularly demanding**.
6 We went for **an invigorating** walk at the weekend, ending up at a **delightful** restaurant.
7 The original novel was **entertaining**, but the film they made of it was **dreary**.
8 The meal we had last night was **delicious**, but the wine **was disappointing**.

 ANSWERS

1 came up with
2 get through/across to them   got me down
3 take back
4 put up with
5 brings on
6 held up
7 made up   took   in
8 came apart
9 go along with
10 put   out

Writing Part 1

EXAM PRACTICE

 👥 Encourage students to add to the ideas given in the Student's Book. But make it clear that they will have to leave quite a lot of ideas out to keep to the 350-word limit later.

 1 ✏️ This should be done against the clock, without a dictionary.

2 👥 Suggestions for improvements should be given, not criticism.

16.8 Model version

Should we trust the experts when they tell us how to remain in good health and go on living for a long time? We all know that being overweight and unfit is detrimental to our health. The experts tell us what to eat, how to take exercise, how to avoid stress and not to drink or smoke. How can we possibly do everything they advise?

Of course we should all try to eat a well-balanced diet with plenty of fruit and vegetables, fish and not too much red meat. Not too much fat and sugar and salt. And over-eating is clearly bad for us and will make us fat. We can follow expert advice on diet, but not too rigidly. Healthy food may be more expensive, and not everyone can afford it.

We can keep fit by walking or cycling, but walking and cycling take time and, with the traffic and pollution in our city, they may be dangerous too. On the other hand, going to the gym or jogging can be too energetic. A more gentle form of exercise may be preferable: my recommendation is swimming regularly. Swimming is a wonderful way of exercising many muscle groups — and it helps you to relax. But not everyone has time to take exercise, if they have so much else to do.

A certain amount of stress is necessary in modern life. People work harder and are more productive if they are under pressure. But if this stress is carried over into your leisure time and weekends, then it's certainly bad. We all need to learn how to deal with stress and then be able to "switch off" and relax by spending time alone and with friends. But not everyone can avoid stress, if it's caused by personal relationships and family life.

We know that drinking heavily is bad for you and can lead to alcoholism. But, some experts say, a glass of wine helps to reduce heart disease. If we do drink, we should drink in moderation, and never get drunk.

But if none of the recommendations fits in with your life-style, there's just one thing that will help you to stay healthy and live longer: don't smoke! Smoking is expensive, it's pointless, it's unhealthy and it's dirty. Anyone can stop smoking, if they have the will-power. And if they do, they'll save money and live longer.

Leo Jones *New Progress to Proficiency*

16.9 Reading Part 3: Taking the waters · EXAM PRACTICE

Discuss suitable techniques for tackling this part of the exam either before or after everyone has done the exercise. Also allow time for everyone to discuss their reactions to the ideas and information given in the article.

ANSWERS

1 B   2 E   3 D   4 C   5 G   6 A (F doesn't belong anywhere)

16.10 Use of English Part 3 · EXAM PRACTICE

Most students find this kind of exercise is quite enjoyable!

ANSWERS

1 count   2 operate   3 founder   4 exhausts   5 show   6 type

16.11 Use of English Part 5: Floating · EXAM PRACTICE

 Students should compare their answers before you discuss them with the whole class.

SUGGESTED ANSWERS

1 To suggest stupid, senseless talk
2 Shabby and unfashionable
3 To evoke 'new age' music or hippies
4 To emphasise the non-sexual nature of the procedure
5 Drugs have a detrimental effect on your body; meditation is extremely boring
6 Because of the contrast between the tranquillity and serenity of floating, and the noise and commotion of going out into city streets
7 Loud recordings of waves breaking and whale noises are played to them
8 The effects of floating were discovered by an American scientist researching sensory deprivation. He found that spending time in salt water in complete darkness and silence enabled people to meditate, which induced feelings of extreme happiness.
   The craze swept across the USA after its appearance in a movie. In Britain, over forty have opened in the last six years, encouraged by recommendations from celebrities and doctors alike.

LOOK AFTER YOURSELF!

 SUGGESTED ANSWERS

1 speaks frankly
2 freedom from anxiety
3 telling him off
4 promised
5 decide
6 couldn't decide
7 get a chance to speak
8 believe me
9 in my imagination
10 I forgot to do it
11 the ultimate
12 final decision

 ANSWERS

1 word perfect
2 picked your brains
3 go back on his word
4 brainwave
5 take your mind off
6 have a good mind to
7 word for word
8 it's their/his word against ours
9 had something on your mind
10 play on words
11 change your mind
12 racking my brains

And here are some more related idioms for you to have up your sleeve:

She has **a good head for figures**   I can't **make head or tail of** this
Let's **put our heads together**   He is **off his head**
They found it hard to **keep their heads above water**   Success **went to his head**
In a crisis, try to **keep a cool head**   You've **hit the nail on the head**

You must be **out of your mind**   I've **half a mind to . . .**
Bear it in mind that . . .   **To my mind**, . . .

She was **as good as her word**   Could I **have a word with** you?
You'll have to **take my word for it**

The endings have been rearranged in order of vividness with the most vivid one first – the order is open to discussion.

Extra activity: Illustration and allusion WRITING SKILLS

When telling a story or describing your experiences, illustration and allusion can help to make your writing more vivid, especially if you can give personal examples or make interesting comparisons.

A 👥 **Look at these examples and decide which of the alternative endings sounds most vivid:**

1 The weather was so hot that . . .
   . . . a river of sweat was pouring off him.
   . . . he was sweating like a pig.
   . . . he felt very uncomfortable.

2 They were so unfriendly that . . .
   . . . I wished I had stayed at home.
   . . . I regretted having left home.
   . . . I felt unwanted and unwelcome, as if I was an outsider.

3 The lecture was so dull that . . .
   . . . we found it hard to concentrate.
   . . . we could hardly keep our eyes open.
   . . . we all started to nod off.

4 I was so looking forward to the holidays that . . .
   . . . I couldn't keep my mind on my work.
   . . . I was very excited.
   . . . I couldn't sit still.

5 There was such a lot of rain that . . .
   . . . we were soon soaked to the skin.
   . . . we soon looked like drowned rats.
   . . . we got extremely wet.

6 She was so beautiful that . . .
   . . . he kept on looking at her.
   . . . he couldn't keep his eyes off her.
   . . . his heart skipped a beat every time he looked at her.

B 👥→👥 **Decide how to fill the gaps in this story about 'A visit to the doctor'. When you've finished, compare your ideas with another pair.**

> I woke up feeling as if .... : my head was throbbing and my joints were aching so much that .... And I felt so dizzy that ....
>
> I called the doctor to make an appointment. Over the phone the receptionist spoke to me as if .... , but when I walked in she treated me as if ....
>
> I found a seat in the corner of the waiting room, which looked like .... Sitting there waiting for my turn among the other patients reminded me of .... Looking round, my eyes came to rest on a young man smoking a cigarette, who looked as if .... He had such a bad cough, that it sounded as if .... With him was a little girl who looked so unhealthy that ....
>
> By the time my name was called I was feeling rather better – it seemed as if .... I stepped into the doctor's surgery.
>
> 'What seems to be the trouble?' asked the doctor in such a .... voice that I .... I described my symptoms to her, feeling a bit like ....
>
> 'You've just got the flu.' she said, 'Go home, go to bed and don't waste my time.' I felt so foolish that ....

C **Match the words in the middle with the endings on the right to form suitable idiomatic expressions:**

drink too much alcohol	He drinks like . . .	wildfire
drive fast	She drove like . . .	cat and dog
have a row	They fought like . . .	a sieve
good memory	He has a memory like . . .	a fish
forgetful	I have a memory like . . .	a fish
run fast	She ran like . . .	a house on fire
sleep well	I slept like . . .	the wind
extravagant	He spends money like . . .	the wind
swim well	She swims like . . .	an elephant
be good friends	We got on like . . .	a log
very quickly	The news spread like . . .	water

Leo Jones *New Progress to Proficiency*

This document may be photocopied.
© Cambridge University Press, 2002

A **ANSWERS**

1 . . . a river of sweat was pouring off him.
   . . . he was sweating like a pig. (*not very elegant-sounding*)
   . . . he felt very uncomfortable.
2 . . . I felt unwanted and unwelcome, as if I was an outsider.
   . . . I wished I had stayed at home.
   . . . I regretted having left home.
3 . . . we could hardly keep our eyes open.
   . . . we all started to nod off.
   . . . we found it hard to concentrate.
4 . . . I couldn't keep my mind on my work.
   . . . I couldn't sit still.
   . . . I was very excited.
5 . . . we soon looked like drowned rats.
   . . . we were soon soaked to the skin.
   . . . we got extremely wet.
6 . . . his heart skipped a beat every time he looked at her.
   . . . he couldn't keep his eyes off her.
   . . . he kept on looking at her.

Ask the class to suggest alternatives.

B **SUGGESTED ANSWERS**

I woke up feeling as if **I was dying**: my head was throbbing and my joints were aching so much that **I could hardly move them**. And I felt so dizzy that **the room was going round and round as if I was on a roundabout**.

I called the doctor to make an appointment. Over the phone the receptionist spoke to me as if **I was some sort of idiot** but when I walked in she treated me as if **I was a long-lost friend**.

I found a seat in the corner of the waiting room, which looked like **an airport departure lounge**. Sitting there waiting for my turn among the other patients reminded me of **the last job interview I had attended**. Looking round, my eyes came to rest on a young man smoking a cigarette, who looked as if **he had been through some awful experiences**. He had such a bad cough, that it sounded as if **he didn't have long to live**. With him was a little girl who looked so unhealthy that **I felt really worried for her**.

By the time my name was called I was feeling rather better – it seemed as if **I had completely recovered from my illness**. I stepped into the doctor's surgery.

'What seems to be the trouble?' asked the doctor in such a **stern, abrupt** voice that I **started to panic**. I described my symptoms to her, feeling a bit like **a naughty schoolchild who was wasting her time**.

'You've just got the flu,' she said, 'Go home, go to bed and don't waste my time.' I felt so foolish that **I left the room without another word and went straight home**.

C **ANSWERS**

drink too much alcohol	– He drinks like a fish.
drive fast	– She drove like the wind.
have a row	– They fought like cat and dog.
good memory	– He has a memory like an elephant.
forgetful	– I have a memory like a sieve.
run fast	– She ran like the wind.
sleep well	– I slept like a log.
extravagant	– He spends money like water.
swim well	– She swims like a fish.
be good friends	– We got on like a house on fire.
very quickly	– The news spread like wildfire.

17

The past is always with us

17.1 Use of English Part 1 and Reading Part 2 EXAM PRACTICE

A 👥 The people in the photos are: Napoleon Bonaparte, Joseph Stalin, William Shakespeare and Mahatma Gandhi.

B
> **SUGGESTED ANSWERS**
> **1** style   **2** name   **3** made/woven/manufactured   **4** native   **5** emigrated
> **6** joined   **7** business   **8** idea/notion   **9** reinforcing/strengthening   **10** history
> **11** product   **12** century   **13** rest/whole   **14** storm   **15** example

C
> **ANSWERS**
> **1** D   **2** D   **3** C   **4** B   **5** D

D 👥👥 Ask each group to report on its ideas. Also exchange ideas on how to deal with Use of English Part 1 and Reading Part 2 in the exam.

17.2 War poetry

READING AND SPEAKING

Background information about the three poets can be found in **Activities 9**, **25** and **30** on pages 201, 206 and 207.

A 🔊 The poems are recorded.

B 👥 The questions are intended for discussion and should not be considered as a 'test of understanding'.

> **SUGGESTED ANSWERS**
> **1** C   **2** C (or A?)   **3** C   **4** C (though it is arguable that all the answers are true here)
> **5** B (again a case could be made for the other answers)
> **6** A   **7** B   **8** B (or A?)   **9** B   **10** A   **11** C (or B?)   **12** C (or A?)

C 👥👥 Students find out more about the three poets by looking at **Activities 9**, **25** and **30**. Then there are questions for discussion.

17.3 Modifying adjectives and participles

VOCABULARY DEVELOPMENT

A **1** Both *extremely pleased* and *extremely important* are OK. The others are wrong: it would be better to use *absolutely* instead.

2
> **SUGGESTED ANSWERS**
>
> absurd ✗ preposterous ✗ improbable ✓
> intelligent ✓ sensible ✓ brilliant ✗
> amazed ✗ surprised ✓ astounded ✗
> terrifying ✗ frightening ✓
> fatal ✗ hazardous ✓ deadly ✗
>   harmful ✓
> happy ✓ euphoric ✗
>
> genuine ✗ believable ✓
> identical ✗ similar ✓
> priceless ✗ valuable ✓
> interesting ✓ fascinating ✗
> worthless ✗ futile ✗ inexpensive ✓
> delightful ✗ pleasant ✓
> essential ✗ important ✓

SUGGESTED ANSWERS

1 He was **quite** determined to succeed, and he was **extraordinarily** disappointed when he didn't. We were **highly** amused, but pretended to be **really** sympathetic.
2 The amount of work that is required is **considerably** greater than we expected, and we'll have to make a(n) **really** great effort to finish it on time.
3 We were **absolutely** delighted to hear he was getting married, especially to such a(n) **exceptionally** nice woman.
4 He was feeling **thoroughly** depressed after his illness, but he made a **remarkably** quick recovery, and was **unexpectedly** cheerful after that.
5 We felt we had been **badly** let down when they told us our application had been rejected. We were **deeply** embarrassed because we'd told all our friends.
6 I'm sure her business will be **highly** successful, as she is a **remarkably** capable person, even though it's **perfectly** true that most new businesses don't succeed.
7 It was a(n) **absolutely** wonderful film and I thought the performances were **deeply** moving. It was **totally** different from any other film I've ever seen.
8 The role of women in history is not **fully** recognised by many historians, who tend to be **utterly** traditional in their attitudes.

SUGGESTED ANSWERS

1 Some people find that it is quite impossible to remember historical dates.
2 We should be absolutely delighted to accept your invitation.
3 It happened so long ago that it has been completely forgotten.
4 It's quite futile to ask him to be tactful.
5 She was absolutely livid to find out about our plans.
6 It is totally improbable that he will succeed.
7 It is absolutely essential to remember to check your work through for mistakes.
8 We found the lecture quite fascinating.

17.4 The end of the war

READING

Background Robert Graves (1895–1985) served in the First World War as an officer. *Goodbye to All That* (1929) is an autobiography describing his war experiences. Graves was nineteen when the war began, and many of his friends and fellow-officers died in the fighting. His prose works include *I, Claudius* and *The Greek Myths*, and his poems are to be found in any anthology of modern poetry.

ANSWERS

1 C   2 C   3 C   4 C   5 D (the 'best' answer)   6 C

Here is the complete Siegfried Sassoon poem, of which Graves quotes the first three lines:

Everyone Sang
Everybody suddenly burst out singing,
And I was filled with such delight
As prisoned birds must find in freedom . . .
Winging wildly across the white
Orchards and dark-green fields; on; on; and out of sight.

Everyone's voice was suddenly lifted,
And beauty came like the setting sun.
My heart was shaken with tears; and horror
Drifted away . . . O but every one
Was a bird; and the song was wordless; the singing will never be done.

👥 If necessary, reassure everyone that there won't be any poems to read in the exam, by the way!

A 👥 One suggested meaning for *it* or *them* is in **bold italics**.

> **ANSWERS**
>
> 1 Drink up: it's good **for** you.
>   – This *medicine* will have a good effect on you
>   He was very good **about** it.
>   – He behaved in a kind, calm way in spite of *the problem or difficulty* he had been caused
>   She is very good **at** it.
>   – She has a talent for a *particular sport or activity*
>   She was very good **to** them.
>   – She was kind to *the children*
>
> 2 She was angry **with** them.
>   – Her anger was directed at *the people who had done wrong*
>   He was angry **about** it.
>   – He found *the situation* (of being passed over for promotion) annoying
>
> 3 I knew I was right **about** them.
>   – My intuitions about *those people* were correct
>   The choice was right **for** them.
>   – *The people* who made the choice made the right one
>
> 4 We were pleased **with** them.
>   – We were delighted that *the children* had performed well, which made us feel proud
>   He sounded pleased **about** it.
>   – He had been *promoted* and from his voice I gathered that he was glad
>   We were pleased **for** them.
>   – *The team* had done very well, and we tried to share their pleasure (even though it had done us no good)
>
> 5 She was sorry **for** them.
>   – She felt sympathetic towards *the people who had suffered*
>   He was sorry **about** it.
>   – He regretted what he had done (*broken the window?*)

B 👥 Note that *different from, different to* and *different than* are all used in English, though some purists have strong feelings about the relative 'correctness' of some of these. As all are used, none would be considered incorrect by an examiner. Certainly no question would hinge on this in the Use of English Paper.

> **ANSWERS**
>
> | | | | | | | | |
> |---|---|---|---|---|---|---|---|
> | ahead | ashamed | aware | capable | conscious | critical | devoid | envious |
> | guilty | intolerant | proud | scared | short | unworthy | wary | weary | *of* |
>
> | | | | | | | | |
> |---|---|---|---|---|---|---|---|
> | accustomed | allergic | comparable | courteous | cruel | devoted | equivalent |
> | hurtful | identical | impolite | indifferent | inferior | irrelevant | kind | loyal |
> | preferable | sensitive | similar | superior | susceptible | unfaithful | *to* |

C The ones in *italics* can be used with more than one of the prepositions – see below.

> **ANSWERS**
>
> | | | | | | | |
> |---|---|---|---|---|---|---|
> | *annoyed* | apprehensive | bewildered | curious | dubious | fussy | guilty |
> | *indignant* | sceptical | vague | | | | | *about* |
> | *absent* | famous | responsible | | | | | *for* |
> | *absent* | far | free | | | | | *from* |
> | dependent | intent | keen | | | | | *on* |
> | *annoyed* | comparable | compatible | consistent | conversant | familiar |
> | *indignant* | level | patient | | | | | *with* |
>
> He was absent from class / for the test.
> She was annoyed with me / about what I'd done.
> They were indignant with us / about our behaviour.

D

SUGGESTED ANSWERS

1 apprehensive   sorry
2 kind   proud   annoyed   impolite   guilty   good
3 critical   accustomed   responsible
4 indifferent   sensitive   sceptical   aware   hurtful
5 intent   capable   sorry   wary

17.6 Listening Part 3: Emigration   EXAM PRACTICE

 A

🔊 To simulate exam conditions, allow everyone 1 minute to read the questions through. Then play the recording, rewind it and play it again after 10 seconds' pause.

ANSWERS

1 D   2 D   3 C   4 D   5 B   6 B   7 A   8 C

TRANSCRIPT   *7 minutes 15 seconds*

NARRATOR: You'll hear part of a lecture.

LECTURER: . . . and in the nineteenth century huge changes in population took place which affected the entire world. Er...the world population grew from 900 million in 1810 to 1600 million a hundred years later. So throughout the 19th century a pattern of voluntary and enforced emigration developed, reaching its peak...er...during the hundred years from 1830 to 1930.

   Now, there were many reasons for this. Er...the famine caused by the failure of the potato crop in Ireland, and other harvest failures in agricultural regions all over Europe, er...religious persecution such as that suffered by the Jews in Russia, unemployment in urban areas and so on. But they all had one thing in common: the emigrants had nothing to lose. All right? So whatever happened to them at the end of their journey, it just couldn't be worse than what they were experiencing at home.

   But there were also, of course, the advertised attractions of the New World, a place where, a...according to advertisements and rumour, cheap or even free agricultural land was on offer, where a...a...a penniless immigrant could 'become a millionaire'. [Haha!] Um...but, of course, as we know, the reality was different. The streets were not paved with gold, and reality for a poor immigrant could be...um...trying in vain to grow crops on semi-desert land in Montana, or...er...living ten to a room in New York and working for eight cents an hour in a clothing factory. [Oh!] Yes, really. Eight cents an hour. But...er...still there *were* opportunities, and it was probably better than the life they had left behind them in Europe. And the countries of the New World encouraged immigrants to come with promises of a better life. Yes, in the front there.

1ST STUDENT: Er...w...where did they come from and where did they go to?

LECTURER: Well, the largest number of emigrants in the nineteenth century was from Great Britain: eleven million went to the USA and Canada, two million to Australia and New Zealand. Ahh, the next largest . . . just give me one second . . . the next largest number was Germans: over six million emigrated mainly to the USA, but also to Canada and even Southern Brazil. Er...five million Italians emigrated to the United States and many more Italians went to Argentina. Four million Irish people went to the USA, many as a result of the Famine in the 1840s and its aftermath. Yes, that's...that...that...that was the...er...when a million people had died of starvana...um...starvation when the potato crop failed. [Mm.] As I'm sure you know. Two million Russian emigrants, many of them Jewish, went to the United States. And then from Spain, most Spanish emigrants went to Argentina. Um...and from Portugal especially to Brazil. Oh, and large numbers of French people...um...emigrated, mainly to Canada and to North Africa, particularly Algeria.

2ND STUDENT: Er...excuse me.

LECTURER: Yes.

2ND STUDENT: Wh...what about Africans? Erm...the slaves weren't emigrants but they did settle in new countries too, didn't they?

LECTURER: Good point. Yes, we mustn't forget that the slave trade was still flourishing during the first half of the 19th century. Africans were still being shipped to the United States, to South America, and to the Caribbean – where their descendants now form the majority of the population on...on virtually every island if not all . . .

3RD STUDENT: Um...so . . .

LECTURER: Yes.

3RD STUDENT: So it was the USA which received the largest number of immigrants?

LECTURER: That's right, it was. Between 1830 and 1930, er...let me just get this right, yes, 35 million immigrants entered the United States. Proportionally, Australia certainly beats that: Australia's prop...population grew from a few thousand in 1800 to five million by 1900. Yes, on the left there.

4TH STUDENT: Um...er...so far you've...er...you've mentioned only...only the New World, but...um...I...I take it i...it wasn't just Europeans who emigrated?

LECTURER: No, by no means. Um...many people from India went to East Africa and South Africa, firstly to work temporarily as labourers on plantations. And...er...many of them never returned home. Er...the Chinese went all over the Pacific, particularly to the various countries of South-East Asia and also to the United States, where they…they hoped to make their fortunes in the Gold Rush and…and worked subsequently as labourers building the railroads – and…and most…um…stayed on afterwards.

5TH STUDENT: You're talking about what happened a hundred years ago. [Mmhm.] I was wondering what are the effects of all this on the countries today?

LECTURER: Ah, well that's an interesting…interesting question. Er…the number of second and subsequent generations grew and grew of course. There are well over thirty million Chinese people scattered around the world outside China and Taiwan. In the USA, because of the so-called 'melting pot' effect, the descendants of the early immigrants became English-speaking Americans. But more recent immigrants have retained their cultures and languages. Er…for example if you go to Argentina, there are districts in Buenos Aires where you can still hear Italian being spoken. Just as there are…er…German-speaking communities in…in Southern Brazil, where even second and third gener…generation immigrants still speak German as well as Portuguese.

Yes, in fact, almost every country has received immigrants at some time in its history. Some of this has happened more recently. Many Greeks, for instance, emigrated to Australia in the…in the fifties and sixties: the largest…er…the third largest, excuse me, the third largest Greek community in the world is in Melbourne.

And huge numbers of people from Mexico and Central America and the Caribbean have been emigrating to the USA since the 1940s. Cubans in Florida, Mexicans in California. And there was also a big influx of Koreans in the seventies and eighties: the world's second largest Korean community lives in Los Angeles. Yes?

1ST STUDENT: Um…but how can you tell what nationality someone is descended from? I mean, if they're Korean Americans they'll probably look different, but what about the Europeans?

LECTURER: Well, actually, a good way to find out the origins of people, if you go to a North or South American country, is to look in the…in the local phone book. [Oh? Haha!] Yes, strange but true! You see…you see Swedish surnames in the Mid-West of the USA, Italian surnames and Jewish names in cities like New York, er…Ukrainian names in Pennsylvania, Chinese and Korean names in California. In Canada there are many Scottish surnames. And all over North America you'll notice Irish names, Polish names, Hispanic names and so on in the phone book. And, interestingly, even if the grandchildren don't speak their grandparents' language, they often still do eat their national dishes at home or in restaurants. And this variety makes life for everyone in the country more diverse and interesting. Um…so, many people in North and South America can trace their ancestry back to another country – and, rightly, are proud of their origins.

B 👥 After the discussion, ask each pair to share their most interesting ideas with the rest of the class.

17.7 Listening Part 4: What if?   EXAM PRACTICE

This is the very last **Listening** section.

🔊 To simulate exam conditions, allow everyone 30 seconds to read the questions through. Then play the recording, rewind it and play it again after 10 seconds' pause. Allow a minute at the end for everyone to check their answers. (In the exam there are 4 minutes' silence at the very end – this gives candidates time to check their answers to all four parts of the text.)

ANSWERS					
1 A	2 J	3 J	4 B	5 B	6 A

TRANSCRIPT *6 minutes*

NARRATOR: You'll hear part of a broadcast.

PRESENTER: And in the studio today are Alan Forster and Jane Watson, both experts on early 20th century history. So, Alan and Jane, could the First World War have been avoided?

ALAN: Probably not. Er…John Keegan says 'the First World War was a tragic and unnecessary conflict' but I believe that the question in 1914 wasn't so much *if* a continental war would break out, so much as *when* it would happen, what form it would take and who would be the winners – and losers. But it could have been confined to a scale that wasn't worldwide in its events and influence.

JANE: I think it could have been avoided if things had turned out differently. At the very least it could have been much shorter by years, with the savings of millions of lives, if things had happened differently. And it could of course have turned out differently: Germany could have won.

ALAN: Also no one could have foreseen which nations would take part in the conflict. Nobody could foresee that the conflict would be so enormous or change so much or last so long. At the start of the war in August 1914, people said, 'It'll all be over by Christmas'.

PRESENTER: It all began when Austrian Archduke Franz Ferdinand and his wife were assassinated in Sarajevo on June 28th 1914, right?

ALAN: Yes, um…and on July 29th the Austrian army started to attack Belgrade, the capital of Serbia. On July 31st Austria, Russia, Turkey and France mobilised their armies – but Great Britain seemed ready to watch from the sidelines and remain neutral. It was a European affair, the British government thought. Relations between Britain and Germany were actually improving. Well, then Germany began

PRESENTER: to mobilise and declared war on Russia, Serbia's ally. France was Russia's ally, so they were committed to supporting Russia.

PRESENTER: And so that made France and Germany into official enemies, then?

JANE: Yes, and so what Germany did was to march through Belgium to attack France from the north. It was at this point that the British government joined the war knowing that this would bring the Germans a mere 30 kilometres from the English coast on the other side of the Channel.

ALAN: Yes, they could have put all their efforts into attacking Russia in the East, but this was considered to be the responsibility of the Austrian army.

PRESENTER: What if the British had delayed this decision by a week? And not started moving troops across the Channel when they did?

JANE: Well, the German army would have reached the coast but the French could still have prevented them from reaching Paris. It would have been too late by then for the British to move sufficient forces to France. This would have given Germany an overwhelming advantage. At this stage some sort of deal might have been reached.

ALAN: Yes, the Battle of the Marne was the major turning point. It was after this that semi-permanent trenches were dug and the Western Front was established – a front which would hardly change for four years.

JANE: Mm, in August 1914 the Germans should have won. The mistake they made was to remove men from the right wing (the western wing closest to the sea) and send them to the Eastern Front to protect Germany from Russian attack. They also strengthened the left wing – to protect Germany from attack from France. If they had maintained the strength of the right wing, their plan would have succeeded and the French army would have been contained inside a sort of sack with the German forces all around them. The right wing was too weak to complete this manoeuvre.

PRESENTER: And then there was a lost map, wasn't there?

ALAN: Ha, yes, on September 1st, a French patrol captured a German dispatch car, killing all their soldiers. They found a map which showed the German military plans for their next attack, which would bring the Germans to within 30 kilometres from Paris. This knowledge enabled the French to anticipate the next attack and stop it and to keep the Germans over 100 kilometres from Paris – a stalemate that would continue for another four years. The Front moved back and forth a few metres in various places, but in most places it never moved at all. Millions of lives were sacrificed for a gain of a few metres.

JANE: Mm, and the war might have been won by the Germans when on October 31st they attacked the British line at a place called Gheluvelt, near Lille in Northern France. They broke through the line and started to advance. But then they stopped for further orders. None came. 1,200 untrained Bavarian reservists waited for further orders instead of continuing the attack, which would have taken them to the sea, cutting the British army in half. An English Brigadier, Charles Fitzclarence, who was on the spot, made a swift decision. He sent all the men he had, a mere 370 men, in an attempt to stop the Bavarians. Against all odds they forced them to retreat and ended the German advance. Many of the Bavarians were killed, many were captured, but some managed to get away. One of those who escaped was a private from Austria – Adolf Hitler. What if he had been among the soldiers killed? Just one bullet would have changed . . .

ALAN: Well, also if the Germans had won – and they could have done this by reaching Paris – the war could have been over by Christmas. Millions of lives wouldn't have been wasted.

PRESENTER: What if the war had ended sooner? If Germany had made peace with France and Russia in 1914?

ALAN: Well, in Russia, peace would have allowed the Russian industrial economy to flourish, instead of being tied up in supporting the armies. And there would have been further moves towards democracy, which had been stopped by the war. There would have been no sealed train arranged by the Germans from Switzerland to St Petersburg to carry Lenin to start his Revolution.

PRESENTER: And if the war had ended sooner? So many lives would have been saved.

JANE: Mm, exactly, writers like Wilfred Owen and Rupert Brooke would have lived. There would have been an Ernest Hemingway but no *Farewell to Arms* and the most wonderful opening paragraph of the century: 'Troops went by the house and down the road and the dust they raised powdered the leaves of the trees.' [*See 11.9 for the continuation of this paragraph.*]

ALAN: Without the events of 1914 with its trench warfare, remorseless killing and disregard for human life, men like Adolf Hitler wouldn't have repeated this cult of death twenty years later.

PRESENTER: So, without the First World War, there would have been no Treaty of Versailles in 1919, no Second World War. And with no Bolshevik Revolution, there would have been no Soviet Union and no Cold War.

17.8   Writing Parts 1 and 2   EXAM PRACTICE

This section can be treated as a mock exam. To save time, it's best for everyone to do this at home, not in class.

A & B   Ask everyone to do both compositions at home under exam conditions (against the clock and without dictionaries).

Finally . . .

Discuss approaches to the Writing Paper with everyone. Has anyone got any useful tips to share?

Writing Paper General Mark Scheme

In the exam, this mark scheme is used in conjunction with a task-specific mark scheme for each question.

Each composition is placed within a 'Band' and awarded one of three performance levels within that band: ·1 = weaker, ·2 = average, ·3 = strong. 'Acceptable' performance at CPE level is Band 3.

Band	
5	Outstanding realisation of the task set: • Sophisticated use of an extensive range of vocabulary, collocation and expression, entirely appropriate to the task set • Effective use of stylistic devices; register and format wholly appropriate • Impressive use of a wide range of structures • Skilfully organised and coherent • Excellent development of topic • Virtually error-free Impresses the reader and has a very positive effect.
4	Good realisation of the task set: • Fluent and natural use of a wide range of vocabulary, collocation and expression, successfully meeting the requirements of the task set • Good use of stylistic devices; register and format wholly appropriate • Competent use of a wide range of structures • Well organised and coherent • Good and ambitious development of topic • Minor and unobtrusive errors, arising from attempts at complex language Has a positive effect on the reader.
3	Satisfactory realisation of the task set: • Reasonably fluent and natural use of a range of vocabulary and expression, adequate to the task set • Evidence of stylistic devices; register and format generally appropriate • Adequate range of structures • Clearly organised and generally coherent • Adequate, though unambitious, coverage of topic • Occasional non-impeding errors Achieves the desired effect on the reader.
2	Inadequate attempt at the task set: • Limited and/or inaccurate range of vocabulary and expression • Little evidence of stylistic devices; some attempt at register and format • Inadequate range of structures • Some attempt at organisation, but lacks coherence • Inadequate development of topic • A number of errors, which sometimes impede communication Has a negative effect on the reader.
1	Poor attempt at the task set: • Severely limited and inaccurate range of vocabulary and expression • No evidence of stylistic devices; little or no attempt at register and format • Lack of structural range • Poorly organised, leading to incoherence • Little relevance to topic, and/or too short • Numerous errors, which distract and often impede communication Has a very negative effect on the reader.
0	Negligible or no attempt at the task set: • Totally incomprehensible due to serious error • Totally irrelevant • Insufficient language to assess (fewer than 20% of the required number of words) • Totally illegible

This is the very last **Speaking** section. If possible, before the exam, enlist the aid of another teacher and carry out a Mock Speaking Paper with all your students (in pairs), using the Assessment Guidelines below. Suitable Speaking Papers can be found in *Cambridge Proficiency Examination Practice 1*.

Part 1 of the Speaking Paper consists of 3 minutes' general conversation between the Interlocutor and each candidate in turn. The candidates are encouraged to give information about themselves and express personal opinions.

A 👥 Part 2 is a conversation about pictures (4 minutes).

B 1 👥 Part 4 begins with two long turns (2 minutes each).

2 👥 Part 2 continues with 8 minutes of discussion on topics related to the long turns.

Assessment guidelines

In the Speaking Paper, candidates are assessed on their own individual performance and not in relation to each other, according to the following analytical criteria: Grammatical Resource, Lexical Resource, Discourse Management, Pronunciation and Interactive Communication. Assessment is based on performance in the whole test and is not related to particular parts of the test.

Both examiners assess the candidates. The Assessor applies detailed, analytical scales, and the Interlocutor applies the Global Achievement Scale, which is based on the analytical scales.

Grammatical Resource   This refers to the accurate application of grammar rules and the effective arrangement of words in utterances. At CPE level a wide range of structures should be used appropriately and competently.

Lexical Resource   This refers to the candidate's ability to use a wide and appropriate range of vocabulary to meet task requirements. At CPE level the tasks require candidates to express precise meanings, attitudes and opinions and to be able to convey abstract ideas. Although candidates may lack specialised vocabulary when dealing with unfamiliar topics, it should not in general terms be necessary to resort to simplification.

Discourse Management   This refers to the ability to link utterances together to form coherent monologue and contributions to dialogue. The utterances should be relevant to the tasks and to preceding utterances in the discourse. The discourse produced should be at a level of complexity appropriate to CPE level and the utterances should be arranged logically to develop the themes or arguments required by the tasks. The extent of contributions should be appropriate, i.e. long or short as required at a particular point in the dynamic development of the discourse in order to achieve the task.

Pronunciation   This refers to the ability to produce easily comprehensible utterances. Articulation of individual sounds is not required to be native speaker-like but should be sufficiently clear for all words to be easily understood. An acceptable rhythm of connected speech should be achieved by the appropriate use of strong and weak syllables, the smooth linking of words and the effective highlighting of information-bearing words. Intonation, which includes the use of a sufficiently wide pitch range and the appropriate use of contours, should be used effectively to convey meaning.

Interactive Communication   This refers to the ability to take an active part in the development of the discourse, showing sensitivity to turn taking and without undue hesitation. It requires the ability to participate competently in the range of interactive situations in the test and to develop discussions on a range of topics by initiating and responding appropriately. It also refers to the deployment of strategies to maintain and repair interaction at an appropriate level throughout the test so that the tasks can be fulfilled.

Global Achievement Scale   This refers to the candidate's overall performance throughout the test.

18 Modern life

18.1 Reading Part 2
EXAM PRACTICE

(A)

> **ANSWERS**
> 1 D   2 D   3 D   4 C   5 B   6 D   7 D   8 C

(B) 👥 Ask the groups to report on their discussion at the end. Also, ask for their reactions to the stories in the articles: which one amused them most and why?

18.2 Use of English Part 3
EXAM PRACTICE

Part 3 of the Use of English Paper is 'Which word fits?'

(A)

> **ANSWERS**
> 1 sound   2 sharp   3 notices   4 fair   5 land   6 square

(B) 👥 Ask the groups to share their advice with the rest of the class.

18.3 Use of English Part 4
EXAM PRACTICE

Part 4 of the Use of English Paper is 'Key word transformations'. Each gap must be filled with between two and eight words. A partly correct answer can get one mark, only a fully correct answer gets two marks.

(A)

> **ANSWERS**
> 1 of crime prevention depends on
> 2 didn't/did not scream for fear of waking
> 3 a gradual increase in the
> 4 had their flat broken into / break-ins at their flat
> 5 journey to work takes an/one hour
> 6 is some doubt about the exact
> 7 not be able to rely on
> 8 of modern life are what I

(B) 👥 Ask the groups to share their advice with the rest of the class.

18.4 Reading Part 3
EXAM PRACTICE

(*Design flaws* in **12.3** is also by Bill Bryson.)

(A)

> **ANSWERS**
> 1 F   2 H   3 G   4 A   5 B   6 E   7 C

B 👥👥 Ask the groups to share their advice with the rest of the class. Also, ask for their reactions to the article: what amused them most about it?

18.5 Use of English Part 5 EXAM PRACTICE

Part 5 of the Use of English Paper is two passages with questions and a summary-writing task. Before writing the summary students should make notes – or maybe highlight information in the passages.

A
> **SUGGESTED ANSWERS**
> 1 She has no real friends
> 2 Destructive, causes a lot of damage progressively
> 3 There is something for everyone to enjoy in a healthy city
> 4 A small amount attaches itself
> 5 For people who find it hard to make friends, life in a city can be terribly lonely. The more people there are around, the more a lack of companionship leads to their feeling of isolation. But cities are thrilling places, full of so many different things to do which appeal to so many different tastes. Some excitement is dangerous and even unhealthy, however.

B 👥👥 Ask the groups to share their advice with the rest of the class. Also, ask for their reactions to the articles: did they strike a chord?

18.6 Writing Parts 1 and 2 EXAM PRACTICE

A This can be treated as a mock exam – best done at home under exam conditions. Back in class, form groups and ask the students to read each other's work before handing it in for marking.

B 👥👥 Ask the groups to share their advice with the rest of the class.

Further practice using the *Cambridge Proficiency Examination Practice 1* is recommended, together with discussion of right and wrong answers.

Refer to *Cambridge Proficiency Examination Practice* TEACHER'S BOOKS for a detailed marking scheme together with sample compositions and Examiner's comments.

18.7 One last word . . .

Share some of these ideas with the class.

> ### Finally, twelve more tips for the exam:
> 1 In the Speaking Paper, don't keep interrupting each other: wait until the other candidate has finished his/her sentence. The examiner will make sure you both get a chance to have your say.
> 2 Read the rubrics carefully and make sure you follow the instructions exactly – especially in Paper 2.
> 3 Use a highlighter or pencil on the exam paper itself – you *are* allowed to make notes on it.
> 4 Check through everything you have written for mistakes: grammar, spelling, punctuation and vocabulary.
> 5 Don't skimp on paper in the exam: leave plenty of space for amendments and corrections. Leave a wide margin, a couple of blank lines between paragraphs and even a couple of blank lines at the end of each page. Write clearly.

6 Stay calm – use your time wisely. If there's time to spare, re-read and re-re-read your work, looking for places where it can be improved.

7 Don't spend too long on the hardest questions to the detriment of the rest of the paper. Do the easier questions first and come back to the trickier ones later. Make a pencil mark beside any that you're missing out, so that you can spot them again quickly later.

8 Although the exam tends to follow a predictable pattern, don't panic if there is a 'new' item. Expect the unexpected.

9 Don't worry if parts of the exam are unexpectedly difficult – they're probably equally difficult for everyone else.

10 Don't leave any blanks – if you don't know an answer, first eliminate any obviously wrong answers and then guess!

11 Go to the exam armed with all the equipment you'll need: several pens, pencils, highlighters, rubbers, rulers – at least TWO of each!

12 Read the rubrics carefully AGAIN. Make sure you follow the instructions exactly!

PLUS ...

Your own tips, based on the foibles and proclivities of your students:

13

14

15

Remind everyone to look through all the Exam tips in the Student's Book before they do each paper in the exam. Perhaps insist that each student writes down the six main points he or she must remember in the exam.